Women, Religion and Tradition

Women, Religion and Tradition

The Cult of Jogins, Matangis and Basvis

Vakulabharanam Lalitha

Indira Gandhi Rashtriya Manav Sangrahalaya, Bhopal
(National Museum of Mankind)

RAWAT PUBLICATIONS
Jaipur • New Delhi • Bangalore • Hyderabad • Guwahati

ISBN 978-81-316-0395-6

Published by
Indira Gandhi Rashtriya Manav Sangrahalaya
Shamla Hills, Bhopal-462013 (Madhya Pradesh)
email: directorigrms@gmail.com

Prem Rawat for **Rawat Publications**
Satyam Apts, Sector 3, Jawahar Nagar, Jaipur 302 004 (India)
Phone: 0141 265 1748 / 7006 Fax: 0141 265 1748
E-mail: info@rawatbooks.com
Website: www.rawatbooks.com

New Delhi Office
4858/24, Ansari Road, Daryaganj, New Delhi 110 002
Phone: 011 2326 3290

Also at *Bangalore, Hyderabad* and *Guwahati*

Typeset by Rawat Computers, Jaipur
Printed at Chaman Enterprises, New Delhi

Dedicated to

Madari Bhagya Reddi Varma

who initiated pioneering efforts in eradicating the
Jogin system in Andhra Pradesh
and
Jogins, Matangis, Basvis, Muralis, Bhavins and Mariyammas.

Contents

Foreword

I have great pleasure in writing the foreword to the book on the life of *jogins, matangis* and *basavis* of Andhra Pradesh by Smt. V. Lalitha.

This book is the result of painstaking fieldwork and study by the author for more than two decades, from 1985 to 2006. The objective of the study is to trace the origin and diffusion of the *devadasi* culture in India; to find out differences in temple worship between the so-called Great Tradition and Little Tradition; and to critically evaluate the impact of reformative and rehabilitative measures undertaken by the government, voluntary organizations and legislations. Consistent with this objective, the book examines in detail the varied manifestation of the social practices concerning the communities of *jogins, matangis* and *basavis* in Andhra Pradesh and other southern regions of India.

A young woman, more often a girl child, was customarily dedicated or 'married' to a local deity called Yellamma or Poleramma, to perform rituals that evolved over time by such dedication. This is an obnoxious practice with consequences as inhuman as the practice of untouchability. Author's case studies and narration of life histories of such women are a poignant description of their sufferings of women and indignities heaped on them. This study adopts a comparative perspective, and draws similarities and contrasts between the afore-mentioned communities in Andhra Pradesh and the *devadasis* of Karnataka, *muralis* of Maharashtra, *bhavins* and *deviles* of Goa, and *thayammas* and *mariammas* of Tamil Nadu. A detailed account of the Yellamma temples at Saundatti and Chandragutti in Karnataka, and Khandoba temple at Jejuri in Maharashtra, where women dedications took place every year is also provided. It is instructive to note that the system does not exist in Kerala.

During my stint in the Indian Administrative Service (IAS) in Andhra Pradesh, I got the valuable opportunity to work among the poorer sections of the society, particularly with people of the Scheduled Castes (SCs), Scheduled Tribes (STs) and Other Backward Classes (OBCs). I was quite shocked when I came across for the first time during the 1980s while my travelling through the villages and towns of Andhra Pradesh poor women variously called *jogins* or *basavis,* most of them hailing from the untouchable groups. This practice persisted almost until the end of the twentieth century. Poverty is said to be an important reason why parents endorse the ritual dedication of their girl child. If poverty is the only reason, we might ask why boys are spared, and why only girl children are targeted. The system is then obviously also based on gender discrimination and patriarchal practices.

Over the recent decades, some people's organizations have started working for the eradication of this social evil. There are now laws enacted by the various state governments prohibiting the practice and making any association with it punishable. A detailed account of the endeavours of various reformist organizations is also provided in the book.

I compliment Mrs. Lalitha for writing this invaluable book which will not only greatly help in arriving at a proper and contextual understanding of this social evil, but also in devising a variety of measures in ensuring that the pernicious practice is eradicated.

S.R. Sankaran, IAS
Former Principal Secretary,
Social Welfare Department, Andhra Pradesh

Preface and Acknowledgments

Taking stock of past achievements is a normal exercise, especially at the beginning of a new century or a millennium. As we look at what women achieved during the last century, it appears as if those achievements left their indelible mark on every dimension of social life today.

The origins of the *devadasi* system can be traced back to the practice of ritual dancing as part of service to gods and goddesses. Temple dancers were dedicated to gods, supposedly to give them worldly pleasures. The *devadasi* system in course of time degenerated into prostitution, and as a result of relentless battle waged by reformist individuals and organizations, the Andhra Pradesh Devadasi Prevention of Dedication Act of 1947 (Act No. XXXI of 1947) was promulgated on January 21, 1948.

Lower caste women were illiterate and oppressed in economic, social and cultural terms. Some Scheduled Caste (SC) women converted as *jogins, matangis, basavis, muralis, bhavins* and *mariammas* were exploited in the name of cultural traditions. These traditions are by no means confined to extra-domestic sexual gratification nor can we argue that there is an explicit intent as such of that kind in them. It may be argued that by making the connection between divinity and extra-domestic sexual gratification, patriarchy legitimized and strengthened its norms of sexuality within the domestic spaces.

By attaching divinity, the chosen woman's sexuality was controlled in particular ways that were decreed by society. Though a *jogin* or *murali* is dedicated to some local god or goddess, she is in practice slave to a rich and influential man in the village and later made available to any man in the village. Thus, these women are inducted into prostitution with social sanction.

The *jogin* system has caught the attention of journalists, film directors, etc., and has also provided poignant material for novelists and fiction writers. However, not many professional or academic research works have been published on the subject, though some studies of the *devadasi* cult in Karnataka and Andhra Pradesh are available. The present book hopes to bridge this gap.

Many organizations have been working for the uplift of these unfortunate women in Andhra Pradesh such as Samskar at Varni (Nizamabad district), Andhra Pradesh Jogin Vyavastha Vyatireka Porata Sanghatana (APJVVPS, Mahabubnagar district), RISE and Stree Shakti Sanghatana (Chittoor district), and Duties (Nellore district). Similar organizations are also operating in other states such as Maharashtra, Karnataka, Goa and Tamil Nadu.

Funding for the research was provided by the Indian Council of Historical Research, New Delhi, while Mahatma Gandhi National Institute of Research and Social Action (NIRSA), Hyderabad granted me affiliation to their institute. I am grateful to founder president, Professor D. Swaminathan and the Registrar, Mr D. Suresh. Sri S.R. Sankaran, IAS (Retired), who has just passed away, clarified issues at every stage of the research and agreed to write the foreword. Samskar, the NGO based in Nizamabad district, led by the well-known reformer couple, Late Hemalatha Lavanam and Sri Lavanam, and later by Dr KHSS Sundar, allowed me to speak and spend time with several *jogins* involved in the process of rehabilitation. My niece Hema accompanied me on my field visits to Maharashtra. I am thankful to her.

The publication of this book is made possible due the initiatives taken by Professor Kishor K. Basa, former Director of the Indira Gandhi Rashtriya Manav Sangrahalaya (IGRMS), and the present Director, Professor K.K. Misra. I am especially grateful to both for their encouragement. I would also take this opportunity to record my deep appreciation for Sri Sudhir Shrivastava, Publication Officer, IGRMS, who kept in touch with me all through the process of publication of this book.

I am deeply indebted to Professor M.L.K. Murthy for keen interest that he evinced in getting this work published.

I am also grateful to Rawat Publications, for their promptness in bringing out this book in a nice format.

I have also benefited from constant advice and guidance provided by Professors K. Laxmi Narayan and P. Venkata Rao of the

University of Hyderabad. Sri Harnoor helped with copy editing of the book, Bharat Bhushan and Mallesh typed the manuscript, and Sri Madari Ramachander brought out the final soft copy of the book. D.M. Premavathi, Anandalakshmi, Malli Gandhi, M. Rani, C. Sarada, Nirupama, Vamsicharan, Nishant, Vidya, Shailendra, Irfan, Rukmini and Rajagopal contributed in ways they will realize and in ways they may not.

Finally, my husband V. Ramakrishna was always there for me when I needed him and readily offered helpful advice to make this book happen and improve its quality.

V. Lalitha

From the Director's Desk

In pursuance of the mandate of the Indira Gandhi Rashtriya Manav Sangrahalaya (IGRMS), Bhopal to promote research, scholarly works are published by the Sangrahalaya from time to time, written and edited by distinguished scholars from various disciplines. The present volume on the Jogins, Matangis and Basvis of Andhra Pradesh by Dr V. Lalitha is a welcome addition to the series of such scholarly books.

In this well-researched book the author has demonstrated how the 'sexploitation' of the women, largely belonging to the lower rungs of the Hindu society, is legitimized under the garb of tradition and religion. It is indeed a sad saga of the downtrodden women in rural India. Dedication of young girls to a god or deity is an old and universal practice under various nomenclatures, for various purposes, and in different forms. In India, this practice is generally known as the Devadasi system. Besides, there are also different forms and terms of this 'great tradition' wrapped in many 'little traditions' at the local level. However, one can understand these devolved forms and functions under the domain of the Devadasi, which is a popular form of great tradition. Dr Lalitha, in this book, has not only traced the origins of this practice, but also extensively examined the systems of the Jogins, Matangis and Basvis in Andhra Pradesh and Karnataka, and other such systems existing in Maharashtra, Tamil Nadu and Goa as well. In the course of her discussion, she has also shed light on the reformation and rehabilitation dimensions of this social evil and how it can receive the attention of the government, media, intellectuals and the voluntary sector.

I am indeed grateful to Dr Lalitha for agreeing to get this volume published by IGRMS, Bhopal. My sincere thanks are also due to late Shri S.R. Sankaran, IAS, for writing the Foreword, Shri Pranit Rawat for expediting its publication, and my colleagues at IGRMS for making this venture successful.

K.K. Misra
Director, IGRMS

CHAPTER 1

Introduction

Religion is a complex phenomenon which pervades a vast range of human activities. The purpose of religion is to help us to grow from this world of intellect and divided consciousness, with its discords and dualities, to a life of harmony, of freedom of life. Describing man as a participant in this process of cosmic evolution, Dr Sarvepalli Radhakrishnan had said that man has to achieve this goal.

India is famous for its temples, shrines and sacred places. In these places, the devotees conduct different religious activities. They express their devotion by singing songs, performing dances and serving god with other activities like fanning and sweeping. At these temples, fairs and festivals are celebrated in honour of their respective presiding deities. Several types of offerings, fire rituals, prayers, sacred baths, observances of sacraments and festivals take place. The popularity of a temple depends upon the influence of the deity of that place. Some deities are called Jagartha deities because of their power of fulfilling the wishes of the devotees. While the devotees belonging to Great Tradition offer more to that particular deity, those belonging to Little Tradition offer food, meat, blood and inflict wounds on their own bodies to express their devotion. However, devotees from both these traditions take vows according to their beliefs and visit these temples once or twice a year.

The numerical growth of the temples coincided with their structural evolution. Temple construction started spreading in pre-Pallava times and continued upto 12th century AD. The cult of devotion (bhakti) saw all major religions take up temple-building activity. Everybody, irrespective of whether he was high or low, used this opportunity to serve god and get liberation or salvation. There are instances to show that many devotees who belonged to the lower strata of society attained salvation by serving god. Nayanar saints also popularized temple construction. Tiruvalluvar cautioned the king that he would decline in position if service was not done to god. In the beginning, temples and shrines were constructed. Later, the rich landlords and kings built choultries and provided all facilities to the devotees. Inscriptions are the main source of information regarding the construction, renovation and maintenance of the temples. We are not going to discuss temple construction and other factors here because our main concern is what is called the Little Tradition.

Devotees belonging to different traditions and religions take vows according to their religious beliefs. Devotees belonging to the Hindu faith come under the Great Tradition, and take vows in the way prescribed in holy scriptures. They are usually in the form of offering worship, going on a pilgrimage, doing penance and giving charity. On the other hand, the vows taken in the Little Tradition are non-sanskritic, that is, in the form of offering cooked food including meat and blood to the deity and self-flagellation.

Devotees from both the Great and Little Traditions visit the temple of their family deity once or twice a year and attend annual fair or festival; their main object of visiting the shrine is to offer something to the deity for fulfilment of a vow or vows.

The Little Tradition evolved as a result of the Brahmanical form of worship in Great Tradition temples where Brahmin priests played a very important role in their maintenance. Devotees belonging to the lower rung of society, especially the so-called untouchables, were not allowed to step into these temples. These 'untouchables' were deprived of education and suffered from the stigma of untouchability. They were not allowed to draw water from the common wells and they had exclusive washing ponds. As these people were not allowed to enter the temples, they went to the outskirts of the village and started constructing their own temples which were crude and enshrined within them tough unhewn stones representing the 'amma' or 'mother' sacred to that village. These people used to provide manual labour for the construction of the temples of the Great Tradition.

They have many deities such as Yellamma, Pochamma, Matamma, Maisamma, Mariamma, Sunkalamma and Ulagamma. These deities are of two types, namely, benevolent, protecting the devotees, and the malevolent inspiring devotion by frightening people or causing harmful diseases to the devotees. In the case of malevolent gods and goddesses, the devotees have to appease the deity by offering animal sacrifices. Most of the devotees visit Yellamma Jatara at Kokatnur, a village of Karnataka.

Yellamma in Karnataka state is called by different names such as Ellavva, Renuka, Saktimata, Jagadamba and Elukolladavva. In Andhra Pradesh, Yellamma is called Ekavira, Hemalamma, Renuka and Jagadamba. 'Jagadamba' means goddess of all, an incarnation of Parvati.

The mode of worship in a Yellamma temple is a Dravidian ethnic tradition, not sanskritic. Sanskritization is the process by which a 'low' Hindu caste or tribal or their group changes its customs, rituals and way of life in the direction of a high and frequently 'twice-born' caste. Generally, such changes are followed by a claim to a higher position in the caste hierarchy which the local community traditionally conceded to the claimant caste.

Thus, the position of castes in the hierarchy as it actually exists is liable to change, whereas in the varna model the position of each varna is fixed for all time. The varna model of caste is really a hierarchy in the sense that the priestly varna is placed at the top and the criterion of ranking is derived from religious consideration.

Yellamma is a local deity. Priests are non-Brahmins. Just as girls from backward class communities were bought and dedicated to the temples which followed the Brahmanical order, likewise, women of Mala and Madiga communities began to dedicate their daughters to Yellamma temples. A majority of these devadasis serve only the local feudals and go for 'Joga' or begging. It denotes their poor economic condition. They do not attach any stigma to the profession of prostitution after dedication.

How do the young girls dedicated to the village deity survive? What is the process of rehabilitation of these victims of circumstances? What are the institutions that safeguard them legally, socially and economically? We need to analyse these factors and make a comparative study of the Jogins, Matangis and Basvis of Andhra Pradesh, Devadasis of Karnataka, Vaghyamuralis of Maharashtra, Bhavins and Deviles of Goa and Thayammas and Mariammas of Tamil Nadu.

Purpose

The female dancers and singers attached to the temples are referred to as 'Devadasis' which literally means 'female servants of the deity'.

They are not allowed to marry any mortal man and are called 'Nitya Sumangalis'. They are ritual specialists.

The culture of dedicating girls to temples is a universal phenomenon in India. Generally, the devadasis dedicated to the temples of Great Tradition are experts in music, dance and literature. Devadasis at the lower rung of the hierarchy are dedicated to Yellamma. They also know music and dance which we call folk dance and it has its own rhythm and spontaneity.

Some Facts about the Devadasi Tradition

- The Devadasi system of the Little Tradition is still alive and is undergoing a traumatic change, i.e., it blends into commercial prostitution. In spite of this, these women are still identified as 'Devadasis'.
- Dedication is a sort of licence for the practice of prostitution and is sanctioned by the society.
- Poverty is the main reason for the parents to dedicate their girl children to the deity. The dedication, thus, serves as a measure of protection to the parents in their old age.
- Socially, the devadasis enjoy more sexual freedom than the other women of their community. What is more, during 'Kolupulu' or festival these women are treated as goddesses.
- Ignorance is bliss for them. There are superstitions and the devadasis do not suffer psychologically from what has happened to them.
- The whole act of worship may be divided into: (a) rituals, (b) symbols, and (c) sacraments and sacrifices. This is an offshoot of the sanskritization process.

Objectives

The main objectives of the present study are:

- To trace the origin and diffusion of the devadasi culture in India.
- To find out the differences between the worship in the temples of Great Tradition and Little Tradition.
- To find out the factors for the persistence of this culture in the Deccan area even after the Devadasi Act was passed in 1947 abolishing the system.

- To critically evaluate the impact of reformative and rehabilitative movements by the government, voluntary organizations and legislation passed by the government.
- To know the actual position of these women subsequent to the legislation and the implementation of the rehabilitation programmes.
- To know the present status of the devadasis and their impact on the future of their children.

Process of Dedication

The process of the dedication is as follows: The priest ties a bead necklace around the girl's neck singing the praises of Goddess Yellamma. After this ritual, as a mark of respect all the villagers offer her kumkum and betel leaves and wash her feet. She then has to visit five houses to beg for food grain. This marks the end of the ceremony. Next day, the food grain collected by her is used in the preparation of 'Prasadam' to Yellamma. Every morning, after bath, the girl has to go to the temple to watch the worship of Yellamma. Though she is allowed in the sanctum sanctorum, she bows to the goddess from outside. She is trained by the senior devadasis. Singing and playing musical instruments is the main function of a devadasi.

Methodology

The approach and methodology adopted for this study are mainly anthropological and historical. For this purpose, an analysis is made on the basis of religion and its impact on the lives of the village people. Hence, various techniques of data collection have been used in the study. To trace the earliest form of this culture, historical or archival research is inevitable. The historical approach helps in knowing the society as an ever-changing organism.

Another technique of data collection is fieldwork which was conducted from 1985 to 2006. The main idea in doing the fieldwork was to contact the informants and interview the devadasis, their parents and elders of the community to seek information from them. This fieldwork covered more than a decade's experience in the three different systems – Jogin, Matangi and Basvi – their evaluation and interpretation of the past, present and future. Frequent formal and informal interviews with people who could provide information about these systems, their relations with landlords and community members, their status in the society and the reformatory methods adopted both by governmental and non-governmental agencies. Some non-governmental organizations (NGOs) like 'Chelli Nilayam' are doing active service in areas where the Jogin, Matangi and Basvi systems are prevalent. The author visited Varni in Nizamabad district, Sangareddy in Medak district, some villages in Mahaboobnagar district and some areas in Ranga Reddy and Hyderabad districts of Andhra Pradesh. The Matangi system is prevalent in Nellore, Prakasam and Chittoor districts and parts of Nalgonda district. She discovered that the Basvi system exists in Adoni town of Kurnool district and in more than 20 villages of Anantapur district. An organization known as 'Aasha' is working for the eradication of this system in seven districts of Andhra Pradesh. She had easy accessibility to material on inter- and intra-caste relations, kinship and rituals. She collected detailed life histories of many devadasis. An opinion survey was conducted covering NGOs, parents, community leaders, landlords and devadasis of the lower strata of society. Although everyone knows that the system is connected with religion and treats the devadasis as goddesses during religious festivities, once the festival is over, they are considered untouchables. This practice in some areas led to commercial prostitution. Otherwise, these women who are dedicated to goddesses are called 'kept women'. Community leaders, however, say that no stigma is attached to them and that they treat them as normal women equal to their own kith and kin. When the researcher asked them whether these women were equal to their wives, she got a negative reply.

The study used the following tools for the collection of data:

- Participant observation,
- Interview schedule,
- Case studies, and
- Interviews – formal and informal.

The field covered by the researcher is not confined to one place, so it is not easy to give a statistical analysis as the study is descriptive and narrative in nature.

An Overview of Literature

Religion has been a universal feature of human life. Students of anthropology cannot afford to neglect its social function. Max

Weber's *Sociology of Religion* is very important to work on the problem of Jogitas.

The idols of the deity Renuka Jamadagni are considered to be self-born (swayambhu) and not carved and installed by human beings. The Yellamma temple is believed to be 600 years old.

The main deity Yellamma is known as Elu Kollada Yellamma, the deity of seven valleys, as the shrine is situated at the meeting point of seven valleys. They are: (i) Sangana Kolla, (ii) Siddam Kolla, (iii) Bairavana Kolla, (iv) Heggolla (big valley), (v) Iruvekolla (valley for ants), (vi) Goravana Kolla, and (vii) Yadravi Kolla.

The mode of worship in the Yellamma temple today is definitely not the original form, but sanskritized. This has evolved from the local traditions and customs. Only the priests are allowed into the inner chamber of the temple. The devotees are supposed to make their offerings to the deity from the doorsteps of the inner hall. The deity is offered vegetarian food, specially cooked and brought by a male member of the priest's family. Thus, at the Soundatti shrine, the temple priests and pujaris belong to the Great Tradition and perform the puja, whereas in small Yellamma temples, the functionaries are the ritual mendicants such as Jogappa and Jogamma. Today, the priests are Lingayats and they claim that they are the brothers of Yellamma and she is their family deity and, hence, they manage the shrine.

In Maharashtra, Muralis are dedicated to Khandoba, the lord of the mountains, and though the Bhavins are not dedicated to any god, they serve the temple not with music and dance but by sweeping the temple and fanning the deity, etc.

To understand the Jogin or Matangi or Basvi system, we should know the traditional elements and social norms that made these women servile in nature, and in the process they were rendered spineless specimens of human dignity and self-respect. Having no control over their sexuality, they suffer the indignity heaped on them by society. Their womanhood is decided by extraneous factors. Being basically illiterate, oppressed and suppressed, they are disadvantaged socially, economically and even culturally. They, therefore, need to be educated and trained in entrepreneurial skills. These women are exploited in the name of tradition. They are either 'public sluts' or concubines of the rich feudal lords. They are expected to obey the village elders. Though deprived of a married life, they can beget children. But the children are not allowed to call their fathers, father. This practice has further burdened the jogins' lives and they live in perpetual socio-economic misery.

There is no normal married family life for the jogin, matangi and basvi women. There is a false belief that when a jogin or her counterpart gets into marriage bond, that person will die, the reason being that since they are married to the goddess, the goddess will get angry and punish them for deviation. Consequently, if she begets children nobody will shoulder the responsibility of the children.

Throughout her lifetime, a jogin is virtually a corpse. When a landlord dies, every jogin is expected to abstain from solid food but drink as much toddy as possible and perform a dance all the way from the house of the dead person to the burial ground. These women do gimmicks such as lifting a toddy bottle with their mouth or picking up with their eyelids the rupee notes thrown by the youngsters. Their behaviour is dictated by the whims and fancies of the people surrounding them. When a man touches a jogin, she is expected to be submissive and not react. This deplorable custom may be an offshoot of Vira Saivism.

When NGOs took up reformation work in Nizamabad and elsewhere, they faced many obstacles and protests. In spite of the obstacles, 'Chelli Nilayam' at Varni has marched forward to achieve its goal. In the beginning, jogins themselves protested vehemently but later on appreciating the laudable goal of the movement, they cooperated. People irrespective of gender used to utter the words, 'Ni Banchan Dora', 'Ni kaalmokta', 'Ni penta thinta'. They used to call her 'Vosey Jogu Posi', a humiliating term.

Some organizations concentrated on the following five steps in order to eradicate the Jogin system. They are:

1. Empowerment of jogins and dalit women.
2. Protests against making of jogins.
3. Propagation of the Act of 1988.
4. Development of leadership qualities.
5. Self-confidence to be instilled in these women.

The reason why we need to instil confidence in the jogins is that they mainly comprise the outcaste people who are treated as 'untouchables'. They had a dubious identity in the past. They were segregated and treated as virtual slaves. They were not a homogeneous group. Economically, they are at the lowest rung of the ladder and work either as landless labourers or construction workers.

At the end of the 19th century, social mobility became somewhat easy due to Western education, changes in the traditional economy, rise of new professions, introduction of communications, etc. Opportunities were created to develop social intercourse between the different castes. Caste associations sprang up and consequently the non-Brahmin movement united the lower caste people and they were provided with economic and employment benefits.

The issue of women was the focus of attention during the colonial period. Women occupied a pivotal place in the social reform movements in India because they had lived in social bondage for centuries. As a contemporary writer, R. Venkata Subba Rao puts it: "Deprived of all education, confined within the four walls of the house, seeing little of the world and knowing little of it, immersed in superstition and opposed by customs, our women – to our shame be it said – are no better than slaves".[1] The backwardness of women was attributed to their ignorance resulting from the lack of education and exposure to societal problems.

Certain concepts essential for understanding this deep-rooted evil practice are discussed below:

(1) Dedication: Dedication means the performance of any act or ceremony by whatever name it may be called by which a woman is

Plate 1 A potharaju is preparing for the act of dedication of a girl (some location in Nizamabad district).

dedicated to the service of any deity, idol, object of worship, temple or other religious institution or place of worship. Not only a girl a boy is also dedicated to a god or goddess. Such a boy is known as Jogappa, Vaghya or Potharaju.

Along with the dedication of girls as sacred prostitutes, there were instances of dedication of boys as potharaju and eunuchs as jogappa and vaghyas. The initiation rites to make a girl a divine prostitute start with the taking of a vow. Sometimes, dedication takes place even before the birth of the girl or when she is just a few years old. As a vowed gift to the deity, the girl becomes the property of the temple. The landlord or village head visits her on a fixed day as a sex mate and rewards her in cash and kind for her services. In Karnataka, the ritual starts with a bath in the Jogu-bhavi.

In Telangana areas, the initiation is pathetically dramatic. The young girl, usually between the ages of five and nine, is married to potharaju, the brother of Yellamma. She is smeared with turmeric powder from head to foot, dressed in yellow, which is considered an auspicious colour, decked with flowers and treated every bit as a bride. The priest performs her marriage to potharaju by tying a 'mangalasutra' around her neck on behalf of the goddess. She is then called 'Nityasumangali' and treated as a privileged person. In Karnataka, the girl's dedication ceremony is called 'Jogipattam'. The nuptial ceremony with the landlord or any person who undertakes to give her financial support is called 'Mailapattam'.

It is unfortunate that these girls are forced to eke out their livelihood as 'village sluts' or 'common women'.

(2) Goddess: Any V-shaped stick smeared with turmeric and kumkum and buried in the ground can serve as the goddess for the purpose. Even a stone can be used. Usually, pre-puberty girls are dedicated. They are unaware of what is in store for them when they are dedicated to the deity.

(3) Potharaju: Proxy husband who ties a mangalasutra around the neck of the girl who is to be made a jogin. He is the priest who officiates on behalf of the goddess at every function. He has a tuft of hair, a whip in his hand, wears kada around his wrist and chungru around the leg. It could be the potharaju the priest, the girl's maternal uncle, or the 'Pedda Goud' who is the leader of the Gouda caste, representing the dominant landed castes of the village. In some areas, older jogins themselves tie the mangalasutra. This

Potharaju system is a striking feature in Telangana and the potharaju performs 'Ora panduga' to appease the goddess.

Plate 2 Potharajus, traditional priests of Jogin system, are seen performing one of the ritual acts (1998).

Plate 3 Potharajus.

Potharaju is the brother of the Seven Matrikas or Seven Sisters. Bishop Whitehead says of him: "Potharaju is a mysterious person in the Telugu country, sometimes he is described as the brother, sometimes as the husband of the village goddess and sometimes as only an attendant". Sacrifice is never offered to him alone, but always in conjunction with one or more of the goddesses. It is a humiliating factor that potharaju has to be naked and wear neem leaves to cover his body. He is expected to wear the nerves of the buffalo which he has sacrificed. Some parts of the sacrificed buffalo are kept in his mouth. The animal's dung is kept in a basket which he has to carry. There is a risk to his life – he may get cancer, asthma, TB or other diseases.

(4) Funeral dances: The heinous practice of jogins in the Telangana region of Andhra Pradesh is reminiscent of the feudal system and a living example of exploitation of women in the name of custom and religion.

A detestable feature of the Jogin system is that jogins are expected to dance before the corpses of the feudal lords and collect the small change people throw on the corpses. At the mock funeral

Plate 4 A Jogin sister dancing before the dead body in Medak district (1990).

ceremony of a landlord, the author saw the jogins doing all sorts of gimmicks while dancing before the 'corpse'. For instance, a jogin picked up with her eyelids a 10 – rupee note a youngster had thrown at her. It is an amazing skill. How did they acquire this skill? This has come through the sanskritization process. Among devadasis, the skill was exhibited while dancing. Some of the dancers would pick up needles with their eyelids. In Eluru, a devadasi demonstrated this skill while being interviewed by the author.

(5) Gavupattu: During the initiation ceremony of jogins, all the jogins worship Yellamma in the shape of a stone decorated with flowers, turmeric powder and kumkum. While chanting mantras, the pujari with one bite separates the neck and body of a goat or lamb. This is known as Gavupattu.

During village festivals, a potharaju is called upon to kill a young lamb with his bare teeth. While doing so, he may lose his teeth or even life.

Plate 5 Animal sacrifice by Potharaju popularly known as 'Gavupattu'.

(6) Kolupulu: Kolupulu is performed for a period of seven days. If Kolupulu is not done, the whole village feels that Goddess Mathamma will get angry. It is believed that distresses or mishaps in the family are due to a visitation of the goddess and the remedy is to dedicate a girl in the family as 'jogin' or 'matamma' or 'basvi'.

The obsession to dedicate girls as jogins or matangis is so intense that even for petty causes the future of the girl is ruined. If there is an epidemic in the village, it is attributed to a lack of enough jogins or matangis in the village. Or if a village bull gets sick, one girl must be made a jogin or matangi to 'appease the goddess'. Even if some disease afflicts their crops, the first thought is to make one girl a jogin. The slightest pretext is enough to turn a good-looking girl from the Harijan community into a property of the village. They expect rain on the second day of Kolupulu. During the seven days of Kolupulu they have the following programmes:

(a)	Tuesday	:	Kapu Kattuta, i.e., the starting of festival.
(b)	Wednesday	:	They go to an ant-hill and recite the story of Yellamma or Mathamma.
(c)	Thursday	:	Saka Poyadam – design is done in the name of potharaju and Parasuram.
(d)	Friday	:	Meditation of Jamadagni and Parasuram's war with Renuka and preparation of Renuka's design.
(e)	Saturday	:	Design is drawn on Gauramma, reciting the story.
(f)	Sunday	:	Fire-walking by matangis and others.
(g)	Monday	:	Animal sacrifice.

The village purohit fixes an auspicious day for Kolupulu. The village spends Rs 30,000 to 50,000 on this festival.

Every year before the start of Kolupulu, a Pedda Golla ties mangalasutra around matamma's neck. Matamma is expected to dance. Pedda Reddy, the feudal lord, draws matamma towards him and she has to fall at his feet. It is the proud privilege of the landlord to do so. If there is no matamma in that particular village, a matamma from neighbouring village comes and plays this role and collects rice, money and sometimes a saree and blouse for performing Kolupulu. For this enjoyment, Reddies spend a huge amount of money. In the Matangi system, three people are important; they are the girl's maternal uncle, Pedda Madiga, who is an elderly person among Madigas, and Pedda Golla. Pedda Golla ties mangalasutra around the neck of each girl on the occasion of Kolupulu. Some people climb up the tree, shower lime fruits, incense and bandaru on the people below. The belief is that those on whose heads these things fall will be blessed with male issues and they will become wealthy and lead a comfortable life.

Matangi Chindulu (steps) is very important because the village will get rain and Mathamma rescues the people from diseases and wards off the evils. Matamma would dance wearing only neem leaves. Matammas come from Kodiyam bidu, Adavi Kodiyam bidu, Kota Katur, Jogi Kandriga and Pallamala villages. Matammas attending the Kolupulu give a dance performance.

(7) Jatara: The Lingampalli Yellamma jatara in Narayanapeta mandalam of Mahaboobnagar district is famous. People from Andhra Pradesh, Karnataka and Maharashtra attend this jatara. The devotees carry cocks, neem leaves and bonam pots and womenfolk go into a trance and begin to dance. The jatara takes place on a Tuesday. Thousands of people attend it. The devotees believe that if they worship the Yellamma of Lingampalli, their desires will be fulfilled. At least once in three years, the local people have to attend this festival. The role Baineedlu play is important in this jatara. Baineedlu are a dependent caste for Madigas. They recite the story of Yellamma. They propagate Saivism. These are known as Bhavanis, Baineedlu or Baindla people. They belong to a scheduled caste. They play the musical instrument Jamadika. They are pujaris and some of them are found in Nizamabad also.

Sayamma is a devotee of Yellamma. Smeared with turmeric powder from head to foot, she wears neem leaves, a garland and a

Plate 6 Jatara.

darshan (shell chain). Her mouth is sealed and she is taken around in a small procession in the temple itself. Then they go to the Parasurama temple and go round it three times.

The pujari of this temple carries the bonam pot. Sayamma follows him and every devotee tries to touch the seal on Sayamma's mouth. This is a trying situation for Sayamma. She is expected to perform a dance with a lighted lamp on her head. The devotees offer to the deity toddy, bonam, neem leaves, curd rice, brinjal curry and a liquid dish made with tamarind. Another noteworthy item of the programme is that a woman tied with a rope around her stomach is suspended in the air from a long wooden bar while the other end of the bar is bolted to a chariot to make five 'pradakshinas' around the temple. Other girls swing rhythmically in 'Sigam' in Telangana. This jatara used to attract curious visitors from Canada, England and the USA.

A similar jatara takes place at Janumpalli (once known as Polepalli) in Bommapeta mandalam. Just before Sivaratri, the girl or woman who is going to become a jogin does 'Sidi ekkadam' or pole-climbing. This, however, was stopped by 'Velugusamstha' and some other NGOs. There is another jatara on Janumpalli outskirts, in Koderu mandalam. It is known as Manthralamma jatara. Here, it is not a 'jogin' but a Kuruma pujari who does this work. In Polepalli, the girl sits in a basket whereas in Janumpalli she is tied with a towel to the pole. Neem leaves, turmeric powder and kumkum are thrown at the people. Violence takes place in the name of devotion to the goddesses. Some devotees hit themselves with iron rods. After pujari's Sidi is over, the devotees remove the loops from their bodies.

Mantralamma is the goddess of Yadavas. It is believed that she came from the Nallamalai forests and settled in Janumpalli. Another jatara known as 'Banda Yellamma' takes place in Kodangal.

(8) Darshan: Darshan is a cowry shell chain used by jogins, matangis and basvis. Its significance is that it is related to the Dravidian goddesses. There are two types of goddesses – benevolent and malevolent. To ward off evil spirits, worshippers of Yellamma and Mathamma use the cowry shell chain, neem leaves and incense. Yerukala women use the cowry shells and sing a hymn to goddesses such as Kanchi Kamakshi and Kasi Visalakshi.

A cowry shell symbolizes creative power as it comes from water and is therefore concerned with the fertility cult. Almost all the goddesses of India are fertility goddesses. There is an affinity between cowry shells and the goddesses. That probably is the reason why matangis, basvis and others use the cowry shells as necklaces. They, thus, serve both ritual and fertility purposes.

(9) Ant-hill: One of the characteristics of mother goddess is that she is located underneath the neem trees, and an ant-hill. Called Uppala Maisamma, she is worshipped as a snake. Posamma, Yellamma and Mathamma came out of the ant-hill. According to a legend, Jamadagni ordered his son Parasurama to kill his mother Renuka. After carrying out his father's order, Parasurama cut his own hand. While Renuka's head became a cobra, Parasurama's hand became an umbrella.

Grama devatas are known as the Seven Sisters (seven mathrikas). Devasena was the sister of Nageswara and the mother of Nagamata, Nagabhushana, Naga Bhushita and Naga Sai. Her youngest sister is Yellamma whose symbol is a snake. She is known as Nagarupini and Nagalokavasini.

Yellamma was born in an ant-hill and ant-hill is considered gold. She is adorned with different kinds of snakes such as Kodenagulu, Balanagulu, Kuntena Pamulu, Avula Masanu, Pinzarlu and Jerripotulu. When Yellamma came out of the ant-hill, the ant-hill was divided into two parts. There was nothing for her except Korra grain and so she went to Mamuralapatnam.

The father of Yellamma and Mathamma was Siva and the mother was Parvati. All goddesses are related to Siva and Parvati. Snake worship is considered to be the worship of Yellamma.

(10) The cult of Jogappa and Vaghya: The dedication of boys as jogappas was a practice prevalent in Karnataka. In the southern Maratha country, a eunuch dedicated to goddess Yellamma was known as Jogappa/Jogavva and Vaghya. In Maharashtra, vaghya is dedicated to Khandoba. It was a popular belief among eunuchs that they could regain their virility by dedicating themselves to the goddesses or gods. Those who were born as eunuchs or who were in some way malformed were dedicated to goddess Huligamma whose temple is on the left bank of the Tungabhadra river in Raichur in Karnataka. The eunuchs dress like women, carry on their head a circular basket, the centre of which is called kalisam, representing the goddess. The young eunuch to be dedicated is taken to the temple to the beats of the drum. He is then married to a sword and this constitutes his dedication to the temple. He is asked to stand on a heap of rice placed on a wooden board in front of the deity. In Hinduism, myths are centred on the concept of chastity and celibacy. Though there is some abnormality about a eunuch's role, yet on religious and ritualistic occasions his role is rationalized. The jogappas or vaghyas belong to outcaste communities. Dedication of male children to temples is in fulfilment of certain vows taken before the god concerned. In Andhra Pradesh, there is the Guravaiah tradition, the followers of which beat and wound themselves and sometimes behave as if they were the dogs of Mallanna (Siva). They drink milk like dogs and quarrel like dogs. Vaghyas in Maharashtra are also called Kalabhairavs and are regarded as the dogs of Khandoba. Vaghya, a mendicant dedicated to Khandoba, belongs to the Dhangar caste. Over his shoulders are a blanket and a chain, a pinch of turmeric powder and in his hands, a spear and a begging bowl. Thus, we have the Jogappa tradition in Karnataka and the Vaghya tradition in Maharashtra.

(11) Jagaran: Breaking of the chains represents a ritual which may offer some immediate relief and joy. A newly-wed couple goes to Vaghya Muralis at the Khandoba temple at Jejuri in Pune district of Maharashtra. It is immaterial whether the vaghya and murali are man and wife. They chant mantras and, with their help, the chain-breaking ceremony takes place. It is an auspicious occasion for the couple to be blessed by Vaghya Muralis on one hand and breaking the chains of bondage on the other.

(12) Jogipattam: It is the dedication ceremony of a girl or the marriage of a jogin girl to the goddess or local deity. This takes place when the girl is five or six years old. The girl does not know what is in store for her.

(13) Maila pattam: It is the consummation ceremony with the landlord or any person who undertakes to provide economic support for the girl's initiation into joginhood. He is the first person to be informed of the date of the ceremony. He sends gifts to the jogin girl.

The practice of dedicating young girls/women to deities has been prevalent throughout South India in some name or other. Invariably, these dedications were purportedly done for the common good of villages, such as averting a calamity or overcoming it. They often degenerated into various forms of ritualized and religiously sanctioned prostitution.

It is an age-old tradition in South India to dedicate young, innocent and illiterate women to the local deity. After the initial ceremony, the girl forfeits her right to marry and is condemned to a life of sexual slavery. After the second phase, she is passed on from one man to another and gradually becomes a 'public woman' in that village, earning a little more than subsistence wages from her patrons. This is nothing but sheer exploitation of the lower castes by the upper castes in the name of religious tradition. The practice persists in remote villages. "I went to school and passed my high school examination and did not want to join this profession (as potharaju) but the landlords put pressure on my father and so I had no choice but to join it", said Shankar, a potharaju of Nizamabad district.[2]

Superstitious and religio-cultural sanctions, such as the Jogin system, are being perpetuated. The hierarchies of the caste structure and their stronghold on the people play a prime role in this system. A mangalasutra made of yellow thread with two small leather tablets in the shape of the feet of the goddess has significance in the dedication ceremony. It varies from region to region. A notable feature of this system is that the girl dedicated to the goddess is not ostracized by society. She lives with her natal family and is integrated with the village community. It is estimated that 10 to 15 per cent of the girls are pushed into prostitution. However, there are no middlemen in this system.

The Jogin system gives us an insight into how the patriarchal ideology operates. The jogin, being a scheduled caste woman, is marginalized because of her caste and subordinated not only within the community but also outside it. She is bound, dominated and controlled by the dominant religious and caste superstructure and her own sub-caste plays an active role in perpetuating the system. It is a fact that patriarchal ideology binds all the castes together in their attitude towards women. Generally, the subordination of women is a part of the dominant brahmanical culture and though women of lower castes enjoy more freedom, they are an integral part of the Jogin system.

The institution of family plays an equally important role in such subordination. Superstitions, the lack of proper social security, lack of understanding and natural calamities compel the poor families to subordinate their own girls. Once the jogin or her counterparts are made, they have a crucial role and status in society. The changing mores and values and pathetic economic condition have made them vulnerable and degraded their status to that of mere prostitutes.

One of the major aims in the reform process is to ensure a life of dignity, self-respect and equality for the jogins. In order to eradicate the Jogin system and rehabilitate the jogins, awareness camps and health camps for both jogins and their children should be organized. Residential schools for the jogins' children and vocational training for the young jogins are required. Leadership qualities should be developed in these women. In the words of Hemalatha Lavanam,

> Burn this evil Jogin system to ashes,
> Belch fire at this wicked Basvi custom,
> Bury it unheard in the sands of time.
> Oh! Sister, Oh! Jogin, awake and arise.[3]

Notes

1. R. Venkata Subba Rao, ed., *Kamala's Letters*, Madras,1902, p. 19.
2. Potharaju is the instrument in making the girl as Jogin. Potharaju system is also followed in certain families. It is a hereditary post. Shankar wanted to study but, the feudal lords of Nizamabad district brought pressure on him. So he could not escape his duty.
3. After taking up the responsibility of Jogin's system in Nizamabad district of Andhra Pradesh, late Hemalatha Lavanam, a well-known reformer of Andhra Pradesh wrote a poem on Jogins in Telugu and she herself translated it into English. She is also the daughter of Gurram Jashua, a Dalit poet in Telugu literature.

CHAPTER 2

Historical Background

It is hard to say exactly when the Devadasi system started. There is no doubt that it originated in India and is probably as old as the hills. This can be traced to the matriarchal system which was in vogue in the entire Dravidian India.

Corresponding systems were prevalent in Southern Europe, Asia Minor, Egypt and Mesopotamia, etc. Herodotus, the Greek historian, wrote about the system of offering the chastity of women in the temple of Mylitta in Babylon. Lucian, the Roman writer, mentions a similar custom prevailing at Blus in Phoenicia. There was a goddess who resembled a fish from her waist downwards. There was a pond of sacred fish close by the temple of this nymph goddess. Women offered their hair to this goddess and those who did not like to give their hair were required to expose their bodies and submit themselves to the embraces of strangers in a public place throughout one full day. They were expected to spend the money earned during this process in the service of the goddess. The same practice was observed in Syria too. Likewise, the Argive maidens offered their hair to goddess. Megara women offered strands of their hair at the tomb of Iphinoe; women and youths in Doles offered their hair at the tomb of the Koruba maidens in the sanctuary of Artemis; at Titave near Corinth, the hair was offered to the goddess of health. At least one lock of hair was offered at Trojan by women in the temple of Hippolytus.

Offering hair to deities indicates the close relationship that exists between hair and fertility. The practice of offering hair to gods and goddesses is in vogue in many temples in South India. For instance, devotees, irrespective of sex, offer hair to Lord Venkateswara of

Tirupati. At the Dargah of Mirza Saheb at Nagore in Tanjore district of South India, even Hindu women offer their hair in fulfilment of their vow to the Muslim saint. A similar practice existed at the Phoenician colony of Sicily on the North African coast. In Syria, women prostituted themselves with certain religious motives. At the temple of Aaitos in Armenia, virgins of reputed families prostituted themselves, according to the prevalent custom. This was done in the name of the goddess. They were later married as there was no stigma attached to their act. In other regions like Phoenicia, Canaan, Paphos and Cyprus, the cult of the great Mother goddess was prevalent. She was known as Ashtart, Ashoreth and Astrate. Her attributes resembled those of Eshtar, the goddess of maternity, fertility and war. In Arabia, the cult of mother goddess was At hat or Al-Uzza, and her worship was accompanied by the system of divine prostitution. In Western Africa, young men and women dedicated or affiliated to a god are termed Kosio. Once they were dedicated, they were lost to their parents. A female child would become the wife of the god to whom she was dedicated and, hence, to prostitution. Such girls were given education and trained in dancing and they satisfied the sexual urges of the priests and inmates of male seminaries. In due course, they would become public sluts. Children born to these women belonged to the god. In India, these women were barred from marrying men because they were supposed to be the wives of the immortal husband, that is, god who has no death. So, there was no widowhood for them. Similar institutions existed in other parts of the world such as Peru, Mexico, Borneo and Japan.

On the basis of the prevalence of divine prostitution in several places, we can infer that:

- Man enjoys sexual pleasures; so, god also requires concubines. Women dedicated to god are expected to render divine duties.
- These are fertility goddesses under whose care grows vegetation. Women should assist the function of procreation performed in the temples.
- Sacrifices are essential to placate the goddesses. The most important thing in women is chastity. On account of this practice, dedication of girls and yielding to strangers in temples came into practice. Nagendra Kumar Singh, an anthropologist, says, "when human passions enter into rituals, the votaries and followers of deities or cults are of an excitable and considerably

temperamental, natural and climatic conditions instigating orgiastic activity. It is more probable that the religious part of the ritual plays a minor part."[1]

In the Devadasi system, a woman dedicated to a deity or a sacred object draws the attention of scholars and journalists, but they seem to lack a deeper understanding of the problem and how it affects human beings who comprise half of the universe and their status in society. Before trying to understand this custom, we must understand how this has come into the life of human beings.

'Devadasi' means a woman enslaved to the service of some deity or sacred object. This term is the feminine form of 'devadasa' which means a man who is enslaved for the service of a deity. Though the term 'devadasi' occurs in Sanskrit literature, this custom is not related to gods or goddesses. In South India, there was no temple associated with devadasi. In fact, there are some temples which have more than one devadasi attached to them to render several types of services to the deities.

Several factors are responsible for the origin of the Devadasi system. One of the factors is the demand of a few deities for the services of these women. Some devotees voluntarily offered services to the deities; but, an important factor that encouraged the practice of dedicating women was the dominance of the upper castes or rich people and their craving for extramarital relations. The war situation also drove these helpless women into enslavement. We have to probe these aspects of the origin of the custom.

Devadasi denotes a particular woman who is enslaved for religious work. Such enslaved women are known as 'Jogins', 'Matangis' and 'Basvis' in Andhra Pradesh; 'Basvis', 'Boyasanis', 'Rangasanis', 'Gangasanis', 'Huttukatti kondavalu', 'Kesabi', 'Harake Hottavalu', 'Devara sule' and 'Devadasis' in Karnataka; 'Muralis' in Maharashtra; 'Bhavins' in Goa and 'Thayammas' in Tamil Nadu. These terms differ from tradition to tradition and region to region. Therefore, many names have come into existence. These are dedications to different deities to render different services depending on the region.

Even now, girls are dedicated to different deities. Since this has come to the notice of the government, public and the media, the activity has become a bit specialized, secretive and mechanized. Awareness among the exploited groups also has brought about a change in the scenario. In order to have a discourse on the custom, we should have a deep understanding of the word 'dedication' itself.

To understand the problem of the relationship of a woman to god or goddess, it is very important to understand gender relations in any society. The rich tradition of 'bhakti' is very important for a human being, more so for women. As Uma Chakravarthi points out, "The descent movements of the sixth century BC had virtually accompanied the construction of a caste, class and gender-stratified social order". Here, a very important aspect is that what will be the possibility of salvation of women among all religious currents. Buddhism first denied space to women, later conceded it and provided institutional means to enable them to pursue their religious goals. The social dimensions of early Buddhism are discussed in an article published in *Manushi* in 1987. We can cite the examples of Andal, Avvaiyar, Karikalammaiyar (12th century) and Akka Mahadevi who had experienced bhakti or devotion to god. Avvaiyar lived in the Sangam period. She was born to a dalit woman Athy and a Brahmin by name Pagavani. She was the first abandoned child of her family and was adopted by a family of Panars whose traditional profession was singing and praising the king. She prayed to Ganesha, "only good things should emanate from my lips. Grant me the boon of birthlessness ..."[2]

She took to the life of a preacher and wrote thirteen books. Her brother Tiruvalluvar wrote *Tirukkural* comprising the perfect code of morals for the universal man as well as the state. These women of devotion protested against marriage to a mortal man and ended their life in that fashion. Like these people, in North India, Meera, a devotee of Krishna, broke the barriers and considered Krishna her husband and escaped from the earthly marital relations. Thus, these bhaktins were completely immersed in their devotion and became 'Nitya Sumangalis'. We can also cite the character of the pretty girl 'Girika' in Viswanadha Satyanarayana's great novel *Veyipadagalu* who identified herself with Venugopala Swami and joined him as a mortal wife.

The sixth century was notable in the areas of architecture, religion, culture and models of kingship. All these factors are closely linked to the evolution of Hindu temples and religious institutions in early South India. This period was one of Hindu revivalism through the bhakti tradition. This bhakti ideal of renunciation appealed to the people of all castes. Kalpana Kannabiran says that shift in the language of worship from Sanskrit to the vernacular created space for women to give expression to their creativity. In addition to Saivism and Vaishnavism, post-bhakti ritual incorporated folk deities into its pantheon like Murugan and Subrahmanya and, to some extent, even Krishna. The institutionalization of dedication of women to a life of service to god was a byproduct of the movement.

The Devadasi custom has a religious connection. The devadasi had a very prestigious status. Devadasis were sometimes drafted from leading or ruling families. They were called Kalavantulu, as they were good at singing and dancing. This custom gradually degenerated. For the sake of attaining Suryaloka, the kings or the rich people would buy girls from poor backward class families and dedicate them to the deity. Brahmanical culture was followed in the day-to-day rituals of the temple. According to the Vedas, there were four varnas (castes) and those who did not belong to any of the varnas of Panchamas were treated as untouchables. They were not allowed to draw water from the wells used by the upper castes and they were forbidden to walk in the same lanes when upper caste men and women were walking.

Let us quote the dalit poetry written by Sambuka:

> Do not use our corpses as raw materials to your politics.
> Don't speak standing amidst our corpses.
> Your walk commenced from one Karamchedu to another.
> Now it has reached Tsundur in a big way.
> The government's response to protests and reactions was only oral promises.
> Don't interfere in our lives unnecessarily,
> Let us not worry about these interventions, we are going to die as we like.

This is the humiliating situation they were facing in society. Among them, women were and are the most oppressed and highly exploited people. As B.R. Ambedkar said, women in dalit families are 'dalits among dalits', 'weakest among the weaker sex'.

The illiterate dalit women are forced to prostitute themselves and satisfy the needs of the landlords. The Hindu religion has legalized prostitution, exploiting a majority of dalit women in the name of Devadasi system. As 'maidservants of goddess', they are made to work as dancers, singers and prostitutes. A beautiful dalit woman is the target of attack. These women suffer on two counts – being dalit and being women.

Unfortunately, in our society, birth determines the status of an individual. That means the caste system operates on a principle of hierarchy and distinction-denial of public resources and the basic needs of life, differential punishments are given on the basis of caste restrictions imposed on dining and marriages. That is the main reason why the issue of violence against women cannot be seen as either a 'caste issue' or a gender issue. It is the foremost duty of all educated women to educate, organize and unite all deprived women to make them conscious of their rights and privileges. They should have sympathy towards undergraded professions like flesh trade, Devadasi system and beggary.

Human rights in the contemporary world are universal. They include the right to development, the right to education, the right to housing and the right to preserve cultural traditions which are the ingredients for democratic growth. The Constitution of India guarantees equal rights to all its citizens. These are embodied in the Universal Declaration of Human Rights. In a society such as ours, indivisibility and interrelated quality of human rights, whether civil, political, economic, social or cultural, is self-evident. This link is not strictly followed in respect of scheduled castes (SCs) and scheduled tribes (STs). These people, due to historical reasons, have been suffering from social, educational and economic disadvantages.

The establishment of an egalitarian social order, with equity for all sections of society, free from any kind of discrimination on grounds of religion, race, sex and place of birth, is the cherished goal of our nation. Equity for the weaker sections of society is the moving spirit of the constitutional schema. Unfortunately, SCs have been forced to occupy the sub-stratum of the traditional socio-economic structure of society. As B.D. Sharma puts it in his report on SCs and STs, "the goal of humanists and social workers has thus been to struggle for freedom vis-à-vis slavery, dignity vis-à-vis servitude and justice vis-à-vis injustice". In spite of accelerated development and prosperity, human being has still not reached the zenith.

In India or elsewhere, every day, the mass media is full of lurid descriptions of genocide, infanticide, dowry deaths, rapes, sexual harassments, female genital mutilations, women trafficking and sex-working of different kinds. In this background, we have to study the prevalence of religious prostitution. The devadasi custom has religious and ritual connections. Devadasis who were dedicated to the temples dedicated their daughters to the deity and if they did not have daughters, they adopted female babies and dedicated them to the temples. Very few rich people dedicated their daughters to the temple.

Dedication among the dalit castes has attained high visibility in the post-independence period. One reason is that before independence, the focus was on the freedom struggle; how to shake off the shackles of the colonial administration. Another reason is that these castes do not attach any stigma to the Devadasi system. To them, it is a social norm. The woman who is dedicated to a goddess will automatically become 'Nitya Sumangali' and she need not change her surname and the children born to her become members of the same genealogy. That child can claim the property of his/her father as a rightful son/daughter. After her dedication, she becomes, by established custom, the heir of her parent's property, and can perform their funeral rites as if she were a son. The children of hers belong to her father's family. The daughter becomes a basvi. This change can be seen in their families. In most cases, the girl is dedicated to the goddess before she attains puberty. Men are also dedicated to the deity, but it is altogether a different matter.

In the entire reconstruction of the devadasi tradition, an important aspect that has been left out of the analytical framework of power and the nature of control over the bodies of both men and women through history and connection between religion and the state is maintaining and perpetuating the control. This factor is very important because it is concerned with the nature of patriarchy as a form of dominance. The difference between men and women is that while the control of women involved a control over their sexuality, this is not the case with men. The definition of masculinity and feminity is not merely co-extensive with 'men' and 'women', but extends to every relation of superordination and subordination.

There are nine theories about the origin of the caste system. They are:

- Occupation or Mother Goddess Theory
- Sanskritization Theory
- Religious Tradition Theory
- Racial Theory
- Political Theory
- Matriarchy to Patriarchy Theory
- Lineage Continuity Theory

- Traditional Theory
- Theory of Divine Prostitution

(1) Mother Goddess Theory: According this theory propounded by Hulton (1945), groups which followed certain occupations have become the castes of today. Each occupational group has its own deity to whom the girls are dedicated. These deities have priestesses who negotiate with the nature gods and they, thus, established minor shrines to their caste deities and continued to dedicate girls to them. Society approved this relation since it saved the landlord from disgrace resulting from 'marrying' a woman from another group. It also did not amount to any commitments on his part towards the woman and children born to her out of this union. She is dedicated to an immortal being but she should have a human husband and the landlord served this purpose. This is not regarded as prostitution; it is their belief, their tradition and their devotion to the particular deity.

(2) Sanskritization Theory: This theory posits that the process of sanskritization continued even for the non-sanskritized shrines. Even the dedication to mother goddesses got sanskritized. The Brahmin priests with the help of the ruler or the landlord created myths that these goddesses were the consorts of male deities. As a result, for some generations, the two will exist side by side. The impact of the Devadasi system of the upper castes is felt by the Devadasi system of the lower class as when sanskritization reached a particular level, the religious functionaries started making use of these traditions because they were advantageous for them. Hence came the resultant degradation of the goddesses and the tradition. As the woman in a patriarchal society slipped to the secondary position, the status of goddesses also came down and the priestesses virtually became divine prostitutes.

(3) Religious Tradition Theory: When these unfortunate, illiterate ignorant women went to the shrine with problems like health, poverty, barrenness, the priests would tell them that it was due to the wrath of the deity and that they could appease her only by dedicating a girl from their family to her. The priests would convince them that the whole village would suffer if that girl refused to be dedicated to the deity. They would begin to chant mantras and press their claims. These castes belonged to the Little Tradition and their life was intertwined with these priests, and the landlords give their consent to dedicate their daughter to the goddess. After their initiation, in course of time, the divine prostitute would become a public slut.

(4) Racial Theory: Propounded by Risely (1981), this theory says that during the colonial administration, the officers required local women for their sexual pleasure. The officials would persuade the parents of the girls to dedicate them to goddesses so that they could use these girls. In the name of divine prostitution, no damage was done to the society but the poor dalit women were exploited. Everybody had a right on her body because she belonged to the deity. Patriarchal control continued to prevail and the women served the dominant castes.

(5) Political Theory: When there was a war, the soldiers were not expected to take their life partners with them. In Karnataka, the soldiers belonged to a warrior group known as Nayaka. They did not impose any restrictions on their women-folk as they were not sure of coming back without some disability or other. As a custom, these women were dedicated to the local goddess, sent to the warriors to serve them sexually and provide them with food and render other services. Again, their girl children were dedicated to the deity of their castes. The tradition continued in some way or the other, the victims being the dedicated girls.

(6) Matriarchal and Patriarchal Theories: In the temple dancer's system, matriarchy plays a dominant role. As the father is not known, the mother who is a devadasi dedicates her daughter to the same temple. But, indirectly, the purohit, the landlord or the elder male member in the family, maternal uncle or Pedda Golla, plays a significant role in the dedication ceremony. These people who are supposed to safeguard the village actually become responsible for the degradation of the particular girl into divine prostitution.

The women or girl children remain in the service of the deity as long as they want to maintain their virginity. However, financial position and biological instincts force them to lose their virginity. In course of time, the rulers of the land or the affluent landlords claim these girls as their concubines. All the same, the practice of dedicating the girls continues. But, instead of the immortal husband, mortal husbands began to play a dominant role.

(7) Lineage Continuity Theory: This is a son-preference theory. In other words, if the parents have no male issue to continue their line, they would take a vow that they would dedicate one of their daughters to the goddess or god so that they may have a male issue. That means that the girl who is chosen to a life of shame contributes to the continuance of lineage.[3]

(8) Traditional Theory: Just as Indra the god used to have celestial women like Rambha, Urvasi, Menaka and Tilothama for his pleasure, the lords on earth wanted beautiful girls for their pleasure. This tradition was followed throughout the length and breadth of this nation.

(9) Theory of Divine Prostitution: No evidence has been found to prove that religious prostitution existed in ancient India. Some scholars, however, claim that certain images carved in second and third century temple-like structures suggest that there was religious prostitution. The images were sculpted by Devadinna who was in love with a dancer called Sutanuka.

In a number of icons and figurines of the Indus Valley civilization around Harappa and Mohenjodaro, phallic emblems were found at Quetta. Worship of the mother goddess associated with the bull form was also discovered. Bull worship was quite common in the earlier civilizations. In ancient Persian religion, the 'primal bull' was regarded as the representative of the soul of the world, a generating power to maintain the whole world. Brefault called this the 'lunar bull', and it was the supreme deity.

An interesting discovery was a bronze 'dancing girl' figurine showing a naked woman bedecked with ornaments with the hair done in an altogether different fashion and standing in a provocative posture. As Basham says, "... This dancing girl is a representative of temple dancers who existed in contemporary Middle Eastern civilization and this became an important feature of Hindu culture ... later on".[4] These naked or half-naked figurines represent the mother goddess and each household maintained such icons. The worship of mother goddess is a feature of Dravidian culture. There is a similarity between the Indus valley civilization and South Indian culture. Those who studied the script of Indus valley civilization came to the conclusion that the Indus people spoke a primitive form of Tamil.

Although there is a mention of a dancing girl in the *Rigveda*, there is no evidence to suggest that there was religious prostitution in that period. There were institutions like Samana, Goshti and Sabha which provided scope for free love. There are no clear references to prove the prevalence of temple dancers. The custom of the association of dancing girls with temples is unknown to Jataka literature. Vatsyayana's *Kamasutra* (AD 250) dealt with courtesans only.

In Kalidasa's *Meghadoot*, there are references to dancing girls in the 'Mahakala temple' of Ujjain. *Bhavishya Purana* suggests that the sure way of going to Suryaloka is by dedicating girls to temples, especially to a 'Sun' temple (Altekar, A.S.). There are more such references from the twelfth century onwards. During Muslim invasions, many temples were destroyed in North India and this affected the religious practices of Hindus. Abul Fazl's well-known work *Ain-e-Akbari* mentions 'Shaitanpurah' or 'Devil's Villa'. In North India, instances of dedicating dancers to temple are rare.

The origin of divine prostitution in India may be understood in the background of the early medieval socio-economic formation. Worship of the deity and the religious services rendered by temple dancers were an integral part of that period. Construction and renovation of temples reached its zenith in the tenth and eleventh centuries.

The custom of temple dancing was an integral part of the ritual service to gods and goddesses. Lands were given to Brahmins, religious institutions and officers of state and temple servants. Coinciding with this land transfer was the growth of bhakti movement, which led to temple-building activities. As R.S. Sharma says, "With the puja was interlinked the doctrine of bhakti or complete self-surrender of the individual to his God ...".[5] This movement provided opportunity to the worshippers of all castes to serve the god and aspire for liberation. Service to gods could be of several forms. It might be by building a new temple, renovating old ones, sweeping, washing, weaving of garlands, lighting the temple lamps, singing and dancing for entertainment.

In addition to this, women could be dedicated to gods to become their consorts. These women called 'Nitya Sumangalis' were and are invited to all functions as 'sacred women'. The preaching of Nayanar saints also gave a fillip to temple construction. Tirumular was a great champion of the temple culture. All these factors created a favourable atmosphere for temple construction in South India.

We shall now see how religious prostitution became popular among the lower strata of society. The dedication ritual among the 'untouchable' communities is on a totally different footing. Dedication of the minor girls takes place among the devadasi community. The devadasis dedicate either their girl child or adopt a girl from the poorer strata of society and dedicate her to the temple. A significant characteristic of the institution of dedication among the so-called SCs is that these girls are dedicated to goddesses instead of gods. It is a Dravidian tradition. Dedication among these castes became noticeable in the post-independence period.

Dedication to goddesses is rampant in Karnataka, Maharashtra, Andhra Pradesh, Tamil Nadu and Goa. In Karnataka, the untouchables are divided into four sub-castes: Samagars, Dhors, Madars and Holers. This classification is based on occupation. Scavenging was a caste obligation of the Holers and Madars; the Samagars tanned the hides of animals and the Dhors were cobblers.

Likewise in Andhra, we have Malas and Madigas; but there are several sub-sections among them. There is no marital relationship or sharing of food between these people. It is interesting to know that in Andhra Pradesh, there is a parallel caste system. This comprises main castes and dependent castes. Madigas who are at the lower rung of the hierarchical structure of the caste system have six or seven dependent castes – dependent not in the sense that they literally depend on these people, but they have a right to claim anything from the main caste whenever they require. They cannot have marital relations with the main caste and they are forbidden to enter the portals of the houses of the main castes. These dependent castes are the carriers of culture. They are the real artists, rendering real service in the rural sector. Those are Dekkalas, Chindu Madigas, Baineedlu, Kinneras, Nulaka Chandiahs and Mastis.

Dekkalas are experts in enacting Jambapuranam with the help of palm leaves and other objects. No curtain is used in this play. All actors and musicians sit on the stage. A peculiar feature is that only men take part in the performance and women are not allowed. That may be because of the patriarchal values they have in the day-to-day life or they would like their womenfolk to look after the family.

The second caste is known as Chindu Madigas. They recite the stories of the *Ramayana*, the *Mahabharata* and *Bhagavatam* and prepare their own versions on the basis of plays already available in the market. That means they make minor changes before enacting any play. There are many melams (a group of people combined together to perform a play is known as a melam) among them and there are two varieties based on their dress pattern. Chindula Yellamma was a great actress and her role as Yellamma on the last day of the camp was superb. As an expression, 'Yellamma character' suggests a woman of loose character; the melams have changed this pattern and include their own family women to avoid bad reputation for their performances.

The third caste is known as Baineedlu or Bhavanis. These people perform the Devi Puja in the Madiga community. The Bhavanis who play the Jamidika in their performances are called Jamukulavallu and the stories they narrate are called Jamukula Kathas. Baineedlu means those who sing songs in praise of Bhavani in jataras and wander from place to place. Their names differ from region to region. In Godavari, Krishna and Guntur districts, they are called Jamukulavaru; in Nellore district, they are called Baineedlu or Bainatis; and in the Rayalaseema region, they are called Asadivaru. In Matangi Kolupulu, while the Baineedlu recite the story, the Kommuvaru blow the conch.

The fourth caste is known as Kinneravaru. Kinnera is a beautiful musical instrument made from bottle gourd or 'Sorakaya'. Kinneras are experts in playing this instrument. Hence, they are known as Kinneravaru.

Lastly, there are Nulakachandiahs who are the gurus of the Madiga community. They are adept at reciting Jambapurana.

All these dependent castes of Madigas are performers and they are concerned with the Yellamma culture and the country is rich only because of its myriad art forms and their vibrancy despite the changing trends of the modern world. But the pity is that all these performing artists are 'untouchables among untouchables'. The problem of 'untouchability' is not limited to the SCs; there is untouchability among the tribals also. That means the hierarchical structure is universal in India and we must, therefore, fight all forms of untouchability wherever we see it.

Ritual dancing as part of religious services in a temple has a long history. In India, this practice originated during the early medieval period; but in countries like Mesopotamia, Egypt and Greece, the system flourished several thousand years earlier. In Egypt, temples of Osiris and Isis were crowded with dancing girls. At Corinth, in Greece, we find thousands of women associated with the temple of Aphrodite. The custom was prevalent in Babylonia, Cyprus and other countries as well. In Sumer, beautiful women were attached to every temple. In Babylonia, these women were attached to the temple of Ishtar. In the Babylonian and Assyrian literature, goddess Ishtar has been depicted as a naked woman which indicates that the fertility culture prevailed there.

The same culture is evident in the Alampur temple of Mahboobnagar district of Andhra Pradesh and the Yellamma temple in Shimoga district of Karnataka. It is a pointer to the existence of sacred prostitution. In this context, woman is equated with earth, the logic being that just as land gives us fruits – when we plough it and sow the seeds, so does a woman give birth to children. Woman is also equated with nature – she ploughs the land and sows the seeds, and the yield is plentiful. Also, like the earth woman has great patience. It can, therefore, be inferred that wherever there is a naked icon, it is indicative of the fertility cult.

Among many savage races on the earth, Yellamma is spiritualized as female valour. Some scholars are of the view that this represents a survival from the matriarchate. The first division of labour was between men and women. Women were the first potters, basket weavers and agriculturists. According to D.D. Kosambi, "the cattle are inherited in the male line, being herded by men, while the land is inherited in the female line."[6] Several ethnic groups preserved these mythologies in their oral traditions, centred on gods and goddesses. The mythology, the ritual of Ulka Peddamma (Kurnool district) unfolds some more facts of social, economic and cultural landscape of Andhra.

The worship of the village deity (Gramadevata) forms an important part of the conglomerate of religious beliefs, customs and ceremonies which are generally classed together under the term Hinduism. In almost every village and town of South India, we find the worship of Gramadevatas. All these deities have some common features. Romila Thapar points out that "each village had to protect itself against warring chiefs, plundering raids and cattle-lifting, specially under conditions of environmental duress in the semi-arid dry-farming-cum-pastoral regions of the Deccan."[7]

The village deities and their worship are vastly different from the popular Hindu deities in the sense that:

- they symbolize local history;
- the village deities, with very few exceptions, are female. A notable feature of Dravidian culture was the worship of the female principle in nature. Often, there are no temple

structures, and when these existed, they were simple, enshrining within them rough stones representing the 'amma' or 'mother' sacred to that village. After the advent of Aryans, female deities were relegated to a subordinate position;

- the village deities were almost universally worshipped with animal sacrifices. Buffaloes, sheep, goats, pigs and fowls were freely offered to them, sometimes in thousands; and
- the pujaris, i.e., the priests who performed the ritual were not Brahmins, but drawn from all other castes (including SCs). Sometimes, males dressed themselves as females and performed puja. In addition to these deities, the worship of ancestors was an important feature of the old Dravidian religion, common all over South India.

The names of village deities are a legion. However, in all parts of South India, the Seven Sisters are the most prominent among Dravidian deities. They are known as Saptamatrikas. For example, the names given in Nellore and Prakasam districts are Poleramma, Ankamma, Muthyalamma, Dillipolasi, Bangaramma, Matamma and Renuka. They have a younger brother by the name of Potharaju. Worship of Seven Sisters is typical of the Dravidian worship; Ekavira. Nangamma, Hemalamma, Mahuramma and Matangamma are the common names of the same deity. Also known as Ellamma, Ellammal, Ellamma talli. (derived from 'ella' meaning all, 'amma' meaning mother, the mother of all) and Sarvamba or Jagadamba, the deity is revered as Adishakti.

Shrines of Ellamma are found everywhere in South India. She is represented in a sitting posture with two right and two left hands, a very fair skin and a very bright face. On her head is a crown with a serpent lying over it. Many serpents dwell in her pagodas. People invoke her help in driving away the serpents. In one raised right hand, she has a small drum (damaru) around which a serpent is entwined. In one uplifted left hand, she has a trident and in the other a noose, and in the other severed head of a Brahmin.

According to another legend, Ellamma was the reincarnation of Renuka, the wife of Jamadagni. Renuka and her sister Satya were the nieces of sage Viswamitra. Kartavirya, the Hyhaya king, belonged to the clan of Yadus who were of a foreign extraction. They ruled parts of western India comprising the present Maharashtra, Karnataka and Kerala. Polygamy was prevalent in these areas. In Soundatti of Hubli district of Karnataka, there are two separate temples of Renuka

Yellamma and Satya. People go to Satya after taking a bath in the pond. They then visit the Yellamma temple. Nowhere else in South India do we come across a separate temple for Satya. The original legend of the beheading of Renuka must have arisen from some historical incident, for it is found in Mahabharata, the Bhagavatapurana, Padmapurana and Agnipurana.

According to a legend, when Parasurama beheaded Renuka, the head fell in the house of a Mala and the trunk fell in the same place. In the same stroke, Parasurama unwittingly cut the head of a pariah woman. These heads were said to have been interchanged. Another legend says that Parasurama placed by mistake the head of the pariah woman on the body of Renuka, and that in consequence, Jamadagni did not recognize her as his wife. Here, the author has observed that while Soundatti Yellamma (in her full form) is worshipped by non-Brahmins, Renuka Yellamma of Chandragutti is worshipped by both upper castes and lower castes. In the Tulu country (part of today's Karnataka), Goddess Kali goes by the name of Yellamma and it is a peculiar coincidence that in most Kali temples Parasurama is worshipped in a special shrine. This legend is an offshoot of the sanskritization process.

Yellamma is Renuka and the latter is identified with Ekavira as mentioned in Vallabhamatya's *Kridabhiramam*:

> Mandapakanu, Benupaka, Mahuram
> Nagavanamuna Bolasa Navicheninthi,
> Yoruganti Vasimche Nilotpalakshi,
> Kakatammaku Saidodu Ekavira

and in the same stanza the poet writes

> Jamadagni garapu satiki saranu.[8]

The glory of Ekavira is sung at Warangal by Malas who hail her as a woman of their caste. Her shrine is at Mahuram and is, therefore, known as Mahuramma. In the Rayalaseema region, Yellamma is known as Nangammadevata and in Tamil Nadu as Hemalamma. Nangamangalam, a village in Chittoor district of Andhra Pradesh, is the storehouse of folk traditions and folk songs. The theme of the songs sung by village girls during the death ceremonies is the Nangamma episode.

As already mentioned, at Alampur in Mahaboobnagar district of Andhra Pradesh, two naked images of the mother goddess are found. They are generally called Nagnakabandha (naked torso). In the Alampur image, the headless torso with legs wide apart is that of Lajjagauri, the goddess of fertility, known in the Little Tradition as Yellamma in the Deccan. In the Great Tradition, the goddess is related to the Parasurama-Renuka episode and is a consequence of Sanskritization.

Historically, as Nagarjunakonda evidence reveals, the goddess of the Little Tradition was patronized by the Ikshavaku rulers and accepted by the society. The stone image of the goddess was housed in a temple and the queen and her family worshipped her (*Epigraphica of Indica,* Vol. XXIX, 137). The same nudism can be traced back to ancient Babylonia, Greece and Egypt. Siva himself is a Digambara, so Saivism and, most probably, Jainism also contributed to some extent to this nudism. Maremanda Rama Rao (Andhra historian) says, "Ekavira must have been a Jain goddess who later became a Saiva goddess."

Thus, the Shakti cult has been an important religious component of the Indian civilization since time immemorial. The Yogini culture, a form of Shakti cult, made its appearance in the religious history of Orissa in the early medieval period. There were 264 Yogini temples in Orissa. This mysterious cult was, therefore, a strange amalgamation of Shaktism, Saivism and Buddhism.

Next to Yellamma, there are other deities like Ulagamma, Sunkalamma in the Rayalaseema region of Andhra Pradesh and Karnataka. Basvis of both the states attend the Jataras and festivals of Ulagamma. Some girls are dedicated to Murugan and some are dedicated to Hanuman temples. In Maharashtra, there is Khandoba to whom Muralis are dedicated and in Andhra Pradesh, there is one China Obulesu to whom some Basvis are dedicated.

Khandoba and China Obulesu are pastoral gods. God Mallanna of Andhra Pradesh and Mailar of Karnataka are closely related to Khandoba. The Khandoba cult included all five of the components: (i) the work and the teaching of the Brahmanas; (ii) asceticism and renunciation; (iii) tribal religion; (iv) folk religion; and (v) bhakti. In Karnataka, 'Mailar' is called Murukan. Khandoba may be traced to a prototype of a god found all over the Deccan from very early times. Like Rudra and Bhairava, Khandoba has protective functions. The predominant element in the origin of Murukan and

Khandoba is the worship of the mountain in the forest tracts by hill tribes or pastoralists.

The origin of the god may also be found in the worship of the ant-hill, the seat of snakes, in which form the god may also appear. The ant-hill is the characteristic of forest. The horse of Khandoba is also important all over the Deccan. The special devotees, the Vaghyas, are dedicated to the god's service in fulfilment of a vow for a child. They consider themselves the dogs of the god.

Khandoba is called the lord of the mountains. His two wives, Banu and Mhalsa, always quarrelled with each other. During festivals, when the Lord is on duty, i.e., in his temple, both join together to celebrate the festival of Diwali, and the Kaminis (erotic women) become Yoginis (female Yogis). A representation of Khandoba on the rear wall of the sanctum of the temple at Jejuri shows the Lord as Martanda Bhairava, the form he assumed when he battled the demons. For such a god, the pastoral people dedicate their daughters and they are named Muralis. A Murali wears round her neck a small band of black cloth to which are sewn seven cowries. These cowries are quite common to all the divine prostitutes, devadasis, matangis and basvis. These Muralis had the same custom and lead a life of shame, supporting their old parents with their earnings. As a poet said, "Of all sad words of tongue or pen, The saddest are these, 'it might have been'".

Muralis are girls dedicated to Khandoba, an incarnation of Siva. This custom is confined to the Marathi country, except the Konkan. It has its counterparts under different names in other states of South India as Jogins, Matangis, Basvis and Bhavins. The headquarters of the worship of Khandoba is Jejuri in Pune district and there is another place of worship called Pali in Satara district.

There is a three-foot-high stone column and at the head of it is cut a filthy design. This is called Yeswantrao, to whom poor deluded women promise to sacrifice their first-born daughters thinking that Khandoba will make them mothers of many children. The parents do not feel ashamed to take the earnings of those girls because they belong to Khandoba. The devotees do not consider it a sin. Kunbis, Mahars, Mangs and other low castes make their daughters Muralis in this manner.

In Karnataka, there is the Devadasi custom wherein a girl child is dedicated to Yellamma. Devadasi means a woman enslaved for the service of some deity or sacred object. At present, there is not even a single village where girls are not dedicated to some god or goddess. A virgin is expected to offer her virginity to the deity.

Dedication of a girl as a divine prostitute definitely helps commercial prostitution, in the sense that it provides license for prostitution with religious sanction. There is no stigma attached to it. The derogative nature of their profession attains respectability as they are supposed to be performing auspicious functions. This culture is prevalent in Belgaum and Gulbarga areas of Karnataka. Legislation and rehabilitation programmes have so far made little progress. Officials and non-government agencies have to work to curb this culture.

The outcome of an ethnographic survey of Bombay was a monograph titled 'Bhavins and Deviles'. This deals with the ceremonies and lifestyles of certain divine prostitutes in the Maharashtra region. In Ratnagiri and Kanara districts and Savantvadi, a particular non-Brahmin caste is known as 'Deviles' or 'Naiks' and the women are known as 'Bhavins' or 'Naikins'. These are dedicated to local gods. The dedication procedure is very simple. Non-Brahmin women become 'Bhavins' simply by pouring oil on their heads from the god's lamp in the temple. When a bhavin girl attains puberty, she has to undergo a kind of marriage known as Sesha. The bridegroom is a representative of the temple. On an auspicious day, a puja is performed at the girl's residence. A few temples have more than one devadasi attached to them to render service to gods and goddesses. Though it is a custom, the ultimate aim of the dominant sections of society is to use these girls as sex objects. The girls who are dedicated to goddesses are known by different names – 'Basvi', 'Boya Sani', 'Ranga Sani', 'Ganga Sani', 'Muttu Katti Kondavallu', 'Kasabi', 'Haraka Hottavolu' and 'Devara Sule'. There are regional differences between one tradition and another and from one caste to another.

There is an outcry that the devadasi custom has degenerated. However, some others say that the custom has been rejuvenated after the advent of independence. There is continuity in this activity, but it has become a bit specialized, secretive and mechanized. Women have been exploited in many ways in the name of age-old customs and traditions. The idea of dedicating something to the gods to get a boon or to ward off evil effects existed in the past in all societies and at all times, irrespective of the nature and composition of the society. Hindus are known for their unflinching belief or devotion to supernatural beings.

Till recently, offering of human blood to the deities was common. The sacrifice of a human being has been banned.

A Bhavin's temple duties are confined to sweeping the floor, sprinkling it with fresh cow dung and waving the fly-whisk before the god. She is then allowed to practise prostitution. The difference between the temple dancers and Bhavins is that a Bhavin is forbidden to dance either in the temple or in public. The 'deviles' blow horns and trumpets morning and evening. The daughters of Bhavins are married to the sons of other Bhavins.

In Tamil Nadu, the Mariamma cult is still very popular in almost all districts. The author found that in many temples of Mariamma, the Brahmanical tradition is adopted. Only in one village near Tanjavur, the dalits have their own temple where the girls are dedicated to that god. Generally, in Tamil Nadu, because of various social problems and due to the anti-Brahmin movement, dedication has been stopped to a great extent, although erotic dances are performed at some places. In the next chapter, we will discuss more about gods and goddesses to whom girls are dedicated.

Notes

1. Nagendra Kr. Singh, *Divine Prostitution*, A.P.H. Publishing Corporation, Delhi, 1997.
2. Akka Mahadevi was a devotee of Ganesha. She prayed the ganesha to give her chance of being born as a human being. *Manushi*, Delhi, 1987.
3. P.V. Mahale, *Sanskrutigalalli Sampradaya* (Devadasi Tradition in Different Cultures), Karnataka, 1987.
4. A.L. Basham, *The Wonder That Was India*, New York: Grove Press, 1954. Cited in Nagendra Kr. Singh, *Divine Prostitution*, A.P.H. Publishing Coroporation, New Delhi, 1997, p. 11.
5. R.S. Sharma, cited in Nagendra K. Singh, *Divine Prostitution*, p. 39.
6. D.D. Kosambi, *An Introduction to the Study of Indian History*, Popular Prakashan Private Limited, Bombay, 1975; p. 23.
7. Cited in V. Lalitha, "Yellamma Worship – Village Deity: A Case Study of Jogins in Andhra Pradesh", Proceedings of Andhra Pradesh History Congress, Warangal, 1990.
8. Vallabhamatya's *Kridabhiramam* mentioned about the places of Yellamma as Mandapaka, Benupaka, Mahuram and Nagavanamu, Bolasa, Yoruganti wherein the latest place she is called Ekavira. Yellamma or Renuka is the wife of Sage Jamadagni. This is a prayer song.

CHAPTER 3

Dedication to Gods and Goddesses

Lajja Gauri

Striking images of certain Indian goddesses are referred to as the shameless women, 'the nude squatting goddess', 'the mother goddess',[1] etc. There are more than twenty-five names of goddesses and among them are Aditi, Lajja Gauri, Renuka and Nagna Kabandha. The best-known images of this goddess have a female torso and a lotus flower in place of the head, while her legs are bent up at the knees and drawn up in a pose like one of 'giving birth to a child' or 'self-display', but we cannot call her by one name. Her names vary from state to state and district to district.

Lajja Gauri, in artistic and conceptual ancestry, descends from a group of ancient and popular symbols like lotus and purna kumbha or brimming pot. This according to the scholar like H.D. Sankalia can be traced back to the Indus valley art of 2500–1500 B.C.

Though Lajja Gauri was obviously a popular goddess throughout India, her religious function remains unilluminated by commentaries or any developed set of rites of worship. The artists creating images of Lajja Gauri drew on various ancient symbols such as fortune and fertility symbols.

These Lajja Gauri figures are auspicious, beatific rather than erotic. They are meant to ward off evil. Many images of Lajja Gauri have been published and she is described as a 'mother goddess', a 'nude squatting goddess', or 'a displayed female'. An article by Stella Kramrisch in 1956 related to the physical form of one such image in the Alampur Museum. Sankalia called her a 'shy woman'. The description of Lajja Gauri as a 'shameless woman' is a 'mistranslation and a misnomer'. Lajja Gauri means an innocent goddess. 'Lajja' denotes modesty. It is a manifestation of Parvati, Siva's consort.

An inscribed marble image of Lajja Gauri was discovered atop Nagarjunakonda in 1940. Several Chalukyan images are still worshipped in some temples like the Lakulisa temple at Siddhanakolla and Bala Brahma temple at Alampur in Mahaboobnagar district of Andhra Pradesh. At Alampur, Lajja Gauri is known as Renuka. The Naganatha kolla Lajja Gauri is similar to the one at the Bala Brahma temple in Alampur. There is a large Lajja Gauri fragment at the site of Mahakuta, near Badami in Karnataka.

Similar Lajja Gauri statues are found in Osmanabad district of Maharashtra (3rd–4th century), Ahmednagar, Paunar, Ramatola (Maharashtra); Sannati, Siddheshwara temple in Gulbarga and Belgaum (Karnataka) Bhita and Allahabad (Uttar Pradesh), Sanchi, Bundelkhand and Rewa (Madhya Pradesh); Nagarjunakonda, Kudavelli, Sangameshwara temple, Yellala, Bhavansi and Alampur (Andhra Pradesh); and Datasuram-chakrayi temple in Tanjavur district of Tamil Nadu.

Plate 7 Mother Goddess: The configuration of the purnakumbha, bearing an inscription of the time of Ehuvala Camtamula.

The big number of Rashtrakuta style of Lajja Gauri images at Kudavelli indicates the continued worship of the mother goddess. Images of Lajja Gauri were rarely made after the eighth century and not made at all after the twelfth century anywhere in India, but the worship of the goddess continues in some temples.

Among the names scholars and village folk use to refer to Lajja Gauri are: Anantha Devi, Nagnamata, Kumkana, Aditi, Renuka, Elaba, Yellamma, Kotvi, Prithvi, Belam Kallachema, Nagna Kabandha, Verul, Kamalamukhi, Kamala Gaurima, Kamala Gangamma, Mahakundalini, Adyashakti, Jogulamba, Matangi, Maria, Mahuramma, Ekavira, Yamabai, Yamai, Vyaghreswari, Sang and Sakambari. These names are descriptive of her physical aspects. Nagna Kabandha means 'nude, headless body' (Nagna means nude and Kabandha means torso). Sakambari is a fertility goddess, associated with harvest. Yellamma (goddess of the boundary), Yellala, Yellesvara, Elapura, Alapuri, Alampur and Hamlapuri are all interrelated. Originally, she was worshipped as a Gramadevata. Her main function was to grant family well-being. But from the fourth century onwards, her association with Siva reveals that she was elevated to the status of Parvati. All the ancient sites where images of Yellamma or Lajja Gauri were found were fertility worship centres.

Dhere, the historian, suggests that the name of the famous site Ellora or Eluva, may have been derived from Elapura and Ellamma and that Yellamma is a name of the goddess, who is also known as Lajja Gauri. Dhere explains that a verul or pot was worshipped in South India from ancient times as a symbol of 'Yoni' or womb, which later came to be recognized as a form of the goddess, and that verul is a symbol of Renuka who is the Yoni of Prithvi (earth). The pot, signifying water, is therefore associated with fertility.

The association of Lajja Gauri with Ganesha in the iconographic images is more common in Andhra plaques than in other places. Ganesha, the remover of obstacles, is a son of Siva and Parvati. The association of Lajja Gauri with Ganesha further supports other Saivite association of this goddess. A snake is carved directly below the goddess.

The significance of the lion face is ambiguous. It could represent Kirthimukha, the vehicle of the goddess. The conch, likewise, probably represents Vishnu or it may be an emblem of the goddess as symbolic of water and thereby denoting fertility. Except this in all other figures, Lajja Gauri has association with Siva.

Lajja Gauri's head is either lotus or human, her Uttanapad pose is less stressed in images and she is represented as an equal to the other gods by her equal size.

The concept of fortune underlies the meaning of the forms of Lajja Gauri, specifically as the goddess of fertility and reproduction In Indian art, the lotus is the symbol of fortune, fertility and reproduction. Also, the lotus is associated with ideas of purity and perfect wisdom. It is not surprising, therefore, that many gods and goddesses are depicted with the lotus as their abode, seat or throne.

The extension of the torso to include breasts, and a fully blossomed lotus for head, may have been inspired by purna kumbha.

Yakshas are nature deities, worshipped since vedic times. These are also associated with the fertility cult. The frog as a fertility charm surely is derived from a universal observance of its fertility.

Whatever may be the form, the importance lies in her role as goddess of creative power. Her Uttanapad pose, her purna kumbha ancestry and her lotus head suggest this meaning. Lajja Gauri may have originated on either a tribal or local village level as gramadevata with a pot serving as her original form.

Lajja Gauri entered the Hindu pantheon with minor status. As a mother goddess, she was worshipped for fertility. Thus, the earliest fertility cult icon transformed into a benevolent goddess through the sanskritization process during the 3rd–5th centuries, Lajja Gauri taking the place of Parvati in the sculpture. This is a very important aspect.

Gauri, as a manifestation of Parvati, includes Umå, Rambha, Totala, Tripura and Sri. Another traditional explanation wrongly identifies Lajja Gauri as Renuka.

We will now study in detail how these two names, Renuka and Yellamma, are linked.

Yellamma Tradition

Yellamma is believed to be the incarnation of Renuka, the mother of Parasurama. The central place of the Yellamma tradition in Karnataka is Soundatti and in Andhra Pradesh, Orugallu where the Kakatiya kings reigned. In the story of Parasurama, there is a mention of Yellamma playing on the instrument Javanika in front of the Ekavira temple at Orugallu. This instrument is spelt as Jamadika also.

The Yellamma tradition is a part of widespread culture in Andhra Pradesh and Karnataka. The Baindla caste in Andhra Pradesh and Choudikavaru in Karnataka represent this culture. The Yellamma temples are managed by socially backward classes. The rituals and festivals are peculiar to those castes. The Brahmins and other upper castes cannot face the dreadful sight of animal sacrifice which is common. The goat, cock or any other animal to be sacrificed is not cut with a sword, but is bitten with bare teeth and the blood is tasted by the Baindlas. "The intestine of the goat is worn like a garland by the worshipper round his neck and it is a macabre sight indeed", says R.V.S. Sundaram in his booklet, *Yellamma-Epic Tradition*.[2]

It is widely believed that Yellamma represents Adishakti (primal force in feminine form). In Jambapurana, Adishakti gives birth to the trinity by laying three eggs. She asks them to give her sexual pleasure. Brahma and Vishnu refuse to do this as she is their mother. The last of the trinity, Maheswara agrees and prepares a strategy and takes the Trishula and the third eye from Adishakti and makes her lose everything. She is reduced to ashes and from these ashes the Trinity get their wives. In the story of Yellamma, Siva and Parvati are her parents. That means Yellamma is Adishakti or the feminine power of the world. The reasons for the presence of mother goddess in the Yellamma epic tradition are:

- Dravidian worship of mother goddess is still prevalent in rural India, especially in the South.
- The rituals and festivals of this tradition are quite different from others, as only lower castes participate in them.
- Songs of the Little Tradition are sung by lower castes (so-called untouchables).
- Poverty, illiteracy and ignorance of the lower castes are the causes of their socio-economic and cultural backwardness.
- In the name of tradition, the feudal lords and other rich people exploit the lower caste women.

The Yellamma tradition recognizes the supremacy of the mother goddess and gives psychological satisfaction to its followers. Star Buck says, "Female deities have often enjoyed the highest place among the Gods ..." The mother is the head of that group. There is a close connection between woman and agricultural pursuits. Woman was the first cultivator in the world but with the advent of war, man's power was viewed as a product of war and deities of the weaker sex became the symbols of peace. The myth of the 'weaker sex' is itself a late product of the patriarchal society. Briffault says,

"The differentiation of man as warrior and fighter is certainly not due to any constitutional indisposition or incapacity in the primitive woman, but to economic necessities. The pastoral economy which generated the Vedic pantheon was no longer there in the post-Vedic period". Father's right might have been aggressively imposed on the lives of people, but the remnants of mother's right could not be completely stamped out. The lower castes who were the tillers of the soil were sticking to their mother goddess or Shakti. Marshall, an archeologist, sums up his observations on the Indus valley civilization as follows:

Five thousand years ago, even before the Aryans were heard of, people in Punjab and Sind were enjoying an advanced and uniform civilization of their own, closely akin, but in some respects superior, to that of contemporary Mesopotamia and Egypt.

This affirms that India was equal to Persia, Mesopotamia and Egypt where civilizations developed. At that time, agriculture was women's domain. We can see the strong survival of the matriarchal elements. These elements, according to archeologist Etherenfels, were: (i) the predominance of the pre-Aryan features in Hinduism, and (ii) India owes so many elements, impulses and cultural moulds to this culture.

Here we can say that the 'female principle' in the religious history of India was not the product of the peaceful conditions of the post-Vedic period. This mother goddess concept widely spread throughout Asia Minor. In India, this Shakti or Devi is known as Adi Shakti and Jagadamba, 'the Mother of the Universe'. Interestingly, even in some foreign countries, statues resembling this goddess have been found. For instance, in Austria, an 11-cm-high figurine of a nude woman with arms folded across the breasts has been found. Carved in soft limestone, this paleolithic statuette is known as the Venus of Willendarf. Hundreds of such figurines have been discovered in the Mesolithic and chalcolithic deposits of Central Europe, the Mediterranean region and the Near East.

In the Danubian culture, a few female figurines have been found. Babylonian influence on the figurines of the different parts of the world is noticeable. Apparently, this is indicative of the mother goddess concept. In the same context, mother goddess herself had evolved from the same origin. As Evans said, that in Crete itself, it is impossible to dissociate the primitive images from those that appear in the shrines and sanctuaries of the great mother goddess. In

Greece, throughout the Neolithic and Chalcolithic periods, we find these female figurines in abundance. These figurines generally are crudely modelled.

A number of female figurines made of clay, with exaggerated sex-marks were found in the Neolithic deposits in Java. Female statuettes were found even in the Philippine islands. Playing with dolls was considered to be a rehearsal for motherhood. In South African Valeng, there was a woman called Nyambusti who inherited her mother's office and for generations together, some initiatory symbols were handed over from mother to daughter. They consisted of a drum, a horn, models of the genitalia of both sexes, and male and female wooden dolls, all painted with red ochre (Nyambusti). A band of initiated women performs a nude dance to the beats of the drum, the symbol of womb. In the evening, each girl is pierced with the sacred horn. In the succeeding days, they receive training in the facts of sex life. Together with the genital images, they serve as working models of the sexual act. They are considered to be representatives of ancestral spirits. On the last day again, the girls sing and dance round the dolls:

> Babies elect, babies elect,
> Babies, we greet you because you are beautiful.[3]

In all ancient civilizations, female figurines symbolized goddesses of fertility.

The mother goddess cult did not end with the Indus Valley civilization. Village deities or the Gramadevatas whose names begin with Parvati symbolize fertility goddesses, the relics of whom are traceable as far back as 3000 BC. This is the primeval goddess. Terra cotta representations are at the centre of ancient civilizations.

The mother goddess cult existed in India from a much earlier time, but it acquired an outstanding place in the sixth century BC. These goddesses were known during the periods of Buddhism, Jainism and Brahminism. They were treated as Shakti or energetic female principles and were worshipped with the help of tantric fertility deities. This cult was prevalent in the Deccan area. This idea of female energy as the agent of creation led to the evolution of Guardian spirits as culture goddesses in tribal societies. Silappadikaram states that among the Elnar community, a suitable virgin was chosen and taken in a procession to the temple. After that, she would go into trance and predict the future of the community.

The village deity is regarded as a Jagruta Devata, i.e., she protects and helps the villagers when they are in trouble and she is concerned with the prosperity of the villagers. However, some village deities have malignant powers and they create diseases and calamities.

The culture of 'Seven Akkammas', known as Saptamatrikas, is generally prevalent in South India. In Silappadikaram, they are referred to as the Seven Virgins or Seven Mothers. Their sculptural representation is found in all Saiva temples of South India including the temple of Siddheswara at Haveri in Dharwar district and in the Rameswaram temple. Henry Whitehead says that the goddesses differ only in name. For example, Puttur Ankamma of Chittoor district and Gangamma of Tirupati perform the same functions. In the Tamil country, the deity worshipped in every village is Mariamman or Mary, the goddess of smallpox. Mariamman is not one of the Seven Sisters who are supposed to be benevolent. She can be vindictive and inexorable and hard to propitiate. Though her special function is to protect the village from smallpox, she can also inflict it if she wants. She is also known as Pidari, Kali, Selliyamma, Draupadi and Angalamma. Pidari shoulders the responsibility of protecting the entire village against epidemics. Next to Mariamman, a benevolent male deity known as Iyenar, is worshipped as the protector of the village throughout Tamil Nadu. Next in rank is Kariappamma, a female attendant of the village deity.

In Telugu country, the village deity Peddamma, meaning 'great mother', is worshipped by the villagers with the belief that she wards off epidemics. They propitiate her by sacrificing buffaloes. The Selliyamma temple at Alambakam in Thanjavur district has a shrine for the Saptamatrikas.

Most of the Saivite goddesses have a fearsome appearance. They are depicted as being fond of flesh, blood and wine and intimately connected with goblins, spirits and demons. Some of the ceremonies peculiar to the temples of village goddesses, besides animal sacrifices, are: (i) fire-walking, (ii) swinging on the Sidi (Chakra puja), (iii) lashing oneself with a whip, (iv) piercing a metal wire right through the tongue, (v) slashing at the breast and forehead with swords until blood gushes out, (vi) thrusting a spear through the abdomen, and (vii) carrying on head the Karagam, lamps or earthen pots.

The village goddess is commonly called Shakti. Animal sacrifice is a must to please her. Good earth is compared to a woman as, like land, woman has the procreative power. Some scholars believe that woman invented agriculture. Pregnant women in Nicobar sow the seeds and expect a good yield. Their village deity is a fertility goddess. Woman's fertility power is responsible for rainfall. For example, in Gorakhpur (Uttar Pradesh) in 1873–74 when there was a famine, some women in the nude went to the fields at night to plough the land. Likewise, in North Bengal, during the famine, women danced in the nude before the statue of the rain god. (This custom was prevalent even in some foreign countries like Serbia in Greece and Caucasian Province in Georgia.) Women sing, dance and pray for rain. Men do the planting and women do the rest of the work. After performing Gauri puja, they immerse Gauramma into water. Adding some water to the resultant mud, they pour it on the patriarch. This ritual is done by married women. Harvest is compared to mother and women start the harvesting, not men. The implement used for ploughing is addressed as woman. Woman is equated with nature.

After the Aryans came to India, worship of Durga, Kali and Adishakti came into vogue. The Indus valley civilization has proved that women ploughed land more than 4,000 years ago. Nomadic people from various places after settling down in villages took to the worship of mother goddess, the reasons being (i) the mother goddess cult, (ii) invention of agriculture by women, (iii) without woman, there is no fertility concept, and (iv) she is the creator. There is a world of difference between Aryan gods and goddesses and Dravidian gods and goddesses as indicated in Table 3.1.

The names of village deities differ from region to region and village to village. For example in Telangana, they are known as Pochamma, Mahankali, Yellamma, Edemma, Maremma, Maisamma, Balamma, Suramma, Mutyalamma, and Gundalamma; these names include the Saptamatrikas (Seven Sisters). Villagers name their children after these goddesses. Even men have names like Yellaiah, Maraiah, Mysaiah, Pochaiah and Birayya.

Seven Matrikas, the children of Siva and Parvati, are mentioned in many inscriptions. Amara Kara defined Saptamatrikas as:

> Brahmee Maheswaree Chaiva Kanmidee Vaishnavee
> Thadhana
> Varchee Chaiva Chendravi Chamunda Sapta matharaha.

Table 3.1

Characteristics of Aryan and Dravidian Gods and Goddesses

Aryan	*Dravidian*
Gods are prominent.	Goddesses are important.
Trinity is responsible for the whole world.	Adishakti plays a primary role.
Fertility is not much associated with land.	Fertility goddesses and woman are associated with land.
Brahmins are the priests.	Non-Brahmins are the priests.
Generally pleasant and on rare occasions, ferocious.	Goddess is supposed to be fearful, chaturbhuja (four shoulders), Lambajihvaka, Vikata Danta – all these features denote the fearfulness of the goddess.
Very big structures, icons.	No statues or peans for goddesses. The object of worship is a copper vessel decorated with turmeric and kumkum powder. Called Yellamma, it is placed near a pond, tree or under some roof.
There is no animal sacrifice.	Animal sacrifice is common, particularly in jataras.
No vindictive or protective.	The goddess protects the action. villagers and punishes those who neglect her. She protects and loves children, condoning their mistakes. Village goddess is the guardian of the village.
Devotees are important.	Potharaju is the brother of Seven Sisters.

Thus, village deities are the representatives of the mother goddess. Stories of the deities gathered by folklorists constitute the oral tradition carried from one generation to another. Here, the author confines herself to the Yellamma culture.

Yellamma as a village deity is an important part of the conglomerate of religious beliefs, customs and ceremonies, generally classed together under the term Hinduism. Shrines of Yellamma are found everywhere. There are many legends about Renuka, the wife of Jamadagni.

Pre-historic stories are the encyclopaedias of ancient times. God was the custodian of all living things. People would offer something or other to god to appease him. These stories can be classified into five categories: (i) stories related to village deities; (ii) stories related to caste deities; (iii) stories related to nature and the Shakti cult; (iv) stories related to the Perantalu cult and; (v) stories related to puranas.

India is a land of villages and agriculture is the mainstay of the people. Villagers believe that the villages are governed by some forces which will punish the wrong doers. The village deities act as guardians of villages. If these forces are satisfied, there will be plenty of foodgrain and livestock in the village. Otherwise, floods, cyclones, epidemics and diseases will hit the people. To appease the village deities, the rural folk sacrifice animals, offer naivedyams and hold jataras. The most important deities are the incarnations of Adishakti or Jagadamba. Morgan in 1875 wrote a book *Ancient Society* to depict the customs, traditions and beliefs of the ancient periods. The evolution of human history comprises three phases: (i) pre-historic phase; (ii) uncivilized phase and (iii) civilized phase.

In the first phase, the evolution of man took place. He learnt everything by experience. He developed love for hunting and there were cases of man eating man. Man-woman relationship was not very strict during those days. For example, Greek God 'Zeus' got his children by his own daughter. In the Rigveda times, Yami married her brother Yama. Brahma created Saraswati and made her his consort.

In the second phase, man tried to settle in the river valleys and led a community-based life. Each clan had its own customs and traditions. The child was known through her mother. For example, Diti–Daityulu; Kunti–Kounteyulu; Gandhari–Gandheyulu. The descent came from mother. In this phase, man used to go hunting and woman did the household work, besides collecting fruits and forest produce for their sustenance. Later, woman invented agriculture. When hunting came into vogue, matriarchy transformed into patriarchy. At that time, village deities were women. We can cite the example of Pramilarjuniyam to show how patriarchy superseded matriarchy.

Folks gave an insignificant place to gods. They worshipped goddesses and offered them many things. Among the Nairs, a matriarchal community, mother and maternal uncle played a very important role. The eldest daughter is a kind of prime minister in the family and her brothers are expected to help her. The descent is straight through the daughter. Enfrenfels, in his book *Mother Right in India* says, "Illadevi is an Aryan goddess and she is the goddess of agriculture". In Markandeya Purana and Devimahatyam, the goddess expressed herself as 'Sakambari'.

The instrument used for ploughing is 'para' which is equivalent to woman. This indicates that commodification of woman started in the ancient times.

Village goddesses have no icons. As already mentioned, they are located near ponds or trees. The place is called a 'Gudi' (not a big temple). In the course of time, the four walls and roof came into existence. People worship small stones decorated with kumkum and bandaru. They call such a stone Yellamma.

The village deities have a brother by name Potharaju. Every village deity has some name and 'Amma' is suffixed to it. In Telangana, the village deities are known by various names such as Pochamma, Mahankali, Yellamma, Balamma, Suramma, Mutyalamma, Challalamma, Gantalamma, Yaparamma, Mamillamma and Gajjelamma. In Eluru, we have Gangamma, Poleramma, Sunkalamma, Maremma, Yellamma and Nukalamma.

Yellamma and Pochamma are said to have been born on the seat of Siva. Here, we see a conflict between matriarchy and Saivism. In ancient India, Siva Puja and Shakti Puja existed side by side. Even before the Trinity came into existence, the concept of mother goddess existed. Even today, Mahishasura Mardini (Parvati) is found in Pochamma and Mahankali temples. Let us know the significance of village deities one by one.

The Yellamma cult is popular throughout India. The votaries belong to different castes. The Yellamma tradition has developed so much that it can be considered as a separate epic tradition. A great deal of literature has been written in Telugu and Kannada, the principal languages of Andhra and Karnataka, respectively. During the time of Kakatiyas, the Yellamma story used to be recited by Baineedlu and Madiga women to the accompaniment of the musical instrument called Javanika or Jamuku whose sound pattern is 'juka jum jum juka jum jum'. Over the years, the number of these artists has declined.

Baindla, an untouchable caste, has taken over the responsibility of propagation and performance of the epic. Baindlas are also called Bhavanis. In Karnataka, Choudikavaru and Goudalivaru (migrants from Maharashtra) play the instrument Javanika while reciting the story of Yellamma.

All the artists enacting the Yellamma story belong to backward classes. They recite the story during Yellamma jataras or festivals. Even the funeral ceremony is followed by a performance by Baineedlu. Such is their devotion to this deity. Sometimes, the performers enact and dance dressed as Yellamma and Parasurama.

In Chittoor district, Yellamma is referred to as Renuka Yellamma. Most of the temples of Yellamma and Parasurama are managed by socially backward classes. Animal sacrifice is a must during rituals and festivals of Yellamma. Toddy and other intoxicants flow on that occasion. R.V.S. Sundaram says, "even sexual contact between the performers and other participants is not ruled out."

The Shakti cult includes the worship of the primal power. Yellamma worship is considered to be the basic and primitive level of mother-worship in South India. These goddesses are worshipped to ward off epidemic diseases.

The Yellamma tradition gained prominence when Saivism tried to suppress Jainism and the Mother cult. Kakatiyas were first Jains and later embraced Saivism. Jain temples were destroyed and the idols were transformed into Hindu gods. "Ekavira was probably a Jain Yakshini naked in appearance", says R.V.S. Sundaram.[4] There were places where naked female idols were worshipped in the name of Yellamma. Virasaivas and other upper castes had taken to the Yellamma cult with the motive of exploiting women. In Andhra, the higher castes' participation in Yellamma festival is minimal. This has helped the cult to retain its primitive features. Still, people believe that Goddess Yellamma manifests herself in the form of an ant-hill or a serpent. However, in Karnataka and Tamil Nadu, idols of Yellamma are worshipped.

The main features of the Yellamma tradition are:

- Non-Aryan worship of the mother goddess in rural areas is prevalent in South India.
- Higher castes do not participate in the Yellamma festivals as they cannot stand the sight of animal sacrifice.
- Lower castes sing the songs of Yellamma and Baineedlu recite the story of Yellamma.
- Exploitation of women by the higher castes and the priestly class in the name of tradition is prevalent in the whole of South India.

The Yellamma of Mahuram village is called 'Mahuramma'. Kridabhiramam says that in Telangana, Mahuramma is called Yellamma. For example, an old street in Orugallu is called Yellamma Bazaar.

Stories of Yellamma

Yellamma was the daughter of Siva and the wife of sage Jamadagni. Jamadagni's father was Gautama, who had committed many sins. As Jamadagni inherited all those sins, he was doing penance to atone for them. Yellamma or Renuka went to see her husband and she had to face many tests imposed by Jamadagni. These tests were meant to determine her chastity and greatness. How Renuka's father Giriraju performed her marriage is described in a song:

> Your father was Muni Raju
> He prepared a pearl pandal for her marriage.
> Diamonds 'Saka' was prepared[5]

The song also speaks of the arrangements made for the marriage – the lights, toddy pots, bandaru, shell's darshan, gold plates, etc.

***

In his book, *Janapada Geya Sahityam* (1958), B. Rama Raju wrote on Yellamma.

For non-Brahmin communities, Yellamma, Maisamma, Pochamma, Balamma all are malevolent goddesses. Baineedlu are the priests of these goddesses. The story goes like this.

Sage Gautama's wife was Ahalya. They had seven sages as their children. God asked Gautama for 'Erra Korrala' literature. Gautama wanted to create 'Korralu' by cutting a banyan tree. He found a snake with 12 heads and it became furious and drove Gautama out of that place. He again went with 'Naga Swaram' (flute) and the snake was satisfied with the music. Gautama killed the snake and the next day, he prepared Bonam and cut the tree called Yaduvula Marri which was an abode of snakes and birds. When the tree was burnt, the birds in it got killed. Gautama came home and killed a cat and a cow. He built a well by the name of 'Sobhanala Bavi' in which one Brahmin died. When people went for a bath, two foxes which were together went away in different directions. The people found one boy in that tree and named him Jamadagni.

Siva at that time was in Sivapura. He decided to give his daughter Renuka in marriage to Jamadagni and gave her Maisapuram as 'stridhanam'. Gautama divided all his landed property among his seven sons and bequeathed his sins to Jamadagni. To rid himself of the sins, Jamadagni took to meditation.

Renuka wanted to see her husband. She went to Kalingimadugu and pacified the snake and went to Mahuram to get rice. She prepared 'bonam' to take it to Jamadagni. This is described in a song:

> Pamuloyamma Chinna Pomaloyamma
> Pamulapai Bhushanamulu, Bangaru Gajjelu Thalli,
> Niku Saranu Jetunamma
> Nagabhushanamulu,
> Vannela pattala valu valu. Gattuka,
> Sannapu Seshuni Chetula Battuka
> Nagubamula Nadumunaku Gattuka,
> Jerripothula cheta bathuka
> Kondi pamula Koppuna Muduchuka,
> Yennika Kekkina Yeka Vira.[6]

Yellamma used different snakes as her ornaments. For example, one snake would be in her hand and a cobra would be round her waist.

God created an impediment in her effort to meet her husband. The Trinity asked for food. She did not like to give them food, but Jamadagni asked Renuka to get water in a pot which had holes. She prayed Ganga to help her. She brought a Bonapu vessel only half of it containing rice. The rice was boiled and Jamadagni asked her whether she had met somebody on her way. She said she had met three children. Jamadagni told her to go and serve the children first. Renuka went there and the children asked her to serve them food naked.

When Renuka went to fetch water, she found two frogs having sex. For a minute, she thought she should have sexual enjoyment with her husband. Divining this with his third eye, Jamadagni with his sweat created a Madiga. He went to the pond and asked for Yellamma. Renuka understood his mind and cursed him. Then she brought water in an earthen pot for her husband. After the meal, he asked his sons what type of punishment should be given to a person who has committed a wrong. While the eldest son said that such a person should be condoned, Parasurama said that person should be beheaded. Thereupon, Jamadagni told his son to do the same thing to his mother, which he promptly did. Appreciating his son's deed, Jamadagni told him to ask for two boons. Parasurama said he wanted to save his brothers and the second thing he asked for was that his mother Renuka should be brought back to life. Renuka was told to go to Maisapuram with her children.

In another version there was one Karveti Raju, the king of 'Jembaragiripatnam', who killed Jamadagni. Renuka did not reveal this to her sons. She went to Vysya, Kapu, Malawada and nobody was willing to rescue her from Parasurama. Then she went to Madigawada where she was asked to stay in a 'Landa' (a place where animal hides are kept in water). Parasurama searched for her in the houses of people of different castes and then he went to Madigawada. Dressed like a Pamba (a Madiga person) with a Jamidika in his hand and a snake on his shoulders, he went to Madigawada. He met a Joguvanitha, and found the clues. Yellamma came out of that 'Landa'. Again, Parasurama asked her about his father. He cut his hand when Uppala Maisamma came. There are two types of Uppali – Rakta Uppali and Sweta Uppali.

Renuka then revealed the secret. She blessed her son that his hand should always be on the upper side and his enemy's hand should be in the lower side. Then, Parasurama started his expedition.

***

Laxmi Kanta Mohan has another version of the story of Yellamma. It goes like this: Bhrigu Maharshi was a great sage. His son was Muchikundu and his wife was Satyavathi. Their son was Jamadagni. Sage Vishwamitra was an uncle to Jamadagni. Jamadagni married the daughter of Prasona Jittu. They had five sons – Ramanathanudu, Suseshanudu, Vasudu, Visvavasuvu and Parasurama.

When Renuka went to the river to fetch water for Jamadagni, she saw Chitrasena, the King of Anga, who was bathing. Stunned by his handsome looks, she lingered at the spot for a while and, therefore, returned home late. This made Jamadagni suspect that she had some relations with Chitrasena. Consequently, he told his sons to kill her. The elder sons did not accept their father's proposal, but Parasurama did and beheaded Renuka. Jamadagni wanted to grant him a boon. Accordingly, he accepted Parasurama's request to bring his four brothers to normal. Later, he prayed that his mother Renuka be brought back to life.

One day, Hyhaya King, Kartaviryarjuna, went to the forest for hunting along with his people. He found that there was an ashram close by. It was Jamadagni's ashram. Jamadagni arranged everything for them and made their stay comfortable. Jamadagni served them a feast with the help of Kamadhenu. Kartaviryarjuna sent his minister to Jamadagni to get Kamadhenu. While taking Kamadhenu, he killed Jamadagni. Renuka wanted to do 'Sati' but, luckily, Jamadagni's grandfather Brighu came there and Jamadagni got back his life. Parasurama wanted to ruin the Hyhaya dynasty. Again, Kartaviryarjuna came and killed Jamadagni. Parasurama meditated and got 'Parasum' from Siva. He first killed Kartaviryarjuna and many kings and lastly, Sri Rama vanquished Parasurama.

The Yellamma story is a folk story, not a poet's creation. The same story exists in puranas as well as in literature. The story came from labourers, from their thoughts, from their happiness, sorrows, desires and dreams.

In Telangana, people of all castes worship Yellamma. They also worship Pochamma, Maisamma and Balamma.

The popularity of Yellamma is evident from places named after this deity. For example, there is 'Yellamma bazaar' in Warangal city and 'Yellammagutta' in Nizamabad city. There are Yellamma temples in Rayalaseema and in every village of Karnataka. The Yellamma story is recited by Bavaneellu, Pambalavaru and Kuruma Gollas. They use Pamba or Jamidika while reciting the story.

In Kogula Gutta, there is Yellamma. When she was supposed to be three months old, Muniraju started his meditation. Kodenaganna asked Yellamma to go to Muniraju. Yellamma came out of the ant-hill. There are many kinds of snakes in that snake-pit such as Kodenagulu, Balanagulu, Sudupurugulu and Jerripotulu. All these have become ornaments to Yellamma.

Yellamma went to Waddewada and asked the people there to whitewash her house, which they did. She gave them 'vvalu' (money). On the second day, she went to the potter's house and asked Gundanna for 'Bonalu' which he prepared and gave to her. Then she boiled rice in that pot. When she was carrying the meal to her husband Jamadagni, Kartikeya noticed it. He did not appreciate the idea that she was the wife of Jamadagni. He went to Jamadagni shouting 'Poli poli' and 'Bali Bali' and killed him.

Gangadevi got angry and she made his blood go upwards and made Yellamma drink that blood in seven gulps. Then Yellamma went to Sivalkota, Siva's abode and met her mother Parvati. Siva heard the pathetic situation of his daughter Yellamma and went with instruments accompanied by Brahma and Vishnu. Three hundred lakh Siva Sattulu, Mutyala Posamma, Veedhi Nanchari, Akkapeddamma, Katta Maisamma, Surya, Kilipaka Swami, Allidada

Ramu, Komudari Mallanna, Dammudu of Dappu community accompanied Siva. Siva Parvathulu and Yellamma went to 'Mahuram' city. She was placed comfortably there. They then started their journey leaving Talari Dommanna to safeguard Yellamma.

Yellamma completed nine months of pregnancy. Dommanna was sent to the Yerupulapatnam to bring Jogu Muthu. She was a 'Mantrasani', or a nurse to help Yellamma's delivery. Six sons and one daughter were born to her. The washerwoman washed the clothes of these children. Viswabrahmins prepared anklets and necklaces for the children of Yellamma. Tailors prepared 'Kullalu' and 'Kasalu' for these children.

Yellamma's last son Parasurama sought his mother's permission to play games with the children of surrounding areas. They heckled him as 'Lanjala Koduku', 'Rankula Ramudu' as Parasurama's mother was an unwed woman. Even the mothers of those children harassed him.

Parasurama got suspicious about his mother as she did not tell him about the death of Jamadagni. Yellamma said she had not married anybody. Parasurama went to the Sun God and on his advice got a cremation pit prepared by the Waddars. Parasurama asked his mother to take the test. Yellamma went through the test and proved her chastity. Yellamma could not face these hardships anymore and she went to Madigawada and asked Jamba to protect her from her son Parasurama. Jamba asked her to stay in 'Landa' and he covered her body with a hide. Parasurama came and understood the situation and took his mother to the spot where his father's bones had been found and performed 'Nagavalli' for her and he brought his sister Gauri to help his mother. It was not with contempt or suspicion about his mother that Parasurama went through all these ordeals, but to prove to the world his mother's chastity. (Of course, no one would support Parasurama for what he did to his mother.) This is a reflection of patriarchal society. In spite of the ordeals Yellamma underwent, her motherhood made her do no harm to her son. As mother, she served him food and took care of him. Parasurama, soon after his birth, created problems for the nurse and cut the nose and ears of Jamba. Here we have to cite one song of Yellamma:

Yellamma is born in Kogulagutta - Tandanoo
Yella is there - Tandanoo
Yella, Please come Yellu - Tandanoo

Mamurala Yellu - Tandanoo
Ma Sati Yellu - Tandanoo
Born in ant-hill, Yellu - Tandanoo
Yellu, three months baby - Tandanoo
Muniraju left for meditation - Tandanoo
The ant- hill is gold - Tandanoo
Yellu, start immediately - Tandanoo
Pandumu bandaru - Tandanoo
Poured out - Tandanoo
Seven baths - Tandanoo
Wore neem Sarees - Tandanoo
Wore neem Jackets - Tandanoo.[7]

Yellamma used bandaru for worship and adorned herself with snakes of different types. With Yellamma, Jamadika also was born. Along with her, seven Shaktis or seven Matrikas also took birth. Yellamma started her journey to Mamuralapatnam, a deserted land. Yellamma kept the grain there. Wadderas saw her, invited her and enquired of her about their work. Accordingly, they built the houses and whitewashed them. She gave a present to Upparlu (Wadderas).

Next day, Yellamma went to a potter's house and met Kummari Gundanna. He asked her to sit on Pearl's plant. Yellamma then asked Gundanna to prepare bonam pots, comprising seven levels. These were of different sizes. Gundanna prayed to the goddess to give him strength to prepare the pots required by Yellamma. He did the work meticulously and showed them to Yellamma.

Gundanna prepared the bonalu with one thousand eyes and Yellamma gave him land and other gifts. Yellamma brought bandaru, kumkum and incense and seven sarees.

Pochamma

Pochamma is a village deity who protects the village. Pochamma's idol has some affinity with the idol of Kali. She creates troubles for people if she thinks they are disloyal to her. She creates diseases like measles, smallpox and rashes on the body. Smallpox changes the complexion of the person.

People in villages perform Bonala panduga (festival) and Pochamma panduga. They also organize jataras on the occasion. Baineedlu recite the story of Pochamma. In Adilabad district,

Pochamma is known as Gajjelamma. We can see men in female attire perform puja. Appropriation of female attire by priests is symptomic in matriarchal society.

There are two kinds of Pochammas: (1) Karri Pochamma (Black Pochamma), and (2) Yerra Pochamma (Red Pochamma). Karri Pochamma is believed to be more powerful than the other. Baineedlu recite the story of Pochamma for three or five days. Siva and Parvati did not have children. Depicting that in a song:

Parvati, my Mother, wants to have children,
What does Siva say about it?
People born in Kaliyuga,
Those are our children,
We don't require more children,
Parvati says that she wants
To have her own children.
Siva gives children even to the birds,
For all human beings, poor people too have children.
Why are we deprived of our own children, she asks?
We have twelve forts, we are wealthy
We have 24 kostala people's kingdoms
Fertility Goddess Jagadamba is craving for children,
Laxmi and Saraswati have advised her to adopt their children
Parvati has replied them as
She needs her own children
Parvati said the children should be my own - Rama Rama
Mother's milk is important - Rama Rama
Silver swing is required - Rama Rama
Jasmine flowers garland - Rama Rama
The swing should be decorated - Rama Rama
When we have the Darbar - Rama Rama
All should salute us - Rama Rama
Parvati wants nothing but motherhood - Rama Rama
Siva has reconciled - Rama Rama
Gave jasmine flowers to Parvati - Rama Rama
Parvati has eaten that flower - Rama Rama
Siva has gone to Parvati's Mother's place - Rama Rama
Punishment to Parvati - Rama Rama
Siva suspects Parvati - Rama Rama
He has prepared for her cremation - Rama Rama

Siva has dragged her to cremation ground - Rama Rama
The child in the pregnancy - Rama Rama
What is the reply of that child - Rama Rama
She has asked Parvati not to cry - Rama Rama
She has given her support - Rama Rama
Siva has lighted the fire for once - Rama Rama
Ashes have risen to higher place - Rama Rama
Parvati's hair has not burnt - Rama Rama
Parvati's dress has not burnt - Rama Rama
Parvati has not changed a bit - Rama Rama
Surprisingly an ant-hill has appeared - Rama Rama
Pochamma is born to Parvati - Rama Rama
Pot, Bonala bandlu, Bosullu have come - Rama Rama
7 bangles, 4 toe-rings, 7 snakes have come - Rama Rama
Pochamma has shown her power to Siva - Rama Rama
Declaration of chastity of Parvati by Siva - Rama Rama
She has asked her father for her naming ceremony - Rama Rama
Siva has declined to her proposal - Rama Rama
Then magical power of Pochamma has come - Rama Rama.
There is another song about the bandaru:
Goredu bandari - Rama Rama
Karri Pochamma - Rama Rama
Chanting with five users - Rama Rama
Does that mother know - Rama Rama
On father's stomach - Rama Rama
Boggulu Podustayu - Rama Rama
They are like seeds of maize - Rama Rama
Boggulu podustayu - Rama Rama
Burning pain on the body - Rama Rama
Thirsty feeling - Rama Rama
He has drunk water - Rama Rama
Thirst has not decreased - Rama Rama.

With Siva then agreeing to celebrate the festival of Pochamma, the Boggulu (boils) disappeared. Siva built a temple to her and created a snake with ten heads to support her. Nearby, a neem tree also grew. Pochamma ordained that a ten-day festival be held. Pochamma wants to make her father blind because he gave trouble to her mother Parvati. A song about the festival goes like thus:

Seven Dappu instruments - Rama Rama
Seven bandaru pots - Rama Rama
Jamidika debbalu - Rama Rama
Seven Siva's devotees - Rama Rama
Sing songs - Rama Rama
White sarees - Rama Rama
Jackets with mirrors - Rama Rama
Food is provided for mother - Rama Rama
Toddy kavallu - Rama Rama
Yekula baskets - Rama Rama
Talliki Trisulam - Rama Rama
Behind the baskets - Rama Rama
Yeduti gullalu - Rama Rama
A thousand eyes - Rama Rama
They are mother's - Rama Rama
Meyani orleti - Rama Rama
Meka Pothulamma - Rama Rama
Koyani Aracheti - Rama Rama
Cocks - Rama Rama.[8]

The song describes the various items used in the festival – Dappu, Jamidika, white sarees, jackets with mirrors, goats and cocks. In any such festival, the feast is followed by toddy.

Kudukalu, shells, nuts, date fruits, Iripala biyyam (Odikattu biyyam) are all important for the festival. Only when these things are provided does Pochamma feel happy and transform herself from being a malicious goddess into a benevolent one and does good to the village. If any disease attacks children, it is called Balaposamma and if elders are afflicted, it is called Pedda Posamma.

The husband of Posamma Adavi Mahamuni is the guardian of all animals, insects and trees in the forest. He used to start on his journey on Thursday and reach his wife on Friday. There was no sexual pleasure for Pochamma because of the curse of Siva. In her next birth, she is called Mutyalamma.

In Adilabad district, where Pochamma is called Gajjelamma, her demands are met by her devotees. Gajjelamma idol is made of wood and placed near a neem tree. Her usual dress is a white saree and sometimes yellow. The devotees make small idols of her and keep them in the temple.

There is no particular day for her worship. However, people worship her on Sunday. The devotees have to do 'Jogu' in five houses and perform puja. They take 'bonalu' and do 'Arati' to the idols and go round the temple.

The devotees then keep the bonalu in front of the temple and decorate the idols with white and yellow sarees. The eyes of the goddess are prepared with silver or aluminium. Incense is burnt. The Dappu is played to create a festival atmosphere. Washermen and Muslims behead these animals and offer the blood to the goddess. After the festival, the washermen take the skin and the head part and carry the rest to their homes.

In Adilabad district, Pochamma devotees celebrate a festival known as 'Oradipanduga'. This festival is meant to avoid catastrophes in the surrounding areas. They feed the he-buffalo which is to be sacrificed. In the evening, a Mala devotee pours bandaru on this buffalo and he is afraid of the sound of the Dappu. A revenue employee of the village or Mali patel holds the tail of the animal tightly because if he loses his grip on it, his life will be at stake. They tie the animal on all sides so that it does not give much trouble. All this is done in front of the temple.

Maisamma

Maisamma is also the daughter of Siva. She is the goddess of animals. When animals are affected by diseases, people worship this goddess.

> Maisamma is in front of the village,
> Oxen have gone somewhere, have you seen them? [9]

Maisamma is a fertility goddess. She is mentioned in the Mallanna story. Mallanna goes to Dhana Kota for money and defeats Mahishasurudu. While bringing money to his place, Mahishasuri eats the he-buffaloes. Then she becomes Mahishasura Maisamma.

Matangi

Among the Seven Sisters, Matamma is a special goddess of the Madigas. Madigas are poor; hence, her worship is not so elaborate as that of other goddesses. She is represented by a small stone image in a very poor shrine. Every year or once in two or three years, Matamma's Jatara takes place. A small buffalo is procured and let loose until the appointed day. The image is given a bath, a sheep is sacrificed and there is the usual buffalo sacrifice. On the last day of the function, a Madiga pujari cuts off the head of a fowl before the idol of Matamma. The pujari holds the fowl by its legs, brushes away the Muggu (sacred designs) before the idol, symbolizing removal of the last vestiges of evil.

Matangi possesses the spirit of Matamma. She is invested with the insignia of her position, a basket or sieve, a snake-headed bamboo stick, a branch of neem tree and a cowry shell attached.

The centre of Matangi worship is a village called Malinthapadu near Cumbum in Kurnool district. Every Matangi must go to this place for the initial ceremony.

The Dravidian gods are more commonly connected with Siva's worship than the worship of Vishnu. Siva is considered to be an aboriginal god. The stories connected with Matangi worship are numerous. These stories contain parts of many legends about other deities.

Matangi is depicted as holding the heavens in her left hand and the great serpent, Adiseshu, in her right hand. These are represented by a basket and a stick. She also holds the Sun and Moon as plates in her hands. In one hand, she has the spilt blood and in the other the scattered brains. That blood was used by the goddess as bottu (sacred mark). She marked it on the foreheads of the people. She also had two plates containing saffron and turmeric powder which she used for the worshippers. All the legends connected with Renuka have an affinity with Matangi. When Parasurama interchanged the heads, Jamadagni accepted as his wife the woman who had Renuka's head and considered the other woman as an inferior deity; hence, she became a Matangi. Another version is that Jamadagni accepted neither of them; so, she remained with the Madigas as Yellamma. All these legends are interconnected.

Khandoba

Khandoba is called Mailar in Karnataka and Mallanna in Andhra. He is called Murukan in Konkani literature. He may be traced to a prototype of a god found all over the Deccan from early times. He has protective functions. He is identified with Bhairava who protects the temple entrances, the devi or the village. He is a forest god and in Tamil he is called 'Malaikilavon', the 'lord of the hills'. In the hilly areas, we find the tribal food-gatherers and hunters. So, he is called a hunter, having a spear and an elephant and the peacock as his vahana. He is called a Velan, the carrier of the spear.

Hill tribes and pastoralists worship Khandoba or Murukan. In Kolhapur, he is called Mallayya, 'lord of the mountain'. Veerasaivas have depicted their god in the forests just as Mallanna of Srisailam is located in a forest. Another version is that the origin of the god may be found in the worship of an ant-hill, the seat of the snakes. The ant-hill is also the seat of gold. Today, the ant-hill is worshipped with bandar. The Somvati Amavasya Jatra at Jejuri is famous.

Kapilamuni asked Khandoba to spread the greatness of Martanda Bhairava. The yellow turmeric powder which is a characteristic of this god all over the Deccan is considered to be gold. Birappa, the god of pastoral communities like the Dhangars of Maharashtra, the Kurubas of Karnataka and the Kurumas of Andhra, is another god of the hill, connected with the Sun. The fusion of the cults of Siva and Surya into Martanda Bhairava is reflected in Agnipurana and Matsyapurana. Khandoba is specially worshipped on Sundays like another famous god, the Siddhanath of Mhasvad (Kalabhairava). Khandoba's palanquin is carried from the mountain in Jejuri to the Kartha river where he used to bathe. He is identified with a tree. Leaves of the Bilva or Bel tree are sacred to Khandoba. He resides on the hills and manifests himself in the form of a hill.

Khandoba has two consorts – Mhalsa, the first one, is the daughter of a Lingayat merchant and the second one named Banai is said to have come from Dhangars (shepherds). In the Deccan, while Mhalsa may be identified with Parvati, Banai is never identified with Parvati.

Khandoba's devotees belong to several castes. He has acquired the trishul and a damaru along with the kapala. Another version of the 'god of the Deccan' is the Tamil Aiyanar, who has two consorts and he has assumed protective functions for the village. The function of Bhramappa, a god of Karnataka, is to protect the villagers.

Khandoba is depicted as a hero who protected the Kshetra, cattle and Brahmins for which he used the elephant, umbrella, palanquin, horse, shield and sword. In the course of time, Siva and Vishnu temples disappeared and Khandoba, Mailar and Mallanna's temples were built. From that time onwards, Khandoba came to prominence.

Gunther-Dietz Sontheimer has expressed two opinions. First, the attitude of Hindu rajas towards the villagers, especially tribes and pastoral ones was in tune with the traditional polity. Second, the horse played a significant role. Sometimes, the God is worshipped in the form of a horse. Khandoba is equated with Pasupati. The special devotees of the god, the Vaghyas, are dedicated to the god's service in fulfilment of a vow for a child. They regard themselves as the dogs of the god. For instance, at Devaragudda near Ranebennur in Karnataka and Anantapur district of Andhra Pradesh, some Kurama caste people, the devotees of Siva, consider themselves as dogs of Bhairava and like dogs, drink milk without touching the bowl. The Kuruma devotees perform another act. One person tries to eat the plantain fruit and the other person obstructs him. This is a game generally played by the dogs. This custom is prevalent in the cult of Birappa, the god of the Kurubas in Andhra. Khandoba's dog belongs to Banai, the Dhangar woman.

There is another custom in Karnataka. During the Dasara festival at Devaragudda, the devotees gallop like horses, whipping themselves with horse whips. In Jejuri, during Somvati Amavasya festival, the devotees possessed by the power of the god move like horses in front of the palanquin. Animal sacrifice is done to Banai outside the temple. Khandoba is a Lingayat and he does not tolerate animal sacrifice. Sometimes, the devotees of Siva commit suicide in order to identify themselves with god. This can be seen on memorial tablets in Karnataka where the Padukas of Siva are surrounded by the heads of rams and human beings. Religious suicide or hook-swinging ceremony in Jejuri was abolished by the colonial administration.

As the author has already mentioned, Bhairava, Martanda Bhairava or Khandoba is accompanied by dogs for defeating rakshasas. From time immemorial, the dog is associated with the mythology of the Mallari cult. Seated on a horse, the god is surrounded by dogs. He is smeared with turmeric powder, which is considered a substitute for gold. The bhandar provides the ritual and a linkage between god, devotees and animals.

The devotees of Khandoba who beg in the name of the god are called Vaghyas. The word derives from 'Vyabhra'. In Kannada, it is Vaggayya. They act as dogs during jataras and also perform a circular dance to the beats of drums. In the middle of it, the devotees throw coins on a black woollen blanket and the Vaggayyas pick up the coins with their mouths. It is a sort of entertainment for the devotees. With the money thus collected, the Vaggayyas buy food.

The dog is an indicator of sexuality and licentiousness of the sex. This characteristic is absent in the rites of the Vaghyas.

Vaggayyas of Mailar and the Vaghyas of Khandoba have similarities. These Vaggayyas or Goravaiahs have peculiar long, black, woollen gowns. The Sun and Moon and dog's design are stitched in colourful designs. Same designs are engraved on the brass begging bowls of these Goravaiahs. They carry a trishula or a shula, a cowry necklace, a damaru or a bell. Ram skins are tied around their waists and some devotees wear black skin caps too. They go out for begging. Some practice black magic too.

Murali is a woman married to Khandoba. She is accompanied by Vaghya, a bard of Khandoba.

Rudra or Pasupati is perpetuated in the Khandoba cult. 'Pasu' means cattle. By killing milch animals, Khandoba assimilated their power. Man, tiger, dog, horse, cattle, elephant, bull and ram - all are united in the cult.

Khandoba is preserved in folk mythology even now. Vaghyas and Muralis sing 'padas'. A song on the 'doghood' of Vaghyas runs thus:

> He became the Vaghya of the God
> Into his hand (the God) gave a kotama,
> Barking (like a dog) and roaring (like a tiger)
> He came to the door of Mallari's bhakta.[10]

Khandoba and Dhangars have the ritual Jagaran in which the devotees keep night-long vigil and sing and dance in honour of Khandoba. Dhangar women follow the custom of making a vow to him in case of barrenness. The first-born child is dedicated to the god. If it is a boy, he becomes Vaghya and if it is a girl, she becomes a Murali. Of late, these customs have fallen into disrepute.

In bhakti literature, the initiation of animals like dogs represents the self-immolation of the 'dog' like self before god. Sonthomier says, "Imitation, nearness, possession and identity mark the relationship between the God, whether Rudra or Khandoba, and his followers".

Dhangars follow the procession of Khandoba with spears on Somavati Amavasya. They accompany the palanquin of the god, which is carried to the Karcha river. Other devotees act as god's horses. At the end of the hunt, everybody takes his bath in the same river. This indicates that the devotee is identifying himself with god.

Another feature of the Khandoba festival is the breaking of a thick iron chain. This is called 'Sattva'. Sometimes, violence also takes place. This element of violence suggests that there were ritual suicides in the 12th and 13th centuries.

The Somavati Amavasya festival is held twice or thrice a year. The devotees pour sacks of turmeric dust on Khandoba and in return the God grants their request for protection from all difficulties. This is expressed in a song of the Vaghyas;

> See! The whole world is swinging
> There is a scramble for turmeric dust
> The magnanimous Mallukhan,
> Is giving away mountain of Gods.[11]

The song expresses turbulence throughout the festival. But the festival starts with a procession with the god in a palanquin. The air is pervaded with bhandar. The devotees' shouts reverberate. They pray him as 'Victory to king Khandoba, the leader of Seven Crores'. The musicians follow the procession. These are untouchables belonging to the Mang caste. The Dhangars also carry heavy iron chains over their shoulders. After the chain is broken, the procession continues. The devotees also worship their ancestors and other gods and goddesses besides Khandoba on the river bed.

Khandoba takes his bath in the River Kartha when the powers of the Sun and the Moon mingle. This is echoed in the Somvati song,

> When the lord is bathed in milk
> It is as if the Karha becomes as luminous as the
> Sun and pure as the Bhagirathi ....[12]

Then the lord moves to Rambha, a heavenly courtesan, placed on a temporary platform. Khandoba stays a moment with Rambha and moves to the village. Rambha has become a deified Murali of the tailor caste. Vaghyas sing songs describing Murali's love for Khandoba.

The palanquin is then kept for five minutes on the stone pedestal of Phulai Malin, known to be the first Murali. Then, bhandar and millet seeds are sown in the fields. Khandoba bestows fertility on the crops as well as on human beings. He is Siva himself as 'King on earth'.

Like Khandoba, we have China Obulesu in Anantapur district to whom basvis are dedicated. He is also a pastoral god.

Mariamman Cult

The outcastes are neglected in history. In the past, these communities suffered. Outcaste female sexuality is crucial to explore the dynamics of the caste system. In the name of tradition, prostitution is legitimized.

In the Dravidian culture, women are endowed with sacred power. Due to the concept of sanskritization, the difference between Great Tradition and Little Tradition has cropped up. Hence, the regional tradition has developed. The regional tradition occurs predominantly in Kannada-speaking areas, in Maharashtra and Andhra Pradesh. The position of outcaste women and backward class women was characterized by vulnerability and helplessness in contrast to caste Hindu women.

In Periyapuranam, Mariamman is referred to as Bavaniamman. People consider that all goddesses are one because she manifests herself in many forms.

The author enquired from the pujari whether Mariamman is the goddess of the poor people, especially untouchables, or a Brahmin goddess. Pujari said that Mariamman is a Goddess of Brahmin tradition. Myself and one Divisional Engineer and his friend, we all went to a Tamil Professor at Tanjore. He read a book in Tamil and confirmed that Mariamman was the Goddess of poor people. This goddess in Tiruvelkad is worshipped in the same way as is done in the temples of the Brahmanical tradition. Coconuts are offered to the goddess and the pujari is a Brahmin. This is an effect of Sanskritization.

In the annual festival at Periyapalaiyam, the devotees offer 'Kul', a thick porridge made of ragi, and a sheep to the goddess. Sexual acts are forbidden during the festival time. The goddess does not like to see married couples or pregnant women. A peculiar ritual precedes the marriage of the goddess. The goddess is married to a demon. A tree trunk representing Mariamman's demonic spouse is planted in front of her shrine. Eight days later, the trunk is uprooted and the goddess becomes a widow for one night. The same day again, she is considered married to Siva himself.

In Sivanmalai, Mariamman and Virakaliamman are about 100 yards apart in an open area. The village headman brings a mare in front of Virakali where the mare's feet are washed and a bindi is put on her forehead. He then offers puja to Virakali and the mare and sprinkles the auspicious water on the mare which is expected to shake its head. If it shakes its head, (what happens when it does not shake its head?) it is carried around the village and then to a tank where a he-buffalo is given a bath and adorned with a bindi. The procession continues and stops at a Brahmin's house and from there it goes back to the temple straight. The mare is then beheaded by the priest and buried in the ditch. The pujari goes into a trance for a while. Food is then offered to the goddess. It is called "matu, tirupputal", or bringing back of the cows. A female animal is kept apart from the sacrificial ritual to the goddess. Mare suggests Vedic horse sacrifice.

The mare sacrifice is symbolic of the beheading of Renuka. There are many such stories about the beheading of Renuka. Women's powers of regeneration necessitate decay and death, which are a necessary prelude to rebirth. So, Shakti includes benevolent, auspicious aspects as well as malevolent aspects. The power of the goddess can destroy as well as recreate.

Mariamman is an ambivalent goddess, but how malevolent is difficult to determine. Women devotees worship Bavaniamman for the sake of maintaining their family welfare.

Mariamman is regarded as Vishnu's little sister and praised as the goddess of all the directions. She is the fundamental Shakti, the first mother. She accepts sacrifice of sheep and he-buffaloes. She also guards the boundaries of the village. Mariamman appears 'Swinging on the hook', which has for long been a popular ritual at Mariamman temples. In some of her temples, 'bloodless oblations' are allowed.

Another popular ritual is the 'neem sari' ritual in which devotees take off their clothes, cover themselves with neem leaves strung together and circumambulate the temple. Every person in a neem 'sari' is expected to roll a coconut and prostrate at every step. This ritual is not restricted to the lower castes. Sometimes, Brahmins and other high caste devotees also worship Mariamman wearing the neem leaves garment. This ritual is meant to safeguard the health and welfare of the devotees and their families.

There is another ritual concerning the health and long life of the husband. In this, the wife lays a 'Tali' with a gold or metal insignia. She brings it to the priest who places it on a tray and performs puja. Later, it is taken and put into a 'Hundi' of Bavaniamman, the goddess of fertility. A woman without a child buys a small wooden cradle with a doll in it, keeps it in front of Parasurama and later hangs it from a neem tree. Another interesting thing is that an unmarried girl performs the 'Kutaikalyanam' or 'Pot wedding'. The girl brings a decorated pot and pours neem leaves and milk into it and places a coconut on that. She ties a tali to the pot, a symbol of the goddess as also of a married woman. She worships Bavaniamman and immerses the pot in the river and worships her again.

The Samayapuram Mariamman temple in Trichy in Tamil Nadu is famous for 13-week-long annual festival during which Bavaniamman's utsar murti (ceremonial idol) is taken around the village in a chariot. On the third Sunday, devotees belonging to four villages who saw her when she appeared in the ant-hill dance in front of her image. There was a time when devotees used to curse Bavaniamman for creating diseases, but not any more. Use of obscene words by devotees in front of goddesses is common. For example, this can be seen during the Gangamma festival at Tirupati.

Yellamma and Mariamma are equated with Durga or Parvati. Girls from the so-called SCs and backward class communities are dedicated to them.

The characteristics of these mother goddesses or Jagadambas are:

- The deities are worshipped as village guardians and averters of epidemics and other misfortunes; for example, Uramma and Peddamma.
- Villagers do not consider them as evil spirits, but look upon them as beings of uncertain temper, that is sometimes benevolent and sometimes malevolent.
- The functions of each goddess are not clearly mentioned. While most people think that all goddesses are one and the same, some consider Mariamma in Tamil country superior to other goddesses.
- Next to Mariamma, the deity that is most worshipped among the Tamils is Iyenar, a village god.

Thus, in spite of Aryan influence, the Dravidians have been able to maintain their distinct identity in South India. In most of the Dravidian worship practices, pujaris are non-Brahmins and very rarely do Brahmins serve as pujaris of the village goddesses.

In the next chapter, we will discuss how a jogin is dedicated to Yellamma and what her status and that of her children would be.

Notes

1. Carol Radcliff Bolon, *Forms of the Goddess Lajja*, Published for College Art Association by The Pennsylvania State University Press, Pennsylvania, 1992.
2. R.V.S. Sundaram, G.S. Mohan and G. Linga Reddy, *Studies in Folkloristics*, Folklore Book Trust, Mysore, 1966.
3. In Philippine Islands, playing with dolls was considered to be rehearsal for motherhood. The song was sung by girls who dance around the dolls.
4. R.V.S. Sundaram, "Ellamma-Epic Tradition", *Studies in Folkloristics*, Folklore Book Trust, Mysore, 1986, ps. 106-7.
5. Suresh Kumar K., "Basvi Literature: A Sociological Analysis", Unpublished PhD Thesis, University of Hyderabad, Hyderabad, 2001.
6. Ibid.
7. Ibid.
8. Ibid.
9. Krishna Kumari Nayani, "Janapada Geya Gadhalu", a folklore book in Telugu, Telugu Academy, Hyderabad, 1990.
10. Vaghyas and Muralis sung this song when the author went to filedwork in Jejuri in the year 2005.
11. This is a song of Vaghyas, sung by them in an interview with them in the filedwork to Jejuri in the year 2005.
12. Ibid. A song sung in the Somvati festival in Jejuri, 2005.

CHAPTER 4

The Jogin System

Origin and Growth

The origin of the Devadasi tradition is traceable to the practice of ritual dancing which formed an integral part of the ritual service to gods and goddesses. It was also an important aspect of the people's life from the third century BC. The temple dancers were dedicated to gods to give them worldly pleasures. The king wanted to prove his divine nature as 'Na Vishnu Prithvi Pati'. Hence, he tried to equate his own life with that of the Almighty. In those times, the upper castes used to purchase girls from lower castes and dedicate them to gods.

There is a difference between the devadasis of upper castes and those of lower castes. Although almost all the girls who are dedicated to gods and goddesses are from the lower castes, the upper caste devadasis hail from backward classes. The devadasis of the lower rung of the hierarchy are mainly from 'untouchables', i.e., Malas and Madigas, the SCs in South India. The SCs were denied entry into temples and ill-treated and exploited by the upper castes. According to an ancient custom, the devadasi inherited her parents' property and performed their funeral rites as if she were their son.

In course of time, the devadasi system gradually degenerated into the profession of prostitution. As a result of the relentless battle waged by social reformers like Kandukuri Veeresali Purna, Raghupathi Venkataratnam Naidu, Muthulaxmi Reddy and Yaminipurna Tilakam against the system, the Andhra Pradesh (Andhra Area) Devadasi Prevention of Dedication Act, 1947 (Act No. XXXI of 1947), dated 21 January 1948 was passed.

The amendment in 1956 to the above Act passed by the Andhra Pradesh government was not comprehensive enough to root out this evil. Some pockets, particularly in East Godavari district, took advantage of the loopholes in the law. Having lost all their moorings in the traditional occupation, these women more or less became destitutes in their middle age and struggled hard for their livelihood. Consequently, their teenaged girls were driven into this unlawful and immoral profession. They requested the government to treat them on par with the jogins of Nizamabad district in regard to their

Map of Andhra Pradesh

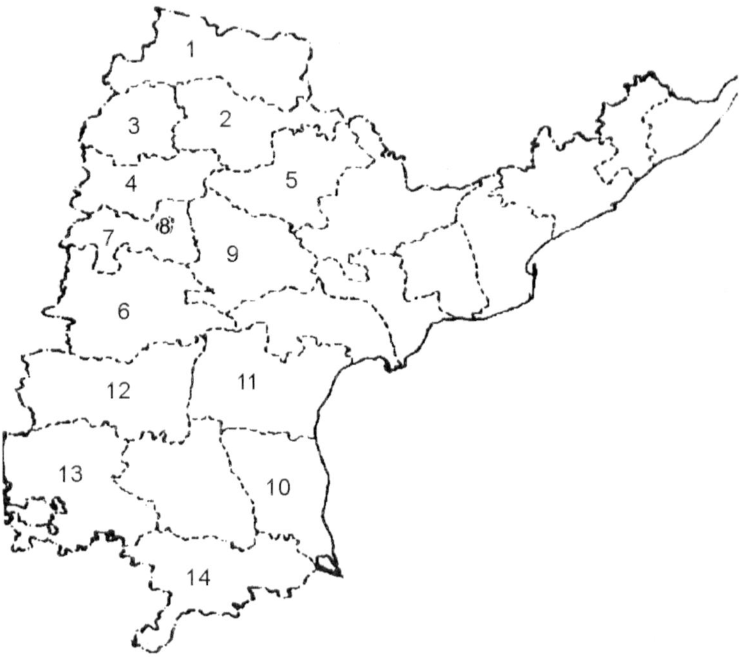

TELANGANA (Jogin System)	COASTAL ANDHRA (Matangi System)	RAYALASIMA (Basvi System)
1 Adilabad	10 Nellore	12 Karnool
2 Karimnagar	11 Prakasham	13 Anantapur (Matangi System)
3 Nizamabad		14. Chittoor
4 Medak		
5 Warangal		
6 Mahaboobnagar		
7 Rangareddy		
8 Hyderabad		
9 Nalgonda (Matangi System)		

rehabilitation. That letter was signed by the then general secretary of the Andhra Pradesh Kalavanthula Sangham, B.A.V.L. Narasimha Rao.

In 1987, the Kalavanthula Sangham requested the government to ban exploitation of women in the name of religion and tradition. They said that the trade in human flesh had been encouraged for centuries by the Hindu tradition. The Sangham said that a few castes should not be exploited as had been done in the case of the devadasis for a long time.

"Behind this sacred and honourable word stands the naked aggression and brutality of consigning the heights of innocence to the doors of the Devil and the flower of childhood to the flames of lust", says Chandramouli, an Indian administrative officer, who was engaged in tackling this problem during the governorship of Kumudben Joshi in Andhra Pradesh.

The word 'Jogin' is derived from 'Yogin', meaning a 'girl saint'. Jogin is defined as a rural girl traditionally or superstitiously dedicated to a village god or goddess.

The Jogin system of the latter day is a variant of the Devadasi system prevalent among the lower strata of society. However, there are differences between these two systems as shown in Table 4.1.

Table 4.1

Differences between Devadasi and Jogin systems

Devadasi System	*Jogin, Matangi and Basvi System*
No particular caste; girls were purchased from all backward class communities.	Girls were purchased from dalit communities like Malas, Madigas and a few other backward classes like Dommaras, Yerukalas, Boyas and washerman castes only.
Patronized by kings and zamindars	No patronage.
Women of letters, fine arts like dance and music.	Illiterates – folk dance is prevalent.
Matriarchal system is adopted; descent from mother to daughter.	Patriarchal system with a few features of matriarchy is observed.
It is prevalent throughout the country.	It is prevalent only in South India comprising the earlier Deccan area.
They are called Temple Dancers.	They are called Matammas or Tayammas in the respective areas.

Cont'd...

Cont'd...

There are two types of temples, viz., Saiva temples and Vaishnava temples. Devadasis in Saiva temples are expected to wear 'Siva Linga' and in Vaishnava temples, they are branded with Sankhu and Chakra.	Gods and goddesses have their own small temples. Yellamma, Maisamma, Mariamma, Mathamma, Sunkalamma and Ulagamma are some of the names of the proletarian goddesses. Murukan, Hanuman, Khandoba and China Obulesu are the gods to whom these girls are dedicated
Brahmin priests perform the puja.	Non-Brahmin purohits perform the puja.
Devadasis lead a life of luxury and pomp.	Some of these women have even become beggars.
It is a temple service.	Any distress or mishap in the family or the village is considered a visitation of God. For every mishap, dedication is believed to be the only remedy.
Devadasi system gradually degenerated into prostitution.	Jogins are inducted into prostitution with social sanction under the cover of tradition.
In the matriarchal system, there is no son-preference. The son is like a pimp. He supports the family by playing instrumental music at the dance performances of his mother or sisters.	Under the Jogin system, potharaju, 'brother' of the local goddess, ties the 'Tali' or mangalasutra to that girl. Among the matangis and tayammas, the maternal uncle, Pedda Madiga (elder member of the Madiga community) or Pedda Golla plays a very important role in the marriage festival. In addition to that, there are Baineedlu who recite the story of Yellamma or Mathamma and they are assisted by Kommuvaru.
Some devadasis are maintained by the feudal lords as concubines and others solicit customers.	Generally, these are 'village sluts' or common women. Sometimes, they also act as exclusive 'concubines' of the feudal gentry in the village.
It was abolished in 1947.	The Devadasi (Prevention) Act was passed in 1988 in Andhra Pradesh.
The marriage ceremony is called 'muttirai'. Five days before this, 'Gajja puja' – initiation into dancing – is performed.	Dance is performed on the day of marriage to Yellamma or her counterpart.

Divine prostitution is an age-old custom in India. This has been a feature of both the Great Tradition and the Little Tradition. The survey of literature on the custom of divine prostitution in India reveals that a hierarchy is maintained similar to the gradation of castes. Some girls still in their infancy are dedicated to the goddesses by their parents. These girls are considered to be of a lower order than the devadasis of the Brahmanical order.

In the absence of a male heir in the family, some would temporarily revert to the system of descent through daughter so that they may dedicate her to the temple as a basvi or matangi or jogin. The children of these women are also dedicated in the same manner. Let us analyse the system of Jogins in Andhra Pradesh.

In Telangana, they are called Jogins (Parvatis in Karimnagar), Matangis and Basvis in both coastal Andhra and Rayalaseema areas bordering Karnataka and Mathammas or Tayammas in Nellore district. They are called Devadasis in Karnataka, Muralis in Maharashtra and Bhavins in Goa.

The basic feature of the Jogin system is that young girls are dedicated to the 'service' of the local deity such as Yellamma, Poleramma or Renukamba. On an auspicious day, the girl is dedicated to a temple. The ceremony is conducted by the Dasaris, Purohits, Jangams and Potharajus. This worship of Gramadevatas forms an important part of the conglomeration of the religious beliefs, customs and ceremonies which are generally classed together under the term Hinduism.

To fulfil their aspirations, the devotees offer to the deity, food, wealth, and sacrifice animals and even human beings.

The institution of Jogins in Telangana is a relic of the feudal system and a living example of the exploitation of women. In the name of religion and custom, the jogins are condemned in their infancy to lead a life of shame and insecurity. According to a report in *The Hindu* (17 December 1987), "the landed classes have for centuries managed to convince the Scheduled Castes that the paucity of Jogins is the cause of their misfortune."[1]

The origin of the Jogin system is shrouded in the mists of history and since the practice has been accepted and institutionalized, it has never been questioned. The girl is dedicated to a temple when her family members are convinced that a sacrifice to god can save the family as well as the village. In the case of parents who are unwilling to make their daughter a jogin, psychological pressure is brought to bear on them and the feudal lords ensure that someone in the village goes into 'possession state' (trance) and express the will of god that the girl be dedicated as a jogin. As stated by Kamala Devi Chattopadhyaya, "Double standard of morality has now come to be recognized, a severe code for women as the preservers of the social morals and an easier standard for men whose fickleness and lapses are to be indulgently treated."

When a girl is branded as a jogin, she is passed on from one man to another who gives her money, paddy, land or sometimes maintains her. She becomes the exclusive 'concubine' of the feudal gentry in that village. When she is initiated, the innocent girl does not know what is in store for her. The jogin is married to any one of the seven matrikas like Yellamma, Pochamma, Poleramma and Maisamma by their brother potharaju who ties a 'Tali' or mangalasutra to the girl in the name of the particular deity to whom she is dedicated.

Unlike in prostitution, there are no middlemen in the jogin system. A jogin lives with her parents, and men go to her house for her 'favours'. She is not ostracized but is accepted as part of the whole set-up. It is a status symbol among the rich to have more than one mistress. This practice has its deep roots in the village life and it has become a part of the village structure.

The children of a jogin cannot be called the children of the landlord. The son of a jogin can marry a girl of his own caste in the normal fashion but the daughter cannot. Like her mother, she should become a jogin to continue the tradition. A notable feature of the system is that 95 per cent of the jogins belong to the SC groups. Poverty makes an SC man subservient to the landlord and accept the initiation of his female child as a jogin.

The initiation process has two phases. The first phase is known as the first Ghattam or Pattam. At this stage,

- the child is very young, she could be just one month old;
- the child cannot comprehend what is happening and what is in store for her;
- potharaju performs the marriage;
- all other jogins perform a dance before and after the marriage of that particular girl;
- the girl becomes 'Nityasumangali' and she has certain obligations and rights which others do not have; and
- before this Ghattam, the girl has to go to Yellamma or Poleramma where the potharaju (a non-Brahmin pujari) bites a goat in one go. This is known as 'Gavupattu'.

In the second phase, known as Jogipatta, the girl, smeared with turmeric powder from head to foot, dressed in yellow and decked with flowers, is married in an elaborate ceremony to potharaju, the 'brother' of the goddess. Before and after this ceremony, the other jogins perform a dance. The marriage is followed by a community feast and drinking.

After the girl attains puberty, consummation is arranged with the landlord or any person who undertakes to give her economic support. This is called the second Ghattam or 'Milapattam'. The girl is then initiated into her actual role by the village patel or chief. Then depending on her physical attractiveness, she becomes the mistress of some rich man or ends up as a one-night stand for all and sundry to keep her body and soul together. There are other arrangements as well. He looks after her for a stipulated period of time after which she is free to go to other men or sometimes he may even take care of her for the rest of her life. At that time, the system of keeping concubines is highly respected.

A jogin is not confined to the boundaries of the temple. She is required to dance at funerals of the feudal lords. At harvest time, she begs for some paddy. This obnoxious practice was known to the officers and social leaders of those days. Everybody looks down on her because she belongs to a dalit community and not being the wife to somebody, she cannot think of a normal life. Every man would want an opportunity to have sex with her.

The Jogin system is prevalent in the backward rural areas of Bodhan, Banswada, Yellareddy and Madnur. This evil practice has almost come to stay as a way of life with the oppressed sections of society. The child of a jogin can marry only the child of another jogin. The following issues call for a serious discussion: the rationale behind the entire system, the superstition surrounding it, exploitation which has driven the jogins into this deplorable condition and the possibilities of weaning the jogins from this shameful life and rehabilitating them in a respectable profession and how can the problem be nipped in the bud and further deterioration can be prevented.

The SC people are the most deprived group of our society. Most of them are landless, their labour is underpaid and they are treated as untouchables. About 90 per cent of bonded labourers are recruited from SC groups, their women are sexually exploited and they are prone to all kinds of diseases. The problem of jogins should be understood in this background.

Now, what are the essential components of this system? They are:

- Almost 95 per cent jogins are recruited from the SC groups. Poverty drives the male head of the family to obey the orders of landlords and initiate his female child as a jogin.
- Invariably, the landlords come from upper castes.
- The legitimization of jogin is derived from her marriage to the village deity. It has social acceptance.
- It is the money power of the landlord that compels the vulnerable sections of the SC to give away their female children as jogins.
- It is again the vulnerability of the jogins that forces their daughters to perpetuate the system.

The jogin is almost a slave to the feudal lord who uses her to satisfy his carnal desires. She also has to work in the fields to maintain her family. It is a sub-system in the larger framework of the bonded labour system.

Thus, the economic condition of jogins is pathetic. They still live in thatched houses; some of them do not even have that. This social evil is still in vogue in all the Telangana districts. The jogin is not given any allowance either for herself or for her children and, therefore, lives in abject poverty. The pathetic condition of jogins was highlighted in a detailed case study of several women published in the July 14, 1986 edition of *Newstime,* an English daily now defunct, under the headline "Women of God and rich men".[2] The Jogin problem is known to the whole nation. How to eradicate the system is the work of the social reformers.

Every year, at the beginning of the rainy season, in every village of Telangana, people celebrate a festival called 'Ora Panduga' to avoid epidemics, floods and famines. The worship of village deities is limited to non-Brahmin communities. The village deities are generally female, but a few gods are also worshipped. For example, in Anantapur district, there is a god called China Obulesu to whom basvis are dedicated. In Maharashtra, 'Muralis' are dedicated to Khandoba, an incarnation of Siva.

In the village festival, there is division of labour among the non-Brahmin communities. Brahmins and Vaisyas generally do not attend these festivals. The feudal lord or the landlord invites all the non-Brahmins, fixes the date for the festival, suggests how to celebrate it and discusses his plan with them. The village head collects money from people and gives his own contribution for the festival. It is his responsibility to arrange everything for the festival, including the supply of country liquor. A man belonging to the 'Niradi' (one who waters wet lands) gives maize and the potter makes five pots and five guragalu (vessels), five plates and other things. A man from the Begari caste supplies mango leaves and wood of the mango tree. The mason prepares the structures for the deities. The people thus share the work. The potharaju's task is to bite off the sacrificial goat. He then marries the jogin in an elaborate ceremony. The priest, who is from the same caste, performs the marriage on behalf of the goddess. The potharaju ties the mangalasutra. Potharaju, Niradi, Mehr, Begari, Kamdaur, Gaini, Jogin and Kolla are some of the surnames of dalit communities. 'Niradi' people supply water to the lands of people in the village through irrigation canals. 'Begari' is a cremation attendant called 'Katikapari' in coastal Andhra.

A question that is often asked is: why are jogins married to goddesses? The answer is that it is a superstition followed by the Mala and Madiga and some other backward class communities.

Why are only Mala and Madiga girls dedicated to the goddess? To find the answer, the Mahatma Phule Pratishthan organized a convention of divine prostitutes of Nipan on the Maharashtra-Karnataka border. The convention was chaired by Devadasi Gaurabai Satware. Gaurabai posed some startling questions: "Why does Yellamma not demand girls from other communities like Brahmins, Marathas, Lingayats and Gujjars? When caste Hindus also worship Yellamma, why do not they dedicate their girls to her? Why should we be asked to dedicate our daughters and sons?" The dalits were forbidden to enter the houses of Brahmins and Vaisyas. In this context, it must be mentioned that dedication among the SCs attained visibility in the post-independence period. It is rampant in almost all districts of Telangana. The name of the goddess differs from place to place, but the practice is identical. This dedication of a girl to the village deity is almost like a marriage. Caste hierarchy, which was strictly observed even during the colonial period, became more pronounced after independence. The practice of dedicating girls is not confined to the Telangana area but prevails all over the state. Since the practice stems from superstition, the first thing to be done is educate the children by setting up Ashram schools in all the areas where this problem is prevalent. The government should also start adult education centres.

It is a pity that, despite the state enforcement authority being armed with anti-Devadasi Act, nothing has been done to end this social evil in interior Telangana, where a number of girls are ending up as prostitutes or kept women. An incident which happened on the night of 18 June 1987 was reported by *The Deccan Chronicle* in its September 13 edition under the heading "A peep into Jogins' lives". The report said: "The priest, locally known as 'potharaju', comes with a vicious-looking whip in his hand. He lashes himself to drum-beats. A girl, Bhagirathi, barely seventeen years old, is brought into the pandal. Potharaju is offered 'Kallu' (toddy) and he is now ready to perform rites which will make Bhagirathi a property of the villagers. She will be a victim to appease their carnal instincts. When this was going on, the social workers wanted to stop the proceedings with the help of the police people. Her mother said that Bhagirathi was already dedicated to the goddess. As usual, the girl was taken into the room of the village head. She was destined to become a Jogin and ... end her life in prostitution in the cover of religion. In rural areas, the girls are the victims of elders' abhorrent practices."[3]

The report also said that the village Panchayat chastised her. One jogin argued back, "If I go to work, I get a few rupees. If I dance in front of a corpse, all that I get is a bottle of 'Kallu' and a few paisa. Why should we go there?"[4] After experiencing several instances, jogins realized that no fault of theirs had made them the victims of circumstances.

Eradication of the Jogin System

It would be pertinent to recall what Mahatma Gandhi wrote three days before his assassination: "We have won political freedom, but we have yet to win economic freedom, social and moral freedom. These freedoms are harder than the political, if only because they are constructive, less exciting and not spectacular." A social worker Lavanam says, "No doubt, we have achieved economic growth. But, that economic growth being very uneven and being devoid of necessary social awareness, instead of generating reason and responsibility, commitment and camaraderie, has given rise to unethical competition, sectarianism, superstition, frustration and indifference.

Unless rational thinking and social responsibility enter into the blood of our national life we will become paralyzed. We dehumanize ourselves and become asocial."[5]

Fortunately, some social workers have endeavoured hard to eradicate the Jogin system. For instance, Madari Bhagya Reddy Verma established Jagan Mitra Mandali in 1906 in Hyderabad to work among the outcastes. That gradually culminated into the Adi Andhra Movement in 1917. The Mandali worked for the amelioration of outcastes by trying to rid them of superstitious beliefs. Bhagya Reddy Verma pleaded against the dedication of girls to deities as muralis and jogins. He advocated reformation and entertainment through dramas and Harikatha Kalakshepams. Other organizations such as Matangi Maha Sabha at Nampally and the Suveetha Bala Samajam founded by Arigay Ramaswami at Secunderabad worked towards the abolition of Jogin or Murali system. In 1922, the All India Adi-Hindu Social Conference took place at Hyderabad. One of the important resolutions adopted at that conference was that dedication of girls to deities should be declared as immoral and that this custom should be proscribed. The conference strove hard to influence the villagers by holding meetings to create public awareness of the evils of this deep-rooted custom. However, the efforts of the conference were not successful because it looked to effective legislative and rehabilitative measures. Owing to the efforts of Bhagya Reddy Verma, legal measures were brought into force to abolish this system in the then Nizam's dominions.

Until 1948, Telangana was ruled by the Nizam. Their religion did not permit freedom to women. Moreover, the majority of Hindus did not concern themselves with the problem. Besides, the religious overtones of the problem did not allow them to take it seriously. Naturally, the ruling classes ignored this social problem. In the post-independence period, as the focus was on the middle class movement, the problems of the downtrodden did not receive serious attention of the government. The Telangana armed struggle was mainly concerned with agrarian issues and other economic problems. Voluntary organizations such as Christian Missionaries and Area Saman concentrated on conversions and re-conversions and other social problems. Madapati Hanumantha Rao and his followers launched movements in regard to political issues. The Jogin problem thus remained largely untouched. The same situation prevailed till 1985. The Jogin problem demanded socio-economic rehabilitation of the victims, not on administrative grounds but on humanitarian grounds.

In 1980, Appa Rao, assistant collector under training at Yedapally village in Nizamabad district, found that dalit women were being used as prostitutes with social sanction under the cover of religion. He wrote a letter to the Principal Secretary, Social Welfare S.R. Sankaran describing the plight of jogins in that village. Appa Rao was thus responsible for bringing the problem to the notice of the government. From 1981 to 1985, correspondence on the matter of jogins was kept up in right earnest and this state of affairs continued until 30 May 1985 when Asha Murthy took over as Nizamabad district collector. She directed her subordinates like the district women and child welfare officer to help the helpless girls by taking steps to rehabilitate them. She started the rehabilitation programme by setting up a centre for the jogins where they were taught sewing, papad-making and book-binding. Twelve jogins were shifted to a colony built for them at Ambam near Nizamabad town. When the first batch of jogins came to the centre, rumours were spread that the jogins had been taken to the centre to be sacrificed to some god. The programme, thus, suffered a setback right in the beginning.

Asha Murthy admitted that there was no master plan, no separate department, no funds and no encouragement. Yet, the scheme survived because it dealt with a major social issue. The government wanted to bring in legislation on the lines of what Karnataka had done to deal with the Devadasi system. It was generally believed that Nizamabad alone had jogins because of the initiative of the district administration to open a rehabilitation centre. When the author visited Ambam in 1986, she found that all the jogins had vacated that centre.

It must be mentioned that Murthy's move was the first bold move to tackle a really sensitive issue as it involved the parents of jogins and village landlords. While the parents thought that they would be deprived of security in their old age, the landlords felt that they would lose their privilege to have these innocent girls as their concubines whom they paid paltry rewards in the form of grain. To Murthy's dismay, most jogins resisted efforts to bring them into the mainstream of society. Only five jogins came to the district headquarters and the administration provided them with the basic amenities.

Even before Murthy became the collector of Nizamabad district, S.R. Sankaran, Principal Secretary of the Social Welfare Department, had come to know about the prevalence of the Jogins system in Nizamabad district. On 14 April 1985, he wrote to the collectors of Nizamabad and Karimnagar asking for a detailed report. He also wrote to the Director, Scheduled Castes and Tribes, Government of India, Hyderabad branch. All of them replied that they had come across the abominable practice of dedication in Yedapally village near Bodhan in Nizamabad district.

Sankaran learnt that a similar system was in vogue in Karnataka where the government had enacted a law to eradicate the social evil. The Department of Social Welfare, Karnataka, proposed to tackle this problem in three ways as under:

(1) Entrusting voluntary agencies with the task of spreading public awareness of the problem; producing a documentary film on this system prevailing in Soundatti, Chandragutti and other places.

(2) Starting a state home for women at Athani and a certified school at Soundatti for young girls to give them shelter and train them in specified techniques.

(3) Granting loans to women to launch income-generating programmes through Gruhakalyana schemes.

The Andhra Pradesh government took the cue from the Karnataka government in deciding to implement rehabilitative programmes. Sankaran realized that concerted efforts were needed to elevate the status of jogins for their social and economic rehabilitation. This required the officials and non-officials including the NGOs to work together. The rehabilitative measures the government considered were:

- Modification of the Andhra Pradesh (Andhra area) Devadasi (Prevention and Dedication) Act of 1947 to arrest the dedication of jogins, parvatis and basvis.
- Extension of the amended regulations to the whole state and their strict enforcement.
- Implementation of the Suppression of Immoral Traffic in Women and Girls Act, 1956 to check migration from rural to urban areas which gave scope to prostitution as a source of livelihood.
- Enforcement of the Beggary Act.

- Stringent action against the violators.
- Provision of pucca houses and pensions to jogins and basvis to prevent them from begging and involving in prostitution.
- Allotment of lands to these women for cultivation.
- Provision of job-oriented programmes.
- Financial assistance to the jogins to open Kirana shops and other income-generating activities.
- Government jobs for the jogins.
- Granting property rights to the jogins who stay with their parents.
- Conferment on the physically handicapped children of the jogins the right to join homes for the disabled run by the government.
- Provision of Ashram schools for the children of jogins.
- Provision of adult education centres for the jogins to study at night.
- Starting state and district-level cells to tackle the problems of jogins.

The then Governor of Andhra Pradesh, Kumudben Joshi, established the National Institute of Social Action (NISA), a voluntary organization, and headed it herself. Under her stewardship, a campaign was launched against the Jogin system in Nizamabad.

With the object of rooting out the evil, the Governor suggested the holding of a state-level social reforms conference. A prompt response came from Samskar, a voluntary organization of Vijayawada devoted to reformation, rehabilitation and upliftment of marginal groups. A steering committee was constituted to organize the conference. The committee headed by the Governor consisted of 18 members. The committee decided that

- young girls not yet initiated into the Jogin system should be adopted by a voluntary organization. They should be put into residential schools so as to protect them from exploitation.
- middle-aged women should be given training in some craft or other and brought into the category of income-generating groups. A separate colony should be provided for them.
- old women or seasoned jogins should be recruited as social workers who could explain to the youngsters the hardships of jogins. The government should give them pension.

Samskar, a voluntary organization, offered to take up the survey of jogins in Nizamabad district in collaboration with NISA. It identified 150 jogins. The Red Cross Society of India expressed its willingness to adopt 25 girls.

The idea of Samskar was conceived by well-known social reformers Lavanam and Hemalatha Lavanam. Samskar started its work in 1974 with the reformation of denotified criminal tribes of Stuartpuram in Guntur district. This experience was the basis for Samskar's subsequent efforts in the reform and rehabilitation of the jogins in Nizamabad district. Hemalatha Lavanam started her survey and estimated that there were at least 10,000 jogins in Nizamabad district alone.

The Government of Andhra Pradesh had introduced a bill in the Legislative Assembly to abolish the Jogin system. Here, I should mention that there were two agencies that did the survey of jogins in Nizamabad district. One was a government agency under the direction of Asha Murthy, and the other was NISA under the stewardship of the then Governor of Andhra Pradesh with which Lavanam and Hemalatha Lavanam were associated. NISA organized the national conference in New Delhi on February 16 and 17, 1987. The conference made the following recommendations:

- This programme might form an important part of the special component plan for the SCs and the state government departments dealing with the welfare of the SCs and the welfare of women should formulate forthwith schemes of rehabilitation of the jogins from the annual plan 1987–1988 onwards.
- The Planning Commission, the Department of Women and Child Welfare, the Central Social Welfare Board, the All India Association of Social and Moral Hygiene, the National Institute of Social Defence and other organizations concerned may be associated with the programme of rehabilitation of jogins.
- Media, particularly, can be the most effective instrument for arousing consciousness among the jogins and the community at large.
- A state-level committee may be formed for the implementation of the programme. It should be chaired by an eminent social worker like Hemalatha Lavanam and it should consist of the principal secretary, Social Welfare Department and some other officials and non-officials. The committee should be given the status of a first-class state advisory committee.

- At the district level, a joint committee of officials and non-officials should be formed for the implementation of the programme. This committee should be given full autonomy.
- Jogins in the age-group of 5–14 years should be taken away from their homes and kept in residential schools outside their district. These schools should also have students from other sections of the society for social integration.
- For jogins in the age-group of 14–30 years, details of schemes for training them in various trades may be formulated on war-footing.
- Special stipends of Rs 150 per month to the aged persons should be granted. Old-age pension scheme may be extended to eligible candidates.
- The adult members of the families of jogins may be given preference in selection of beneficiaries under different poverty alleviation programmes like Integrated Rural Development Programme (IRDP), Rural Landless Employment Guarantee (RLEG) and National Rural Employment Programme (NREP).
- Girl students of schools of social work as well as women students of universities/colleges may be organized for conducting camps in the villages of jogins to educate them and help them in their rehabilitation.

In the implementation of these programmes, voluntary organizations will have to liaise between the government and the people. They can help in making the victims aware of the existing laws and understand the socio-economic exploitation that forces them into the system.

Hemalatha Lavanam realized that such 'quickfix' methods would not solve the problem. She convinced the government to accept her arguments and entrust the rehabilitation programme to her voluntary organization Samskar. Inspired by the vision of the Governor and encouraged by the involvement of government officials, she took up the stupendous task.

For better and easy working at the grass-roots level, NISA, along with Samskar, established a permanent centre at Varni village in Nizamabad district. Christened 'Chelli Nilayam', the centre aimed at providing vocational training for jogins and hostel facilities for children, besides taking care of the old and uncared-for jogins. 'Chelli' is a Telugu word meaning 'sister'. For setting up the centre and Samskar offices, the district collector allotted five acres of government land.

Chelli Nilayam proposed to develop integrated institutional services and training programmes for jogins and their children. The centre provided the opportunity to all jogins and their children to lead a sort of family life and togetherness. All jogins were to be referred to as sisters and men working in the institution or elsewhere as brothers.

The training programme was in non-traditional areas like leather goods, tailoring, aromatic plantation and nurseries and rabilory. These women were provided with hostel accommodation. They were house mothers, dormitory incharges and cooks. Their children upto the age of six years were allowed to stay with them. First, they provided educational facility for 60 children. Chelli Nilayam also took up a social forestry programme. NISA sought an assistance of Rs 13.50 lakh from the state's budget for the welfare of the jogins and Rs 15 lakh from the Central Social Welfare Board, New Delhi.

The survey was conducted in 1987 by Asha Murthy with the help of Nizamabad Sub-Collector Subrahmanyam. Likewise, a survey was conducted in Medak, Mahaboobnagar, Ranga Reddy and Warangal districts of Telangana. It revealed that 85 per cent of the jogins were under 30 years of age and 82 per cent of their children did not have any educational background. Of the 1,251 jogins surveyed, only 106 had permanent houses, and the others lived in huts or temporary houses or had no houses at all. Only seven jogins had more than two acres of land. That means all others were below the poverty line. Nineteen jogins had an average monthly income of Rs 500.

The pathetic condition of the jogins prompted the principal secretary to the government, Social Welfare Department, to write a letter to the collector and district magistrate of each district. The letter said: (i) Please refer to my D.O. Letter No. 86/PSP(SW)/84, dated 26 January 1987 regarding the socio-economic rehabilitation of jogin/basvi women; (ii) It is necessary to take effective steps to prevent fresh dedication; (iiii) To keep a watch in regard to any cases of fresh dedication of women/girls and to take immediate action to prevent such dedication and also put down this practice.

Subsequently, a detailed survey was conducted in 16 districts of Andhra Pradesh. The survey found that there were about 5,000 such women and more than 80 per cent of them belonged to the SC. With the object of putting down the obnoxious custom, a bill called the Andhra Pradesh Devadasi (Prohibition of Dedication) Bill 1987 was introduced in the Assembly. It later became a full-fledged Act. The government formulated a detailed scheme of socio-economic rehabilitation of jogin/basvi women, and allocated funds for this purpose from the year 1987–1988. The principal secretary, Social Welfare Department, requested the district administrators to implement the scheme systematically and send him progress reports from time to time. To monitor the progress, some officers were appointed as members of the district-level committee.

The efforts of the administration in Nizamabad for the welfare of the jogins came in for special praise in an article by B. Sudarsanam, a freelance journalist. In the article titled "New life for Jogins", he noted that the district administration of Nizamabad was taking a keen interest in rescuing the socially handicapped victims of the Jogin system. Rehabilitation of the jogins was an arduous task not only because it was an age-old social practice but also because it was an economic loss for their guardians and sensuous loss to the village social tyrants who exploit them as concubines by paying them paltry rewards.

The numbers of jogins and basvis revealed by the district-wise survey conducted in 1985–1987 are shown in Table 4.2.

In addition, 351 men were dedicated to various gods and goddesses.

The district-wise survey showed that while in some districts, the Jogin/Basvi system existed, a different system called the Devadasi system prevailed in some other districts such as Vizianagaram, East Godavari and West Godavari. These districts have fertile lands compared with Telangana and Rayalaseema regions. The people of the coastal districts being rich have 'concubines'.

In Krishna, Guntur and Prakasam districts, there is a different problem. People of a semi-nomadic tribe by name Dommaras, who migrated to these areas, provide another kind of sexual pleasure to the locals. The people of these areas are not as superstitious as those of the backward areas of Telangana and Rayalaseema. The author's survey in Prakasam and Nalgonda districts showed that the Matamma system exists in some pockets. The elderly people of a village in Prakasam district near Kanigiri told the author that there is a traditional Matamma who identified herself with Mathamma, the goddess. They said that she was very powerful. It was her order that all the people of the village, irrespective of caste distinctions, should attend the jatara. At jatara time, Matamma is treated as a deity and she can spit toddy on the face of anyone including Brahmins and this is regarded as an auspicious sign. She can also push anybody with her buttocks. That is a symbol of her greatness. When she is not performing the duties of a Matamma, she is an untouchable woman. But untouchability is not a bar to have sexual pleasure with her. This is the double standard society follows.

Table 4.2

Numbers of jogins and basvis revealed by the district-wise survey conducted in 1985–1987

Srikakulam	14
Vizianagaram	Nil
Visakhapatnam	Nil
East Godavari	Nil
West Godavari	Nil
Krishna	Nil
Guntur	Nil
Prakasam	Nil to 70
Nellore	70
Kurnool	790
Cuddapah	Nil
Anantapur	556–3000
Chittoor	102–870
Adilabad	324–500
Nizamabad	1251–2300
Karimnagar	9313–12051
Warangal	1551–2500
Mahaboobnagar	1428–3500
Khammam	Nil
Nalgonda	58-
Medak	384
Ranga Reddy	50–350
Hyderabad	387
Total	16,287

The Jogin, Matangi and Basvi systems are there throughout Andhra Pradesh except beyond Krishna district where they have the Devadasi system. Let us analyse the position of these women in various districts of Andhra Pradesh. We start with Hyderabad.

Hyderabad District

In Hyderabad, there are four mandals and jogins live in 29 slums. There were 387 jogins/basvis/parvatis in the district when a survey was conducted for the first time in 1986. According to government records, 740 jogins were rehabilitated between 1987–88 and 2002–03 in Hyderabad district.

This shows that the number of jogins rose from 387 in 1986 to 740 in 2003 – an increase of 353. What are the reasons for this increase? Poverty is the main cause; jogins have not stopped dedicating their girl child as jogin. They think that earning by prostitution will solve their economic problems. The question, therefore, arises whether the rehabilitation work carried out by the government is sufficient for their survival. It is giving them milch cows or buffaloes, opening petty kirana shops or tea bunks and tailoring work – all these do not afford sufficient economic support.

Organizations that are surviving on foreign funds can, to some extent, support the jogins economically. Table 4.3 shows the profile of jogins based on various factors:

Table 4.3

The profile of jogins in 1986–1987

I	**Age-wise classification of the jogins**		
	(a) Below 18 years	—	14
	(b) Below 30 years	—	73
	(c) Below 50 years	—	223
	(d) Above 50 years	—	77
Because of the scheme, the number of jogins aged less than 18 years was only 14.			
II	**Classification based on castes of the jogins**		
	(a) Mala	—	59 persons
	(b) Madiga	—	186 persons
	(c) Others	—	142 persons
Others mean Dommaras, 1 or 2 Rajakas, Reddis and fishermen.			

Cont'd...

Cont'd...

		Boys	*Girls*	*Other dependants*
III	**Age-wise classification of the children/dependants**			
(a)	Below 5 years	46	53	—
(b)	Below 10 years	69	8	—
(c)	Below 15 years	81	80	—
(d)	Below 30 years	—	—	—
(e)	Above 30 years	—	—	—
IV	**Classification of jogins' children based on educational qualifications**			
		Boys	*Girls*	
(a)	No education	140	95	
(b)	Below 5th standard	39	36	
(c)	Below SSLC	15	9	
(d)	Above SSLC	2	1	
V	**Classification of jogins' children based on sex**			
(a)	Boys	—	196	
(b)	Girls	—	141	
VI	**Number of jogins having houses**			
(a)	Huts	—	164	
(b)	Semi-permanent	—	33	
(c)	Permanent house	—	26	
(d)	No house	—	164	
VII	**Classification of jogins based on occupation**			
(a)	Agricultural labourers	—	Nil	
(b)	Contract labourers	—	Nil	
(c)	Other types of labourer	—	Begging - 385	
(e)			Kirana - 1	
(f)			Employee - 1	
VIII	**Number of jogins getting average monthly wages**			
(a)	Upto Rs 100 per month	—	385	
(b)	Upto Rs 200 per month	—	1	
(c)	Upto Rs 300 per month	—	—	
(d)	Upto Rs 500 per month	—	1	
IX	**Number of skilled jogins - 1**			
X	**Number of unskilled jogins - 385**			

Cont'd...

Cont'd...

XI	Major skills available with the jogins		
		Type of skill	*Number of persons*
	(a)	Basket-making	1
	(b)	No skill	385

XII Classification based on types of government assistance received

1.	Land assignment	-	Nil	(1)	Revenue Dept.	-	Nil
2.	Widow pension	-	Nil	(2)	DRDA	-	Nil
3.	Old-age pension	-	1	(3)	SC Society	-	Nil
4.	Others	-	Nil	(4)	Women Welfare Dept.	-	Nil

XIII Number of jogins who have not received government assistance -386

XIV	Classification based on diseases the jogins are suffering from		
		Type of disease	*No. of persons*
	(a)	STD	—
	(b)	Malnutrition	185
	(c)	Defective vision	27

XV	Classification based on physical handicap		
		Type of disability	*No. of persons*
	(a)	Hands disability	1
	(b)	Legs crippled	1

From this data, following conclusions can be drawn:

- In Hyderabad district, Madiga jogins are more in number. Others also dedicate their daughters to different village deities such as Yellamma, Pochamma, Maisamma, etc.
- Superstition is the bane of jogins here. Because of this, almost all of them are afraid of the wrath of the village deity. However, there has been a welcome change. Realizing the importance of education, the jogins have started sending their children, including girls, to school.
- The housing pattern indicates the poverty of jogins. While 164 persons lived in huts, an equal number had no houses. It shows that they worked as daily wage earners or beggars. No jogin had any land at that time (1986). Even today, the jogins are leading a miserable life. The government's rehabilitation programme has not done much to improve their economic condition. Some of the jogins are still engaged in prostitution or they are regarded as keeps. The sum of Rs 200 is insufficient for their sustenance. One or two families are living by basket-making.

- Very few jogins are receiving old-age pensions and others have no scope to get any money. Their plight in a city like Hyderabad, where the cost of living is very high, can be imagined.
- Their poor economic conditions must have prompted the jogins to make their daughters also jogins. That explains the increase in their number.
- The right type of alternative economic system has not been found for them.
- As the NGOs are working for their emancipation, the jogins should come forward and protest against this obnoxious system.

Nalgonda District

In Nalgonda district, except in one place, the researcher did not find any jogin. The collector of Nalgonda district wrote to the managing director of the Andhra Pradesh Scheduled Castes Cooperative Finance Corporation Limited to chalk out a time-bound programme for the completion of the survey of jogins/basvis/parvatis.

The survey revealed that there were 68 jogins/basvis/parvatis. The author found only one Matangi in Nalgonda town and she interviewed her. She said her name was Matamma. She was a true Yogini type. Even as she was talking to the author, she went into a trance. Her kumkum, turmeric powder and her dress indicated that she was a traditional, religious-minded Matamma.

The collector submitted the survey report to the principal secretary and informed him that there were 68 jogins in Nalgonda district, 12 of them in Nalgonda mandal alone. Of these, three belonged to the Madiga caste and the rest were from other castes. None of them had any education.

There were seven girls and five boys as jogins. Their age-wise classification is shown in Table 4.4:

Table 4.4

Age-wise classification of jogins in Nalgonda mandal

		Girls	*Boys*
(a)	Below 5 years	3	3
(b)	Below 10 years	3	2
(c)	Below 18 years	1	—

Only one jogin had a hut and none of the others had any land. Their monthly income was Rs 200. Five jogins knew mat-making. No government assistance was given to them until 1986. Two jogins had defective vision, but no one was disabled.

In Gundlapalli village of Nalgonda district, there were only two jogins. They belonged to castes other than Mala and Madiga. They did not have any education. One girl child aged under ten was dedicated to the village deity. These two jogins had huts. Their income was Rs 200 per month. No assistance was provided to them by the government.

There was no jogin in Kangal Mandal Dorepalli, while there were five in Kurmapalli village. Their age-wise classification is shown in Table 4.5:

Table 4.5

Age-wise classification of jogins of Kurmapalli village

(a)	Below 18 years	—	—
(b)	Below 30 years	—	2
(c)	Below 50 years	—	2
(d)	Above 50 years	—	1

Of the five, two belonged to the Madiga caste and three to other castes. One girl had studied upto the 5th standard and the others had no education. All the five lived in huts. Each of them had a monthly income of Rs 100.

In Serilingatam village of Kangal mandal, there were three jogins, all aged below 30 years.

In Laxmipur village, all four jogins had huts. They worked as agricultural labourers and used to earn an average monthly income Rs 200. To one person, the State Bank had given a loan of Rs 500. Because of poverty, they suffered from malnutrition and defective vision.

In Junampalli village, there was only one jogin and she lived in a hut. She was under 50 years and had no education.

In Peddakur of Mattampalli mandal, there were six jogins of the Madiga caste. They lived in the huts of contract labourers and begging was their occupation. Their monthly income was upto Rs 100. They did not get any financial assistance from the government.

In Gavidepalli village, there was only one jogin and she was aged 50. She was a Madiga and had four children. None of them had any education.

There was one Madiga jogin in Yellapuram village and one in Ganuga bandi village. Kullur, Mukundapuram, Neredcharla and Somaram each had a Madiga matangi. There was one matangi in Chillipalli.

The reason for the low number of matangis/basvis in Nalgonda district was political awareness. Leftist leaders must have worked for the matangis/basvis.

Ranga Reddy District

All the 207 jogins were rehabilitated in the year 2005. The district collector had in 1987 submitted a report to then principal secretary S.R. Sankaran that the number of jogins in the district at that time was 50 whose classification based on various factors is shown in Table 4.6:

Table 4.6

Profile of jogins as surveyed in 1987 based on various factors

I.	**Age-wise classification**		
(a)	Below 18 years	—	2
(b)	Below 30 years	—	10
(c)	Below 50 years	—	18
(d)	Above 50 years	—	20
In the younger generation, the number was only 2.			
II.	**Caste-wise breakdown**		
(a)	Malas	—	14
(b)	Madigas	—	30
(c)	Baindla (Harijan sub-caste)	—	5
(d)	Potharaju (Harijan sub-caste)	—	1
III.	**Classification based on education qualifications**		
		Boys	*Girls*
(a)	No education	32	35
(b)	Below 5th standard	5	—
(c)	Below SSLC	—	2
(d)	Above SSLC	1	2

Cont'd...

Cont'd...

IV. Classification based on the type of houses they had		
(a) Thatched houses	—	13
(b) Semi-permanent houses	—	30
(c) Permanent houses	—	5
(d) No houses	—	2
V. Classification based on land holdings		
(a) No land holdings	—	41
(b) Less than 2 acres	—	9
(c) More than 2 acres	—	Nil

Table 4.6 shows that nine persons had two acres of land, they lived in semi-permanent or permanent houses and sent their children to school. But 16 people had a monthly income of Rs 100 only. Five people had a monthly income of Rs 200. All these people were below the poverty line. They did not have any skill, nor did the government provide any type of assistance to them. Three jogins got old-age pensions and two got loans from the SC Corporation. Fourteen persons aged above 50 years suffered from defective vision due to insufficiency of food.

The increase in the number of jogins from 50 in 1987 to 207 in 2005 is attributed to poverty and the belief system among the Malas and Madigas and also to the fact that there was no non-governmental organization to work for their emancipation.

Warangal District

Of the 1,671 jogins/basvis identified, 1,059 were rehabilitated in the year 2005. In 1987, the number of jogins/basvis/parvatis identified was 1551. Table 4.7 gives details about the jogins in Warangal:

Table 4.7

Caste and age details of jogins in Warangal district

Particulars	*SC*	*ST*	*BC*	*Below 18 Yrs*	*Below 30 Yrs*	*Below 50 Yrs*	*Above 50 Yrs*
Widows	19	5	27	—	—	29	19
Jogins with consent of their sponsors	410	150	350	150	350	410	—

Cont'd...

Cont'd...

Jogins against the will of their sponsors	46	.9 9	82	29	92	46	—
Jogins (unmarried)	40	2	38	12	26	12	—
Any other chronic diseases	8	—	2	1	1	8	—
Jogins for gents	8	—	2	1	1	8	—

After the survey was over, action was taken involving the agencies concerned for giving necessary economic assistance to the beneficiaries. Mandal development officers collected the applications for loans for taking up petty trade. The officer concerned said monthly progress reports would be submitted to the government.

The particulars of financial assistance for the rehabilitation programme were:

(a)	Land assignment for houses	—	176
(b)	Petty traders	—	910
(c)	Old-age pension	—	341
(d)	Widow pension	—	51
(e)	Physically handicapped	—	39

In 1987, the number of jogins was 1,551 and the number now is 1,671, a difference of only 120 in 18 years. This increase of 120 probably includes girls who were born to jogins and Dommara basvis.

In Warangal, we have Ledella, Vangapadu, Geesukonda and in other places, Dommaras are more in number. Prostitution is rife among the Dommara women. Dommaras dedicate their daughters who are known as 'Venkatasanis'. They also worship Yellamma as their village deity.

Medak District

In Medak district, 933 jogins were identified and all of them were completely rehabilitated.

In 1993–94, a survey of jogins was taken up in Medak district. At that time, there were 385 jogins. The rehabilitation of jogins assumed significance especially after the promulgation of the 1987 Act which prohibited the Jogin system in any form. The government took to rehabilitate these jogins but according to the project officer, the rehabilitation package was not sufficient to provide a mode of income of support for them.

The government used to give Rs 5,000 as Social Welfare grant for each jogin. With this amount, the jogin could purchase a sewing machine or open a kirana shop. Those who had crossed 45 years of age were eligible for pension. For the remaining 76 cases, the Social Welfare Department people provided training in sericulture and horticulture. They brought jogins from various parts of the district and built houses for them and named the area Navodaya Colony. Sewing machines were given to some of them. However, the support given to these people was not sufficient. Government officials required periodical assessment to evaluate the impact of the rehabilitation scheme. Awareness programmes were conducted throughout the district and it was found that most of the jogins were unwilling to go back to the old profession. Ambedkar Sangam's youths helped the government officials. The officer felt that there was need to increase the amounts to be given to them and the District Scheduled Caste Corporation supplemented the amount with subsidy. The Social Welfare Department added margin money to match this subsidy. Though the idea of settling jogins in Navodaya Colony was laudable, the jogins faced problems of adjustment to the new environment.

Interestingly, one Kamalamma, a jogin of Madiramaswamipalli, said that the collector had told her that the government was willing to give her Rs 21,000, one acre of land and a pucca house. What she actually got was a meagre amount. The promised land was not given as the cost had increased three-fold.

Mahaboobnagar District

A survey conducted through women by village development officers (VDOs) and ICDS staff found jogins/basvis in 54 of the 64 mandals in the district and their total number was 1,428. They were found predominantly in Narayanpet and Gadwal divisions.

	Age-wise classification of jogins		
(a)	Below 18 years	—	122
(b)	Below 30 years	—	534
(c)	Below 50 years	—	569
(d)	Above 50 years	—	203

Of the 1,428 jogins/basvis, 1,103 were in the 30–50 age-group, 122 below 18 and 203 above 50 years. This shows that middle-aged and old people were custom-bound and were dedicated to Yellamma or Pochamma.

The jogins/basvis were found mainly among the Madiga caste. In 1987, the number of Madigas was 889 while washermen, Dommaras and other backward castes accounted for 475. The number of Malas then was only 64.

The number of children/dependants below 10 years was 60 and the number of dependant girls was 30. From 15 years onwards, they used to work as daily wage labourers to support the family. Only 60 boys and 30 girls had studied upto the 5th class.

The economic condition of the jogins/basvis was very poor and most of them – 1,220 of 1,428 – did not have houses to live in. While 200 jogins had huts, only eight had semi-permanent houses. None of them owned even a small piece of land. The average monthly wage of a jogin was Rs 100. They had no skill to get proper employment. Of the 1,428 jogins, four used to get old-age pensions. The caste-wise classification of the jogins is shown in Table 4.8:

Table 4.8

Caste-wise classification of the jogins

Name of the Mandal	*No. of the Villages*	*Caste*	*Total*
Mahaboobnagar	6	18 Madiga + 24 Others	42
Koilkunta	5	5 Madiga + 10 Others	15
Nawabpet	1	1 others	1
Hanwada	2	3 Madiga + 2 others	5
Jadcherla	2	4 Madiga + 2 others	6
Bhootpur	3	2 Madiga + 1 others	3
Balanagar	1	2 Madiga	2
Shadnagar	1	Mala	1
Kothur	1	Madiga	2
Kondurg	1	Madiga	2
Amangal	1	3 Others	3
Talakondapally	2	1 Mala, 1 Madiga, 3 Others	5
Nadjil	4	8 Others	8
Veldanda	1	3 Others	3
Vangoor	2	5 Others	5

Table 4.9

Division-wise classification based on caste

Nagarkurnool Division

No. of the Mandal	*Name of the Villages*	*Caste*	*Total*
Nagarkurnool	1	8 Others	8
Bijinepally	1	1 Mala, 8 Others	9
Gopalpet	1	6 Others	6
Tandur	1	3 Others	3
Telkapally	4	8 Others	8
Achampet	1	2 Others	2
Lingal	1	2 Others	2
Kollapur	1	4 Malas, 2 Madigas	6
P.K. Pally	2	3 Others	3

Gadwal Division

No. of the Mandal	*Villages*	*Notified*	*Caste*	*Total*
Gadwal	3	81	81 1 Mala, 55 Madiga, 25 Others	81
Ieej	3	8	2 Mala, 3 Madiga, 3 Others	8
Maldikal	7	25	5 Malas, 1 Madiga, 19 Others	25
Dharoor	10	12	1 Mala, 9 Madigas, 2 Others	12
Ghattu	12	27	10 Madigas, 17 Others	27
Alampur	8	39	3 Malas, 28 Madigas, 8 Others	39
Manopad	1	1	1 Others	1
Itikyal	1	2	2 Malas	2
Shantinagar	3	8	2 Madigas, 6 Others	8
Wanaparti	2	2	1 Mala, 1 Madiga	2
Kothakota	5	30	9 Madigas, 21 Others	30
Pebbair	2	4	4 Madigas	4
Addakal/ Moosapet	1	2	2 Madigas	2
Ghanapur	4	4	2 Madigas, 2 Others	4

Cont'd...

Cont'd...

Narayanpet Division

No. of the Mandal	*Villages*	*Notified*	*Caste*	*Total*
Makthal	18	208	192 Madigas, 16 Others	208
Narayanpet	5	82	1 Mala, 43 Madigas, 32 Others	76
Utkur	17	199	13 Malas, 154 Madigas, 32 Others	199
Magnoor	17	138	4 Malas, 129 Madigas, 5 Others	138
Dhanwada	8	36	2 Malas, 16 Madigas, 18 Others	36
Atmakur	17	74	23 Madigas, 51 Others	74
Deverkadra	17	40	7 Malas, 25 Madigas, 8 Others	40
C.C. Kunta	18	117	6 Malas, 66 Madigas, 45 Others	117
Narva	20	87	8 Malas, 48 Madigas, 31 Others	87
Kodangal	9	9	3 Madigas, 6 Others	9
Kosgi	6	11	1 Mala, 7 Madigas, 3 Others	11
Domargidda	3	8	3 Malas, 3 Madigas, 4 Others	10
Doulatabad	4	5	1 Mala, 4 Others	5
Bomraspet	5	10	5 Madigas, 5 Others	10

Why is the number of jogins high in the Narayanpet division? The reasons may be that it is a backward division and is close to the border of Karnataka from where basvis must have migrated. This region is also known for its superstitions.

Because of the proactive role of the NGOs, women of the Mala, Madiga and other castes realized that they should not continue as jogins/basvis. Secondly, they also want to educate their children and not allow even a single girl child to become a victim of this tradition. Thirdly, they have decided to fight for the eradication of the system. Fourthly, they are also aware of the fact that there is no cure for diseases such as AIDS.

Of the 2,087 jogins, 1,967 have been rehabilitated. On 15 June 2004, the Andhra Pradesh Jogin Vyavastha Vyatireka Porata Sangathana, an NGO, organized a Maha Sabha at Narayanpet. This NGO is working for the eradication of the Jogin system in seven districts of the state. At the Maha Sabha, the jogins asked the society to treat them as women first and as human beings next. They said that nowhere else in the world had such a system been accepted.

They demanded an end to this process of dehumanization. They described the rich people responsible for perpetuating this system as devils in human form.

The oppressive caste structure and the resultant social hierarchy in a village ensure that the so-called sacrifice to save the village is made only by a girl from the lowest caste. This is a permanent arrangement, made in the name of tradition to satisfy the lust of upper caste men. According to a survey by the Andhra Pradesh Jogini Vevasta Vetireka Porata Samithi (APJVVPS), most of the 21,281 jogins were from SCs and a few from other backward classes.

Adilabad District

In Adilabad district, 289 jogins were identified in 1987. The taluka-wise breakdown is as follows:

Boath	5
Chennur	43
Khanapur	9
Nirmal	103
Mudhol	129
Total	**289**

In Adilabad, of the 1,097 jogins identified, 798 were rehabilitated in 2005.

Rehabilitation scheme	*No. of Jogins*	*No. of Jogins yet to be helped*
Tailoring Training at Basar	15	—
Financial Assistance for various schemes	57	—
Old-age pensions	44	—
House sites	39	—
Financial sanction or loans	—	124
Total	**155**	

Financial assistance to the 124 jogins was increased from Rs 30 to Rs 1,000 and 83 persons were selected for old-age pensions and house sites. The details of the rehabilitation of the jogins in 1987 by the Woman and Child Welfare Department are shown in Table 4.10:

Table 4.10

Details of the rehabilitation of the jogins in 1987 by the Woman and Child Welfare Department

Rehabilitation	*No. of jogins benefited*	*Total amount spent (Rs)*
Sewing machines for preparing garments	46	44,000
Beedi unit	16	15,200
Vegetable-vending	87	1,02,900
Kirana shops	15	24,700
Milch cattle	15	12,200
Petty business	5	3,600
House sites	39	—
Old-age pension	44	—
Total	**267**	**2,09,600**

The number of jogins identified	—	324
The number of jogins rehabilitated	—	267
The number of jogins to be rehabilitated	—	57

The collector said the Director of Woman and Child Welfare, Hyderabad had allotted to Adilabad district Rs 2,09,600. He requested the government to provide financial assistance to the remaining 57 jogins.

Karimnagar District

In Karimnagar district, we have Parvatis who are equated with jogins. The parvatis are also unmarried women and are dedicated to the Raja Rajeswara Temple at Vemulavada, a pilgrim centre. However, they are different from jogins in that some of them lead an honourable life. They are religious-minded and visit Vemulavada whenever they want to see the god and spend months together there. There may be exceptional cases where religious prostitution takes place.

The girls or women who are dedicated to the god belong to 33 castes including backward castes. All the 1,605 parvatis identified have been rehabilitated.

The practice of marrying parvatis to Raja Rajeswara Swami is centuries old. The marriages take place during the Sri Rama Navami festival. The temple purohit, called Jangam, performs the marriages and gives each woman a trishulam (a trident). The parvatis were regarded as the wives of the god. An interesting feature was that the "mangalasutra" of a parvati had a linga concealed in a small box. Everyday, the parvati would open the box and worship Raja Rajeswara.

Vemulawada has a Hari Hara temple. The marriage of Sita and Rama is performed every year and thousands of devotees attend it. Only after worshipping Sita and Rama do the devotees have a darshan of Siva (*Eenadu*, April 3, 1985).

A discussion of the rehabilitation of the women dedicated to deities cannot be complete without the mention of the remarkable work done by Samskar in regard to the jogins of Nizamabad district.

Generally, the jogin works as a casual labourer and gets paid in cash or kind according to the convenience of the landlord. If she is deserted, another landlord holds her hand. A jogin without a master (Dora) is looked down upon. The sons of a jogin are not accepted as sons of the 'landlord'. While the sons are driven into bondage, the daughter acquires the same position as her mother and is forced to lead an ignominious life.

One can imagine the agony a jogin goes through when she is told to dance around the corpse of the landlord. When she dances, youngsters give out cat-calls and shrieks of joy. At the jataras when she dances for the amusement of the villagers, she exhibits her skill and picks up a ten-rupee note with her eyelids. This is an imitation of the dance done by a devadasi when the deity is taken out in a procession from one house to another. In Eluru, a devadasi, whom the author interviewed, demonstrated her skill in picking up a needle with her eyelids.

Superstitions uphold the Jogin system. When somebody in a family of untouchables falls ill, the news spreads and the villagers conclude that the illness is the result of the wrath of the village deity. They think that the only way to appease the deity is to make the daughter of that family a jogin. This could well be the landlord's idea.

The three-fold suppressive mechanism is:

(i) The religious superstitions will make her follow the custom.
(ii) Because of the economic pressures the family undergoes, the girl becomes a marketable commodity in the concubine trade.
(iii) Her social status adds to the vulnerability.

In regard to the health problems of the jogins and their children, Samskar has chalked out a plan to conduct health check-ups, special services and reimbursement of periodical bills. The scheme has the following features:

- Conducting awareness camps on health including HIV/AIDS through cultural programmes.
- Motivating the jogins and rural women to consult the doctors every now and then.
- Conducting home visits.
- Periodic health check-ups by specialists and provision of free medicine to them.
- Awareness camps on personal hygiene and cleanliness.
- Providing counselling services.

Special services are provided to the jogins to abviate the need to approach the landlords for loans. Reimbursement of medical bills gives them security and makes them go to the doctors concerned.

Three parties – Samskar, the Scheduled Caste Corporation and jogins – came to an understanding that the rehabilitation should be completed in a stipulated period.

The plan of action of their rehabilitation has following features:

- Providing grants for the promotion of micro-enterprises.
- Formation of self-help groups (SHGs) and organizing training to promote vocational and entrepreneurial skills.
- Management of the micro-enterprises and pinning the responsibility of trained leaders to promote the economic standards of these women by developing linkages with DRDA, local NGOs and women groups.

The children of jogins are given training in such vocations as nursing, car-driving, motor-winding, tailoring and computers. Nearly 300 jogins benefited from the S.C. Corporation in small-scale business development.

The objectives of the project are:

- To promote leadership qualities.
- To train 175 jogin sisters and their children in vocational skills.
- To promote additional income-generating sources for jogin sisters.
- To develop entrepreneurial skills among 1,000 women.
- To ensure the access of qualitative training resources and facilities.

Samskar also planned to promote horticulture and collective farming by buying milch animals at a unit cost of Rs 8,000. Samskar also wanted to make 189 acres of waste land cultivable and supply agricultural tools to 200 jogins' families. Samskar also helped in the marriage of 21 jogins in Nizamabad and Medak districts. The aim is to protect the jogins for at least 10 years so that they may get self-respect in society.

Samskar also helped the jogins in getting funds for housing. Of the Rs 12,400 required to build a house, Rs 10,000 was borne by the Government Housing Department and Rs 2,000 by the district S.C. Corporation.

With the idea of making the jogins self-reliant, Samskar started a cooperative society for them in Nizamabad district. The society has 350 members as shareholders. It also started a grain bank for the jogins to fall back upon during the lean period.

To encourage the older jogins who could defy the Jogin system, Samskar started to get them pension. In its efforts to improve the economic well-being of the jogins, Samskar got the cooperation of several other NGOs such as Oxfam, Help Age, and Hamu (of Norway).

Samskar arranged a field study by selecting three researchers who discussed the matter with Lavanam and the staff of Samskar at Varni in May 2003. They also studied documents relating to the evolution of the devadasi culture, the results of the statistical baseline survey, 1986, and the action plan for social development of jogins.

The relentless work of Samskar has brought a new hope in the lives of jogins and there is no need for them to look back or worry about their inglorious past. Out of gratitude for the help rendered by Samskar, jogins call its male members 'Annalu' (elder brothers). The social status of the jogins has improved so much that no landlord has the courage to send for a jogin to satisfy his carnal desires.

After rendering yeoman service to the jogins of Nizamabad, Samskar extended its activities to Medak and Adilabad districts. This NGO has helped the jogins and rural women know the government programmes for their betterment. And this has boosted their morale.

The significance of Samskar's role lies in the fact that it helped the government by ensuring that its funds for the uplift of jogins reached the intended beneficiaries.

As the jogins were worried about their children's future, separate schools were started and their health was taken care of. Timely preventive steps were taken to help the jogins affected, thereby boosting their morale and self-confidence. The frequent interface meetings arranged by Samskar helped jogins to articulate their problems before the government officials and get redressal.

In the first phase of its movement in Nizamabad district, Samskar started its work in only five mandals – Varni, Bodhan, Ganjor, Birkur and Kotagiri – and covered 444 jogins. Its initial efforts helped the jogins to come out of the age-old practice of Joginhood. The then Nizamabad collector allotted one acre of land to each jogin. While some jogins were covered by the housing scheme, the rest got fixed deposit receipts (FDRs) for Rs 10,000 each. They were also provided with agricultural incentives. These measures gave them self-confidence. In 1996, rehabilitation work was taken up in 26 more mandals covering 1,500 jogins. Almost all got FDRs for Rs 10,000 and one-fourth of them got milch cattle. In some mandals, such as Bheemgal, Jakkarapally, Balkonda and Armoor, the families of some jogins have become rich.

A point worth noting is that some jogins have grown with Samskar. We can compare their perceptions of the organization before they became its members and their perceptions now. The time gap of 15 years has enabled them to gain experience. The development indicators now are how many girl children are getting school education, how much have individual incomes improved and how frequently they interact with government officials, and what new skills have the jogins acquired. Today, the jogins can make decisions on matters relating to their community.

It is true that all the girl children of the jogins are not going to school regularly. Nor, for that matter, are all the children of the different tribes and dalit communities as girls are expected to help their mothers in household chores. The girls of many families work as labourers and construction workers. The parents want immediate gain; they can not wait for long-term benefits. The mother understands the importance of education and so sends her daughter to school without any hesitation. Overall, the awareness levels have increased over a period of time. More and more families are sending their children to school due to the efforts of Samskar.

During the last 15 years, there has been an increase in individual incomes and every member is happy. A good deal of the credit goes to Samskar. Doubtless, the training they received to improve their skills has been of great help in their income-generating activities.

Another development indicator is that the jogins are coming forward to solve their community problems working together. The training imparted to the jogins from time to time will be useful even for their occupational mobility. If they acquire skills and are prepared to move to another place, their knowledge and experience will help them to improve their income.

Jogins are one of the marginalized groups among the weaker sections. The advent of Samskar has changed their social life and standard of living. Jogins are no longer condemned to lead a life of shame and insecurity.

A jogin told the author that they were like puppets in the hands of village elders. They were made to dance in front of the dead bodies and beg throughout their life. Now that their mother (Hemalatha Lavanam) and "annalu" have come on the scene, people are treating them with respect. This has motivated the jogins to contribute towards development activities in their respective villages.

They acknowledge Samskar's key role in their transformation. The children of some jogins are pursuing professional courses such as engineering and master of science. This has raised the social status of jogins and paved the way to perform the marriages of their daughters in a dignified manner. Earlier, the children of jogins used to marry children of other jogins only. At present, there are a few cases of jogins' children marrying non-jogins' children. They are learning to forget their sordid past by foreseeing the bright future of their children. Some of them have started petty businesses like kirana shops, bangle stores and vegetable vending.

The tendency of the villagers to treat the jogin as an incarnation of goddess has vanished. They are rid of the false notions that a jogin's marriage leads to her death and that a jogin cannot think of marriage or family life. This has been proved to be a myth as some of the first generation jogins are married and are leading a normal life. For example, Mamidi Savitri of Rudrur (Varni), Agaram Savitri of Akbar Nagar (Varni), Posani (Pavani) of Bodhan and Ganga Mani are leading a normal life. The children born to them are not fatherless. Some of the jogins' children are married to the children of non-jogins. This reflects their social acceptance. The jogins are fighting for justice and boldly facing any hardship to solve their problems and to stop further dedications. They are able to solve the problems at the individual level, community level and at the village level too. They have reached a stage where they are questioning the authorities, and demanding a better deal. The programmes of Samskar have strengthened the jogins, both socially and economically. The have become self-reliant. Gender equality is the visible outcome of the rehabilitation plan. Though some improvement is seen in all directions, a lot remains to be done in some areas. Thus, in a nutshell, we can say that a result-oriented march has begun. Samskar has liberated 2,200 jogins in Nizamabad district alone. Very recently, 20 women refused to accept the money offered to them, still calling themselves sisters, that is, jogins. They certainly want to shed the stigma, as they are leading an independent and respectable life. Self-esteem to them is more valuable than financial aid. This is the social consciousness that the jogins have gained. Returning to the mainstream is itself a reward for them.

However, some changes are needed in the rehabilitation programme. They are:

- The content, curriculum and methodology of the training programmes need to be restructured.
- Evaluation studies need to be conducted periodically to monitor the progress of the jogins' empowerment.
- Feasibility studies are required before any development programme can be launched.
- Re-orientation to new tasks, latest techniques of database management is required.
- Training of women is important and linkage with DRDA and banks for margin money is a must.
- Imparting of skills to jogins on non-farm income generation activity is a better alternative in the present situation.
- Qualitative rehabilitation is of utmost importance.
- Like the first batch of mandals, all other mandals should be oriented in the same way.
- The jogins should be in a position to live on their own and that should be the motto of Samskar.
- All the jogins should be motivated to pay their dues to the government on time.
- The project director should steer the ship carefully and safely.
- Attempts should be made to reduce the jogins' dependence on Samskar as its withdrawal from the scene sooner or later is inevitable.

Samskar plans to launch future activities on the basis of the above-mentioned points. These issues call for a systematic approach to educate the parents, the exploiter and the exploited. Since the whole system revolves around superstitious beliefs, the first step in the direction of rehabilitation is to wipe out the fallacies about the system. Dedicated reformers like Lavanam and Hemalatha Lavanam have tried their best to undo the damage done to these innocent girls of the so-called untouchable families. The growing assertion and awakening among dalits about their rights has become intolerable to the dominant sections of society. As the author has mentioned, the formation of Adi-Andhra Mahasabha in 1917 under the stewardship of Bhagya Reddy Varma and Kusuma Dhammanna was a landmark in the history of dalit liberation in modern Andhra. This movement inculcated a new consciousness in the dalit people.

It would be relevant to mention here that V. Santhi Prabodha's Telugu novel *Jogini* deals with the sorry plight of a typical jogin and how she gradually becomes aware of her rights and succeeds in winning them. The novel indicated that the gap is going to increase between the 'haves' and 'have-nots' in society.

Notes

1. This article appeared before the establishment of 'Chelli Nilayam' in Varni village of Nizamabad district. The feudal lords made use of the services of the so-called lower castes especially the Scheduled Castes and 95 per cent of Jogins came out of them in the rural sector.
2. Jogins are called the women of gods and goddesses. These are dedicated to these goddesses. Once they are dedicated then there is no marriage for them. After puberty when they do 'Mailapattam', one rich person bears the expenses and enjoyes the girl temporarily or permanently. Thus the rich people exploit her sexuality.
3. Bhagirathi is a jogin in Nizamabad district. She has made Jogin when she was a child. Later, after her puberty an auspicious day was fixed and she was taken into the room of the village head. It is the birth right of the village head to enjoy her. All this is done in the name of god under the cover of religion. That is the reason why it is called 'religious prostitution'.
4. After the death of any feudal lord in those villages, Jogins are expected to dance before the corpse. It is an exploitation. After the reformation took place, the Jogins realised that this dance will bring them disrespect in the

society. In that mood she said if she goes to the coolie work she will get the required money and she is going to get in Savayatra is nothing but a Toddy bottle.

5. Lavanam is a social reformer in the Atheistic centre, Vijayawada. Himself and Hemalatha Lavanam were asked to take up the responsibility of eradicating the Jogin system in Nizamabad district of Andhra Pradesh by the then Governor of Andhra Pradesh Srimati Kumud Ben Joshi, Lavan said that there was uneven growth among the people. Social awareness was required. Rational thinking was required in the society. This is only general paper of Lavanam.

CHAPTER 5

The Matangi System

Matangi is a virgin dedicated to Goddess Matangi (one of the many names of Goddess Kali) and who remains unmarried throughout her life but begets children by co-habiting with men of her caste. Previously, this institution was looked upon with respect and reverence. She was a priestess and as such she had to worship Goddess Matamma or Maremma during Kolupulu. The dedicated girl is hailed as an incarnation of the goddess and, therefore, called Matamma.

The word 'Matanga', derived from 'Matangi', may signify 'a tribe of lower caste'. Matanga is a large subdivision of the Madigas called Matangis. The Madigas of Karnataka call themselves 'Matangi Makkalu' which means 'children of Matangi'. In the story of Kadambari, Banabhatta, a Sanskrit scholar who lived in about 606 AD, described Matanga as the leader of the cobras as "he seemed to be made of iron, he had thick locks of curly hair, his brow was broad, his nose was stern and aquiline, he had the heat warded off by the swarm of bees, like a peacock-feather parasol."

The Matangas lived on the outskirts of villages. They were not allowed to walk in the streets, draw water from wells and were forbidden from entering temples. They did 'vetti' (bonded labour). A Matanga used to serve as a watchman in the fields of the feudal lord who treated him as an untouchable person.

Untouchability definitely represents the extreme manifestation of the institutionalized inequality of the caste. The status of a man or a woman is determined by the rank of that caste in the social hierarchy. The deciding factor is birth, not talents or wealth. The caste controls the vital aspects of an individual such as marriage,

Plate 8 Renuka Yellamma temple in Chittoor District.

vocation and social intercourse. In effect, the individual is shorn of personal liberty. The hierarchical structure of the castes has given rise to inequalities. Every caste, in order to retain its superiority, has created its own dependants. In such a situation, people belonging to the lower layers of society will take centuries to rise to positions of power and influence.

The Madigas who are at the lower rung of the hierarchy are suffering indignity inflicted on them in the name of tradition and religion. Under untouchability, the outraging of human dignity reached its high watermark. The problem of untouchability is tied up with the basic socio-economic reconstruction of Indian society. If the Madigas are made a part of the productive process, they will gain self-confidence and will be treated as respectable people.

Plate 9 Matangi – Nalgonda District.

The practice of offering something to please the supernatural being and get divine favour is prevalent in all societies, primitive or modern. To fulfil their desire, the devotees offer sacrifices which include food, service, wealth, animals and even human beings. The thing that a woman considers most precious – chastity – is offered to the goddess.

In the Matangi system, three people play a major role; they are:

(i) Pedda Golla, head of the Yadava community.
(ii) The Matangi's maternal uncle who ties the 'tali' to her.
(iii) Pedda Madiga, head of the dalit community.

The Matangi system is a part and parcel of the extra economic coercion that exists in the relationship between the ruling sections and the exploited lot. In spite of the programmes that the government has launched for the welfare of dalits from time to time, these people continue to be a psychologically enslaved group. There is a story behind the poverty of the Madigas.

Once, sage Vasishtha sought the help of many women to transform sand into boiled rice. He enquired among all castes and found that only Arundhati, a Madiga woman with supernatural powers, could fulfil his desire. Arundhati finished cooking and the sage asked for her in marriage. Her brother created all sorts of impediments. As a consequence, she rose to heaven and cursed all Madigas saying, "You shall be the slaves of all. Though you work hard and toil, it shall not raise your condition. Unclothed and untaught you shall be, ignorant and despised henceforth!"

In Tamil Nadu, there is a similar story of Vasugi who proved her supernatural powers and married the poet Tiruvalluvar. These legends have come from the oral tradition. Madigas in Andhra Pradesh are also referred to as Arundhatiyulu.

The Matangis belong to the Arundhativada. Very few of them are Matangis by occupation. A Matangi's children are considered as members of the Matangi caste. The dedicated woman used to beget children by serving the male members of the Madiga community. The dedication ceremony used to be performed during the jataras of the village.

The ceremony is officiated by an elderly man of the community. He ties a small piece of sacred leather, locally known as 'tholu billa', with a thread around the neck of the virgin who would become a matangi.

An oath of life-long celibacy is administered to her and from that time, she is known as matangi. She is 'Nitya Sumangali' throughout her life because she is married to the immortal goddess or god. She is a member of her father's family. Her children are also heirs of the same family and inherit the right to property of the family. She is required to perform some religious duties relating to the village jataras of Maremma or Yellamma, besides providing extramarital happiness to the men of her community.

The children born to Matamma are considered as members of the Madiga community and no stigma is attached to them. According to Thurston, the origin of the supremacy of the matangi is obscure and shrouded in legends. There is a story that Matamma's parents are Siva and Parvati.

There are no sub-sects in the Matangi community. The caste is divided into a number of clans and each Gotra or clan is subdivided into surnames, such as Kochhari, Bandaru, Pandari, Vannela, Namala, Vaddimanu, Uliddari and Kottacheruvu. Marriage is exogamous. The structure of the family is patriarchal. These people live along with other Madigas. The houses are agglomerated. Though they maintain neatness in their homes, sanitation in their surroundings is very bad. Tobacco-chewing and betel-leaf eating are common habits among them.

The Madigas in Andhra Pradesh have sub-castes called Bhavanis or Baindlavallu or Pambalavallu or Asadulus, Dokkalas, Chindu Bhagavathulu, Baineedlu, Kinneras, Nulaka Chandaiahs and

Mastivaru. The Baineedlu are performing artists and they also act as purohits, preachers and gurus to people of castes lower than their own. They worship Shakti in the form of Yellamma, Maremma, Bhavani, Durga and Kali, and conduct the religious ceremonies of their patrons.

The Baindlavallu are listed in the SCs. Baineedlu means 'one who sings in praise of the goddess in jataras'. Their main festival is Yellamma or Matamma Panduga. After doing puja at home, they go to the jataras organized at the village level to officiate as priests. They believe that Kolupulu brings rain and that the jataras are effective in pacifying the goddesses and bringing peace and well-being to the community. They also cure certain diseases with magic and tantra.

Plate 10 Kollapuramma.

One of the main rituals they conduct on various occasions is making formal sacrifices. This involves the traditional narration of a story to the accompaniment of the jamadika instrument. Sacrifices are done for various purposes. For example, during the Peddamma Jatara when the goddess is worshipped, the Madigas pierce themselves with spears and sacrifice sheep on the way to the temple.

During the Kolupulu, they narrate the story of Mata and a goat is sacrificed at the end which is done in a peculiar manner. First, the goat is laid down on the floor and held tight and a white cloth is spread on it and it is immobilized by chanting a Mantram and is then taken out in a procession to a Mata gudi in Arundhativada. With one bite, the Baineedlu cuts off the goat's head and separates it from the body. This is called 'Gavupattadam'.

When there is a jatara, the whole village participates in it. A jatara involves puja, processions, recital of Mata's story and animal sacrifices. Baineedlu conducts the proceedings as the pujari. Usually, the atmosphere is emotionally charged.

Matangis, being Hindus, observe Hindu customs in all aspects of their life. They consider Hindu temples as sacred abodes of the Supreme Being. They worship the goddess with a spirit of devotion. All the caste deities are the incarnations of Renuka Devi, the wife of Jamadagni. During her pregnancy, Renuka had an intense desire to eat brinjals and potatoes. Despite requesting many people, she could not get them. Later, on learning that Pratapa Rudra of Orugallu had a beautiful vegetable garden, she asked the gardener to give her some vegetables but he refused. Enraged, she destroyed the garden but carried some vegetables which she dropped throughout the way and went into a Matangi hut and disappeared. Pratapa Rudra learnt of this incident and asked his people to cut the ears and hair of the Matangi. Matangi women told this to Renuka who took the whole responsibility on her shoulders and, with her magical powers, restored the ears and hair of Matangi. Renuka wanted to curse them for having denied her the much-desired vegetables. To appease Renuka, the Madigas from then on became her ardent worshippers. Renuka whom they worship was Yellamma.

According to another story, Pratapa Rudra of Orugallu was an ardent devotee of Siva. He did not like to worship the goddess. In fact, he wanted to punish her. Matangi started her journey to Orugallu along with her father Giriraju and father-in-law Gautama, her brother Potharaju and other devotees including matangis. To teach him a lesson, Matangi created green, white, black and red patches on people; in other words, different kinds of diseases. She wore a shell necklace, neem leaves and created a fearful atmosphere. Pratapa Rudra asked her why she, a Madiga, had come to his place. Subsequently, Pratapa Rudra's health deteriorated fast. He realized his mistake. He took a Jamadika in his hand and his wife took up bells and prayed to the goddess Matamma. Satisfied with his behaviour, Matangi restored his wealth and position.

The moral of the story is that if the Mata is appeased, she would grant her devotees anything, otherwise she would punish them. Thus, the Matangi system, though religiosity is attached to it, has become a social evil. As Thurston said, "There are some permanent inam (rent-free) lands belonging to this shrine, and there is always a Madiga 'vestal virgin' known as Matangi, who is the high priestess, or rather the embodied representative of the Brahman Goddess, and who enjoys the fruits of the 'Bonams'." [1]

At present, 'Matangi' denotes the name of a caste and not the institution. The traditional occupation of Matangis is begging by singing songs. While begging, they play musical instruments like Sruthi and Jhonki. They play these instruments at the weddings of other castes. The caste deities of Madigas are Yellamma, Maremma, Holigamma and Laxmamma. One of the pilgrim centres of the Matangis is Adoni in Kurnool district where the temple of Uligamma is situated. They believe that the deities Maremma and Yellamma protect them from epidemics.

There used to be inams (rent-free lands belonging to the shrine of Matangi). In the name of the goddess, the Matangi women who were initiated used to enjoy the fruits of the inams.

Generally, Matangis are agricultural or construction workers. In the Gulbarga and Dharwar areas of Karnataka, they also beg. However, at harvest time, they get work on farms.

The initiation of a Matangi is an interesting process. A matangi, a Madiga girl or woman, is possessed by Yellamma or Adimata, that is, Mother of all. People, be they Saivaite or Vaishnavaite, worship Yellamma. An elder member of the Madiga community enters the Yellamma temple to offer milk, butter and fruits to her. Baineedlu, the minstrel in the Yellamma sect, would recite the story of Yellamma in the presence of the woman. If Yellamma's power comes to the new matangi then she would dance inspired by the goddess. If it is an evil spirit that has possessed her, narration of the story does not affect her. As soon as the minstrel watches the young woman dance, the other women, called the old matangis, begin dancing. This is a sign that Yellamma's power has possessed the whole family.

At one time matangis were rare, perhaps one or two in a mandal. However, due to ignorance and poverty, the number of matangis has increased. A matangi not only earns her livelihood but also serves as a social security for her parents. A new matangi is installed in her office by the village chieftain, but the expenditure on the ceremony is borne by the family.

There are different reasons for dedicating a girl as a matangi. Some people who do not have any children pray to the goddess and if they are blessed with a girl child, they dedicate her to the goddess. If the child is ill, then the parents throw her into a Matangi temple. If she survives, she is called a matangi. For the sake of male issues also, the girl children are made matangis. A girl is made a matangi if there is any mishap in the family or diseases in the village, affecting human beings or animals. The selection of a matangi is generally done at jataras.

In every humble shrine, the goddess is represented by a small stone image. The landlord plays a vital role in making a girl a matangi. After a girl from the community is chosen, she is taken to the temple and dedicated to the goddess. The landlord sends her a yellow saree, and three sea shells or some coins. The three sea shells are taken from a Siva temple. The girl wears the saree and the shells are tied along with a yellow thread and it is called 'Tali'. The 'tali' is tied to her by her maternal uncle, or Pedda Madiga or Pedda Golla. In some places, the 'tali' is suspended from a 'Trishula' by the landlord and then given to the selected girl.

The matangis dance to the sound of Dappu and Jamadika played by Baineedlu. These rituals continue for five days in some places and for 9 to 16 days in other places. The first day they arrange 'Gauramma Muggu', on the second day 'Parvati Muggu' and on the third day, 'Parasurama Muggu', on the fourth 'AdiparaShakti Muggu' and so on. On the last day, an animal is sacrificed. During all these five days, the narrator tells the story of Matamma near a Jammi tree in the form of Burrakatha.

The dance performed by Matangis has a rhythm of its own. In a state of intoxication, they sway their bodies to drum-beats. There are no circular or semi-circular movements as seen in tribal or folk dances, nor is there any song. They carry neem leaves in the right hand and chhatra (umbrella) in the left.

The Matangi system is prevalent in three districts, namely, Prakasam, Nellore and Chittoor. Let us see how it is in Prakasam district.

Prakasam District

Some of the village deities are fertility goddesses, while Indra and other gods are worshipped in urban areas. The goddesses lost their prominence when the gods occupied prime place in the hearts of the people. Like men in a patriarchal society, male deities occupy a prime place and goddesses are given a secondary position.

In this context, it would be pertinent to cite an incident that happened in Garepalli village of Prakasam district. Malas and backward class communities performed Matangi Kolupulu in a Yadava's house. Friends and relatives from various places attended this Kolupulu. The Yadava family sent money in advance to Matamma (Saroja) to perform Kolupulu and gave money to Babbaiah Madiga.

As per the custom, the matangi should go to the Madiga's house. Later, she should go to the house where Kolupulu is to take place. The youths protested against this custom, while others supported Kolupulu and said they felt sorry that they had not been doing the Kolupulu regularly. They thought that was why there was no water in the ponds and the cattle strength had decreased. The youths said that their self-respect was at stake and so they had migrated to towns and cities. Villages, however, still follow the age-old customs. The people who conduct Kolupulu no longer send their girl children to dance in the villages.

When Professor Jayadhir Tirumala Rao met Saroja and talked to her, she felt shy and kept mum for a while. Slowly, she began to narrate how she was made as a matangi. Her father dedicated her to the goddess. Baineedlu took her in a basket near the ant-hill and Kommu people played musical instruments. As she had been made a matangi, she had no chance to marry anybody. Syamaya of Avula Doddi Gedelapalem, tied the tali to her and she bore him children. In spite of this kind of marriage, she was not treated with respect in the society. The whole family depended on her income, which was Rs 1 lakh per year. "I would have suffered a lot if I had not become a matangi", she said. Saroja said that the matangis faced social stigma. Theirs was the only profession hated by one and all. It was not the sex-working that mattered. If they wanted to maintain sexual relations, they need not do Kolupulu. The Kolupulu was their life and they felt that they were the real custodians of the tradition.

When a matangi scolds a landlord, he takes it as the blessings of the goddess. People belonging to all castes including Brahmans consider themselves fortunate if she pushes them with her buttocks. Such acts during the jatara period are outside the scope of untouchability. It shows how hypocrite man is in certain situations. Whether it brings her some good or not, she says she feels happy to do such things. For her acts, the people give her gifts. However, some people ill-treat her. She performs the Kolupulu for her livelihood. Kolupulu is connected with agriculture. The matangis wish all the people a life of prosperity. It depends on the people how they take it. The NGOs and the government are not in a position to reform the sex workers but they want to reform those who are the real carriers of the tradition. They will continue the reforms for some time in order to bring the matangis into the mainstream of life. Under the 'Jivana Jyoti' scheme, the government has given Rs 10,000 to each matangi to open a petty shop to earn her livelihood.

At present, caste revolutions are taking place and they want to reform their community. They are prohibiting matammas from performing Kolupulu.

In an interview with Professor Jayadhir Tirumala Rao, a matangi called Vajramma said, "The Scheduled Castes are enjoying the reservations and their quota of jobs. But, our community has asked us to live on this work. So, we are doing Kolupulu. If we feel that it is bringing us disrespect, we will definitely give it up." The government or the caste organizations should, therefore, show them alternatives so that they may quit the profession.

Solman of Buddareddipalli said that they can stop the Matangi system in their own community. But he wondered if the practice could be discontinued since matangis also come from the Baineedlu community. He said matangis are helping the villages and they are the real goddesses. He requested Professor Jayadhir to try to stop sex-working in other communities too. Why should a Mata who is dedicated to the goddess die from hunger? Penta Mallamma of Maktal village wondered if anyone would come forward to marry a jogin or a matamma. She wanted to know if the social workers were ready to marry these Matas. In Pedacherlopalli village, social workers stopped Matangi Kolupulu, but used video and were satisfied with it.

In Boduguleru, near Kanigiri in Prakasam district, there is an old, traditional type of matamma. In that village Pedda Gollas and Pedda Kapus arrange for Kolupulu. The Pedda Golla ties the tali to the matamma. Then, Baineedlu recite the story of matamma and Kommu people play the musical instruments and the matamma goes into a trance. The people believe that if Kolupulu is not performed, their village will vanish.

There is no village without Kolupulu. Villagers show great respect to matamma during Kolupulu and offer her many things including animal sacrifices. The matamma used to go to Kolupulu in Bapatla, Chirala, Dindi, Mipadu and other places. The Baindla people bite a hen on that occasion.

The author interviewed a 91-year-old man and asked him about the significance of Kolupulu, customs and traditions of the Matangi cult. He expressed himself in favour of the continuance of the tradition. When the author asked him what if the matangi became a sex-worker, his answer was that Matangi Kolupulu should be discontinued. He felt sad that the Matangi system was being neglected. As an elderly person, he thought he should respect the tradition.

One Baineedu told the author about the Kolupulu in Yerraguntapalem of Kandukur mandal. We went to that place and found that both the young and old matammas had already left the village. That night, Baineedlu and Kommuvaru stayed there to recite the story of the goddess under Jammi tree. As usual, the animal sacrifice was arranged. They asked the author why she had come all the way to this place. They said, "We suspect you must be a government official who has come to check our activity. As you worship your god, we worship ours. This is our belief. For the safety of our children, animals and village, we have to perform this puja. They warned her not to interfere in their affairs". The Kommu people went out to drink toddy. We understood the situation and returned to Kavali, the base of our study camp. After a study of the situation, we came to the following conclusions:

The elderly members of the Reddy community support this system and give the village people financial assistance and tell them when and how to conduct Kolupulu. This shows that there is a feudal element in the system.

They are poor, and collect money from the people in the village and outside and do Kolupulu every year or once in three years according to their financial capacity.

Educated youths are in a dilemma. While they would like to stop this social evil, they cannot face the elders. But to protect their village, they support the customs and traditions of their village. Many people from distant places attend this event.

Families involve themselves in the Kolupulu as they believe that it is essential for the safety and prosperity of the village.

At present, there are 26 matangis in Prakasam district and all of them have been rehabilitated. The reason for the low number compared to Nellore and Chittoor districts is that people have been influenced by the leftist parties against the reprehensible custom.

Nellore District

In Nellore district, of the 294 matangis identified, 267 have been rehabilitated. In the economically backward caste communities like Madiga, Dommara, Mala, Yadava, Rajaka and Boya, the Matangi system is prevalent. This practice is confined to Madigas. There is a Matamma temple in Madigavada which is also known as Arundhativada.

The Madiga community people dedicate a virgin girl to Matamma. Later on, she becomes a common property of the men of the upper strata of society and satisfies their carnal desires. But her children do not have a legal father. Laxmaiah, a journalist, said that DNA examination can determine who their father is. The author found that the age of matammas ranged from six months to 80 years.

There is a test for all the girls in the Madiga community in which Kommu people and Baineedlu with their musical instruments make them possessed by the goddess. The girls go to a Siva temple and get the shells chain (Darshan) and they are expected to walk with fire in their hands. Those who are possessed are selected for the Matangi cult. They have to wear a white saree and carry a basket, neem leaves, a small stick and rice dipped in blood.

The heinous practice of the Matangi system begins with the dedication of girls from the SC communities to the village deities. In the continuance of the Matangi tradition, the rich landlords play the major role. Ignorant and illiterate parents voluntarily declare their children as matangis prompted by some superstitious belief or other.

As the author has already mentioned, the matangis are not allowed to marry, but the landlords or the men of the Madiga community can keep them as concubines. Since poverty and illiteracy are the root cause of the Matangi system, the government should provide education and employment to every Matangi family. Unless this is done, the matangis may not be able to stand up independently and change their lifestyle.

In Nellore district, the author visited Naidupeta, Gudur, Chelakuru, Bhudanam, Manubole, Kanuru, Kadveta, Pudur, Chitamur, Nellore, Pudulurpadu, Ghatpalli, Venkatagiri, Veeragumapadu, Koneru, Renukamma – Kondapuram and Kommarilolu Gandavarm and interviewed the matammas.

She found that there were a total of 70 socially deprived women identified as 'Matas'. Previously in 36 villages of 17 and six of the 46 mandals in the district, three girls were below 5 years of age and six girls were in the 6–10 age group. Table 5.1 shows the number of matangis in various mandals of Nellore district.

Table 5.1

Number of matangis in various mandals of Nellore

	Mandal	*Village*	*Number*
1.	Atmakur P.S.		
	Anantha l	Mahimlu	2
	Sagaram Manda		
2.	Indukurpet P.S.		
	Muthukur	Brahmadevan, Rangasaikandriga	2
	Mandalam	Macharlavaripalem, Chinthopu	2
3.	Venkatagiri P.S.		
	Venkatagiri	Venkatagiri	
	Mandalam	Pigilam, Perimidi	5
	Balayapalli	Ammavarupet, Chinannapet	4
	Mandalam		
	Venkatagiri		
	Mandalam		
4.	Vinjamur P.S.		
	Kondapuram	Kondapuram	2
5.	Kota P.S.		
	Kota Mandalam	Kothapalem,Chittedu,Gudali	4
	Chelakuru Mandalam	Annambaka, Kadivedu	2

Cont'd...

Cont'd...

6.	Gudur P.S.		
	Gudur Mandalam	Gudur	2
		Gudur Town	13
		Viduru	3
		Deepalem	1
7.	Chittamur Mandal	Buradagali, Kothapalem	2
8.	Rapur P.S.		
	Sydapuram	Chaganam	2
	Mandal	Giddalur	3
9.	Sullurpet P.S.		
	Sulluripet Mandal	Yerrabalam	1
		Mannematheri	2
		Sridhanamalli	1
10.	Venkatachalam P.S.		
	Manubolu Mandal	Jatlakondur	1
		Manubolu	1
11.	Naidupet P.S.		
	Pellakur	Kamuru Raju, Palem	8
	Mandal	Vinnamala	1
		Pudur	3
12.	Ozili Mandal		
	Naidupet	Pedupariya	1
	Mandal	Annamedu	1
		Annamedu Harijanvada	1

In course of time, the number of matammas increased to 294. Again, this is due to poverty, ignorance and the selfishness of the parents. They want to live on the earnings of their girl children. Sons who are married are unable to maintain the parents because their income is meagre. The trend now is towards nuclear families.

Though all the women or girls who are dedicated to goddesses are called matammas, they have their own surnames, some of them being Somasila, Palthapu, Alluri, Panditi, Pachigala, Pallipati, Dantam, Kummargunta, Kappala, Cheekatla and Miriyala. Generally, the surnames originate from the villages their ancestors lived in; for example, Kurugondla, Mannar, Chegurupati, Valcherla, Tirupati and Paticherla. Some surnames relate to the animals which they domesticate or use for sacrifice to the deity. Though the matangis have their names and surnames, they are all addressed as matammas.

There are 58 Madiga matammas, 8 Mala matammas and 4 belong to other castes such as Dommaras. Table 5.2 shows the classification of matangis of Nellore based on their various factors.

Table 5.2

Classification of matangis in Nellore district based on various factors

	Matangis	*Girls*	*Boys*
I. Educational qualification			
(a) No education	9	8	9
(b) Below 5th standard	12	5	4
(c) Below SSLC	1	—	3
(d) Above SSLC	—	—	—
II. Housing pattern			
(a) Huts	—	28 persons	
(b) Semi-permanent houses	—	5 persons	
(c) Permanent houses	—	3 persons	
(d) No house	—	15 persons	
Forty-three matammas live in thatched houses. This abject poverty drives them to Kolupulu to earn money for their families.			
III. Land holdings			
(a) No holdings	—	49	
(b) Less than 2 acres	—	1	
(c) More than 2 acres	—	1	
IV. Occupation			
(a) Agricultural labourers	—	33	
(b) Contract labourers	—	4	
(c) Other type of labourers	—	14	
V. Average monthly wages			
(a) Upto Rs 100	—	8 persons	
(b) Upto Rs 200	—	23 persons	
(c) Upto Rs 300	—	20 persons	
(d) Upto Rs 500	—	—	

It is clear that most of them were below the poverty line. The matangis did not receive any financial assistance from the government nor did they have any skills to earn more. Only one matangi knew tailoring. Though most of them suffered from malnutrition, their general health condition was good.

It was heartening to know that later, many success stories brought about a welcome change in the life of matangis. Some of them started small enterprises at Gudur. The government built houses for the matammas and gave them financial help. Some of them started petty shops. The Duties organization started schools for the children. The collectors of various districts were favourably disposed towards the matangis and they are helping voluntary organizations to take steps to rehabilitate them. Many high-ranking officials, National Women's Commission members and the governor of Andhra Pradesh sent congratulatory messages to the matammas. It was good to know that two matangis stood for the Legislative Assembly elections, but they lost the election.

Interviews with Matangi Women of Nellore District

One matangi lived with a male relative and begot children, but he left her. She said that if he did not marry someone else his parents would not spare him. Though he loved her, he had a strange fear that he would die immediately after the marriage. She developed a liking towards another person but he died after two years of relationship. Nobody came to her rescue. She had to work hard to earn her livelihood. She had one son and one daughter. She gave her daughter in marriage to her brother's son. She dedicated the first daughter to the goddess. The reason for leaving her first daughter as matangi was that she should follow in her footsteps, and protect her during her old age. Unfortunately, that child died and she could not help her. The author asked her about her 'tali' and what it contained; she showed its contents – Mata's feet and Trishulam. The author enquired her about the significance of shells. The matangi pleaded ignorance. Many of the educated elite are not in a position to tell the significance of shells. But, they are equal to the goddess because they are natural things and come out of water. Another meaning is that shells indicate the fertility cult. Whatever may be the meaning, the Yerukala women who are experts in sooth-saying invoke the help of various goddesses like Kanchi Kamakshi, Madura Meenakshi, Kasi Visalakshi, Bezawada Kanakadurga and Kavali Kalugullamma in knowing what the future holds for their customers. Irrespective of the fact, the women of sacred prostitution use these shell chains and treat them as crucial for their existence.

Another girl was Gauri. She had visited many places and earned money. Each Kolupulu fetched her Rs 600 to Rs 700. Nobody had compelled her to do sex-working because they had no right to do that. One of the jogins said that they want marriage so that the husband might take care of the family.

Matammas use bhandar (turmeric powder) because they have the name of the goddess. One matangi expressed her feeling that her concubinage would result in her begetting children. They were expected to go for coolie work. So, she was disgusted with that kind of life. Their requirements were one or two acres of land to cultivate, a permanent house and education for their children. Actually in the Kolupulu of Matamma, they do fire-walking, reciting the story of Matamma and sacrificing sheep.

Chittoor District

In Chittoor district, the government identified 544 Matas and rehabilitated all of them. In 1986, a survey was conducted in the following 33 villages.

Name of the Village	*No. of Matangis*
Dommarapalem	10
Nallathummapalle	2
Marjepalle	2
Diggomovaripalle	2
Dommaramitta	6
Nakkalalli H.W.	1
Kesavapuram Chinnaddupalem	1
Pannor Adi Andhrawada	9
Vijayapuram H.W.	1
Jambada H.W.	1
Chinnajambada	1
Kalimbakam Adi Andhrawada	4
Ather Madigawada	1

Cont'd...

Cont'd...

Pichatur Adi Andhrawada	1
T.P. Kota	1
Nagalapuram Arundhathiwada	4
Subbaraju Kandriga	1
Batakodiambedu Adi Andhrawada	3
Adavi Kodiambedu Adi Andhrawada	1
Bairajula Kandriga Adi Andhrawada	1
Parlapalli	2
Pallamala Arundhatiwada	1
Katur Arundhatiwada	3
Katur Adigala Kandiga	3
Venugopalapuram Arundhatiwada	1
Talarivettu	1
Karnimitta	1
Srikalahasti Arundhatiwada	2
Kammakothur	1
Pulbareddi Kandriga	1
Thondamandu Caste-wise particulars:	2
Tirupati, Gandhipuram, Tirupati Mandal	10
Rayalapuram	2
Total	**83**

Division based on castes:

Dommaras	—	22
Madigas	—	57
Kamsalas (Goldsmiths)	—	1
Kapu	—	1
Malas	—	1
Rajaka	—	1
Total	—	**83**

No survey was conducted in 15 other villages.

The dedication of Matangi women in Chittoor district was mainly from Madiga and Dommara castes. Though the basic features of the system in these two castes and in other castes are the same, we have to deal with the two categories of matangis or basvis.

Dommara Basvis

Dommaras are acrobatic people. The Dommaras are beautiful and sturdy and earn their livelihood by engaging themselves as sex workers. The survey conducted by the government in 1986 showed that these people used to dedicate one of their girls to the goddess. When the girl attained the age of puberty, the elders of the village would perform a ceremony on an auspicious day and the girl would be dedicated to their deity called 'Gadimanu'. After dedication, the girl was called 'Nitya Sumangali'. All these Dommara basvis were living in Pedda Panjani, Baireddypalle and V. Kota and Palamner mandals in Chittoor district.

Madigavada Matangis

Every Arundhativada has a Matamma temple. It is not compulsory for every family to dedicate a girl to 'Matamma'. If a girl child falls ill, her parents dedicate her to 'Matamma' in the belief that the goddess would save her. After the girl attains puberty, Baineedlu conduct the dedication ceremony, which means the girl should not marry any mortal man. But after the first night with a village landlord, she is considered fit to be a prostitute. She is expected to dance in Matamma jataras.

A survey conducted by an NGO called Rural Institute for Social Education (RISE) revealed that there were a total of 332 matammas in 19 mandals of Chittoor district. Vijayapuram mandal had the highest number of matammas (12.34%), followed by Tirupati (11.14%), Nagdapuram (10.24%), and Satyavedu (8.03%). Karvetinagaram had the lowest number (0.6%).

The mandal-wise details of matamma population is shown in Table 5.3.

Table 5.3

Mandal-wise details of matamma population

Name of the Mandal	*No. of Matammas*	*Percentage*
Buchi Naidu Kandrega	11	3.31
Chandragiri	06	1.81
Erdedu	25	7.5
Karvetinagaram	02	0.6
K.V.B. Puram	20	6

Cont'd...

Cont'd...

Nagalapuram	34	10.24
Nagari	17	5.12
Narayanavanam	03	0.9
Picchatur	24	7.2
Puttur	10	3.01
Ramachandrapuram	03	0.9
Renigunta	08	2.41
Satyavedu	27	8.03
Srikalahasti	21	6.32
Tirupati (Rural)	39	11.74
Tirupati (Urban)	17	5.12
Vadamalapeta	18	5.42
Varadayyapalem	06	1.8
Vijayapuram	41	12.34
Total	**332**	**100**

The survey showed that they all belonged to the SCs, with the Madigas accounting for 70 per cent, Malas 21 per cent, Vadderas 1.5 per cent, Gollas 1.2 per cent, Mutras 9 per cent and Yanadi 0.9 per cent. In 1986–1987, when the government surveyed for the first time, there were only Mala, Madiga and Dommara matangis. Many backward class communities, driven by poverty, dedicated their girl children to the goddess. Table 5.4 gives the reasons for the dedication of girls.

Table 5.4

Reasons for the dedication of girls

Reasons for dedication	*No. of Matammas*	*Percentage*
Oath to have children	20	6.02
Illness of family members	7	2.11
Handicapped persons	17	5.1
Childhood disease	24	85.5
Critical delivery	4	1.02
Total	**332**	**100**

The survey reveals that the matammas belong to different age-groups, with the 16–20 age group accounting for 27.4 per cent, followed by the 21–25 age group (17.7%). What is urgently needed is rehabilitation measures like housing, land and financial assistance to wean them away from the evil system. This is where NGOs can play a protective role. Table 5.5 shows the age-wise distribution of matammas.

Table 5.5

Age-wise distribution of matammas

Age	*No. of Matammas*	*Percentage*
0–5	10	3.01
6–10	45	13.5
11–15	50	15
16–20	91	27.4
21–25	59	17.7
26–30	35	10.5
31–35	15	4.5
36–40	17	5.1
41–45	05	1.5
46 and above	05	1.5
Total	**332**	**100**

Table 5.6

Distribution of matammas based on education

Educational Status	*No. of Matammas*	*Percentage*
Illiteracy	239	71.9
5th Standard	68	20.4
6th–10th Standard	21	6.3
Intermediate	4	1.2
Total	**332**	**100**

The dedication ritual: When a girl is between 8 and 10 years old, she is wedded to the goddess, usually Matamma. The time is fixed by the Pina Pedda (head of the Madiga caste). As the girl, dressed in yellow, is taken to the temple in a procession, navadhanyas (nine different kinds of food grains) namely, rice, wheat, barley, horsegram, greengram, blackgram, bengalgram, beans and sesame seeds are strewn on the girl's path. Old matangis begin to dance, burn camphor and shower flowers and Akshintalu (yellow rice) on her. She is bedecked with flowers and wears a necklace made of shells. She is given a Jogi Karra (ascetic's stick) and treated every bit like a bride. The priest performs the marriage. On behalf of the

Goddess, the tali is tied around her neck by Pina Pedda, maternal uncle or Pedda Golla. This signifies that she has attained the status of matamma. This marks the beginning of her life as a 'public woman' or 'village slut'. After the marriage, non-vegetarian meal and drinks are served to those assembled there.

The elders of the high castes attend these functions. Their presence is reckoned as official sanction to the whole process. In some places, the girl is dedicated to some inanimate object like dagger, sword, drum or bells as personifying the bridegroom.

Every Monday and Friday, the matangi worships the 'Jogi karra' (stick) and Darshan (shell chain). The villagers present her with a silk saree which she wears on special occasions. She has to dance during 'Kolupulu' of Matamma, which takes place between April and June. She is paid Rs 2,000 for every performance. She goes to many places and earns money.

The matangi maintains sexual relations with somebody living in the same house. The only difference between prostitution and the Matangi system is that the matangi does not go out to entice customers. Her existence depends upon the landlord who keeps her. When he loses interest in her, she has to depend upon men who provide her with rice and other provisions. Some matammas are induced into commercial sex with social sanction.

Table 5.7

Occupational Structure of matammas

Type of Occupation	*No. of Matammas*	*Percentage*
No Occupation (Childhood)	102	31.6
Casual labour	93	28
Petty shops	16	4.8
Dance during performance	90	27.1
Dependence due to physical disability	12	3.6
Prostitution	9	2.7
Sheep-rearing	3	0.9
Begging	2	6
Limestone-cutting	2	0.6
Total	**329**	**100**

The economic condition of matammas is miserable. Most of them are agricultural labourers while some are sex workers and some others earn money by dancing during Kolupulu. Quite a few live by begging. Table 5.7 shows the occupational structure of matammas.

Of the 329 matammas, 102 are without any job and 12 are physically disabled. Two women live by begging. Table 5.7 shows that matangis have to live on the earnings of their parents or do Kolupulu.

Just as there is a potharaju in the Jogin tradition, in the Matangi system we have baineedlu and kommuvaru who help the tradition to continue. Bhavanis, Baindla Vallu, Pambala Vallu, Asadulu, etc. are the sub-castes or the dependant castes (Asrita Jatis) of the Mala and Madiga communities of Andhra Pradesh. These are performing artists. They conduct marriages of the poor, attend to the religious needs of patrons as well as the castes lower than their own. They explain the morals, philosophy and the essence of their stories in a simple yet effective manner through their performances and, thus, guide the people. They worship Shakti in the form of Yellamma, Maremma, Bhavani, Durga, Kali, etc. In Telangana, they worship Yellamma, Maisamma, and Pochamma whereas in coastal Andhra, they worship Matamma and Renuka Devi. These people perform Devi Puja among the Madiga people and play 'pamba', a musical instrument.

The words Bhavani/Baineedlu mean one who sings paeans to the goddess in jataras and wander from place to place. The instrument they play is known as 'bhavanika'. In Godavari, Krishna and Guntur districts, they are known as Jamukula varu; in Nellore district, they are known as Baineedla varu or Baintis and in Rayalaseema, they are called Asadi varu.

These people usually live on the outskirts of their respective villages. At present, they are migrating to the towns in search of jobs. Though they live in separate houses, they are like one huge joint family as they are partners in their profession and generally related to one another. Each family has its own Mirasi needs. Mirasi means the artists or professionals have their claim or right in the particular village.

Their main festival is the Yellamma Panduga which they celebrate at home with a small puja and then they go to big festivals like village jataras to officiate as priests. These people are still quite traditional and conservative in regard to their religion.

The tradition of worshipping Yellamma started in the 12th century. Since then, Yellamma stories have been famous in Telangana districts which have an abundance of Yellamma temples. This shows how Yellamma is revered and worshipped in these parts. This cult is also prevalent in the states of Tamil Nadu and Karnataka.

During the annual festivals in Soundatti in Karnataka, naked women with matted hair used to go around the Renuka Devi temple. The goddess is in nude form in the Chandragutti temple of Shimoga district in Karnataka.

In coastal Andhra Pradesh, goddesses like Gangamma, Poleramma, Maremma, Erra Maremma and Mahalakshmamma are considered to be Neecha Devatas or malevolent goddesses and people try to placate them with animal sacrifices whenever an epidemic breaks out.

The Yellamma cult appears to belong to the genre of the Matangi cult where the matangi presides over all purificatory ceremonies that precede all festivities. The origin and supremacy of matangi is described through the legend of Renuka Devi, thus, leading to the premise that matangi is Renuka Devi or Yellamma Devata.

Yellamma belongs to the Little Tradition of the rural and unlettered folk who believe that she has magical powers. Robert Briffault in his monumental work *The Mothers* says, "It does not appear that the universal practice of female impersonation is susceptible of any other interpretation than the magical power was originally associated with women and was regarded as essentially a woman's function."

Yellamma is identified as Ekavira in Kridabhiramam.

Mandapakanu benubaka, Mahuram
Nagavaramuna bolasa navicharity
Yoruganta Vasinche nilotpalakshi
Kakatammaku Saidodu Ekavira.

The glory of Ekavira is sung by the Malas of Warangal. They regard her as a woman of their own caste. In Maharashtra, she is called Mahuramma. In the Rayalaseema region, Yellamma is known as Nangamma devata. In Tamil Nadu, Goddess Matamma is known as Thayamma.

The power of Matamma is described in the book *Janapada geyalu: Social History* edited by B. Rama Raju and Nayani Krishna Kumari.

Siddha Ganas served her
She is the real Goddess
Nirjarulu served her,
She is a shakti and
Eradicated the bad people

Potharaju is the brother of Goddess
He is the guardian of the fort ... [2]

Interestingly, the worship of the goddess was stoutly opposed by the Kakatiya king Pratapa Rudra who was a Saivaite. He wanted to take revenge on the goddess by separating her head from the body with a single bite. Ekavira dreamt of this and asked her brother Potharaju to bring Giri Raju and Sage Gautama. On being informed, both went to the place of Matamma. She welcomed her father and father-in-law and told them what she had done previously and how Pratapa Rudra had reacted to her. She said, she would like to take severe action against him and asked Matangis to join her. They all came to Mahuramma. Mahuram is a place on the Andhra Pradesh-Maharashtra border, Yellamma in that place is called Mahuramma. Five kinds of musical instruments were played and matangis began to sing and dance. Ekavira went to Delhi and created problems for the King. Wearing a crown studded with navaratnas, she attended a meeting of places such as Anga, Vanga, Kalinga, Bhoja, Pandya, Karakuta, Angada, Malwa and Kosala. Potharajus, Matangis, Bhavanis, Nilavenulu, Kommuvaru and devotees all took part in that meeting. In the worship of Matamma in Orugallu, galalu, korrulu, surapunjulu, drums, buragummalu, trumpets, sirita veenas and bells were used. Jamadika was played and six darshans (shell necklaces), pandals were put up and patams (designs) were drawn. All castes assembled there. Pratapa Rudra heard about her in Delhi and prepared himself to snub her. His people disrupted the work of potharajus, destroyed the musical instruments and threw the shell chains into the fire and thus spoiled the whole atmosphere. Everybody felt unhappy about the situation. Matangis wept and they wanted to do 'Jogu' (begging). The King scolded them and said that the goddess was nothing before Siva's power. He told the people who had assembled there to tell everything to their goddess. They informed Renuka of what had happened in Orugallu.

Renuka was a benevolent goddess. She should protect the people. Then people will believe her. She wrote to her sister about Pratapa Rudra. Matangi felt happy after reading the letter. Matangi caused several diseases to people – green spots, white spots, black spots and red spots. She gathered neem leaves and came to Orugallu. For doing all these things, she appreciated her brother Potharaju and asked him to follow Mata. She wanted to convert Pratapa Rudra as Bavaneedu. She wanted to convert them all to suit to her convenience. She asked the people for 'Saka' (design).

At Orugallu, Pratapa Rudra used the symbol of Siva (Linga Musha) everywhere. Saivism spread to every nook and corner of his country. They considered Matangi as not a devotee of Siva. They asked Matamma several questions about her place of birth, place of residence and where she had come from. Unless they knew about her community, the soldiers would not have allowed her into Orugallu. Mata replied what was the caste or clan of Jangams? She would go to Jogu and sleep in the temple and her clan was 'Kasi', she was a devotee, and her native place was Yeleswaram. She entered the portals of the city.

Mata sold some kind of thread (Yekunara) and got herself acquainted with the atmosphere there. The watchmen told her that the Linga symbol was there and no one who was not a Saivite should go there. Orugallu was considered to be 'Siva Kanchi'.

Matangi immediately thought of reducing the city to ashes and she dressed herself as a Jangam lady. She wore the ornaments and rudrakshamala, Siva's favourite ornament, and asked for Jogu.

Pratapa Rudra demanded to know how she, a Madiga woman, could enter the place and expelled her from Orugallu. Matangi thought that Pratapa Rudra was a Sudra and being a Sudra, he had insulted Matangi, a Madiga woman. Pratapa Rudra said he was not willing to talk to a Madiga woman and he wanted to punish her. Throwing the spots at Pratapa Rudra, Matangi went away to her place. Subsequently, Pratapa Rudra and his subjects suffered from diseases, including cancer. Many people died on account of epidemic diseases. Pratapa Rudra thought that all this was not due to Matangi but it was destiny that had brought misery to his kingdom.

A few days later, a woman soothsayer came to the city. Pratapa Rudra was informed of this. She asked for the ornaments of Pratapa Rudra's queens and they were given to her. She asked the people to bring the king. At that moment, Pratapa Rudra did not have legs to walk nor could he see the world and asked his servants to tell her about how he was handicapped.

Matangi felt happy, gave him bhandaru and prayed to Peda Mahuramma. Pratapa Rudra applied the bandaru to his forehead and was able to walk and perform his duties. He expressed his feelings to Siva that his determination to worship only Siva had turned the tables and he then started worshipping the goddess. Women came and presented navaratnas to Matangi.

Matangi made the king a Bavaneedu and his queens were asked to ring the bells and his children, Kolakandru. She told the king that she was 'Jagadamba' and that she had created all kinds of diseases and showed her avatar as Mutyalamma. Yerukala Nanchari asked him to worship her as 'Oruganti Ellu'. Pratapa Rudra came to Matamma and the people prayed

Asleep Mother Asleep
Vira Pratapudu was a hero
He came here to worship you. [3]

The king prostrated before Matangi and worshipped her. Matangi was very happy to receive him and she said that the mother of Bhruguram (Parasuram), i.e., Polasa and he should tell what he had done. Pratapa Rudra immediately responded to her. She prepared designs, brought neem leaves and Drishti was taken and toddy was brought and poured on the King and then he was relieved from all the ailments. They all worshipped Mahuramma. Then he brought gold Jamidika and his wife played Jeganta (bells) and his sons became the 'Kolakandru' of the elephant. Women who wore different saris became matangis.

Musicians played different kinds of instruments like drums, buralu, daralu and ranjalu. Jamidika is another instrument dear to Renuka. Matangi asked Pratapa Rudra to pray to Renuka and he worshipped her with devotion.

O! Loka Pavani O! Jagadamba
O! Adimashakti O! Paranjyoti
You are the creator of this earth
....
You are Brahmandam.
You are Religion and you are Sarvatamulu,
You are Suralu and You are Polusurulu,
....
You are Mohini, the mother of the Trinity.
O! Loka Mata, you have to protect us."[4]

Mahuramma felt happy and blessed Pratapa Rudra saying there was no king in this world comparable to him.

Similar poetry on Mahuramma was collected by professors Nayani Krishna Kumari and Birudaraju Rama Raju. She was hailed as Adishakti who gave birth to Trimurti – Brahma, Vishnu and Maheswara.

In Chittoor district, many organizations are working for the eradication of the Matangi system. In Puttoor, a social service organization called Mesro (Mothers Educational Society for Rural Orphans), is involved in identifying matangis. Another society called Society for Science and Technical Rural Development is also working for the same cause.

The author interviewed matangis in S.R. Puram mandal, Palamaneru near Nidigunta, Dommarapalem, Kotakanuma Jamunapalli and other places. The author learnt that there was no matangi in Nallaguntapalli of Putalapattu mandal. However, every year the villagers invite matangi to perform Kolupulu in that place. Sometimes, they cannot afford to bring a matamma from some other place because they are expected to give her Rs 2,000. The approximate expenditure on Kolupulu is Rs 10,000. The jatra is celebrated for nine days. We came across Matas in many places in Chittoor district.

In the Andhra region, a matangi enjoys the privilege of smearing her face with turmeric powder and carrying neem leaves. The necklace of cowrie shells is deposited in a well for three days before she is allowed to wear it on the day of ceremony. A knife, wooden shoes and trident are also kept in the well and taken out at the time of the dedication ceremony.

All this explains the significance of the fertility cult. Cowrie shells are related to nature, i.e., water. As already explained, the matangi spitting upon the people gathered there and touching them are believed to remove all uncleanness of the body and soul.

At Tumkur in Karnataka, a Vakkaliga priest performs the marriage. The space is cleaned and smeared with cow-dung. Saka is drawn with red, yellow and white powders. Five small pots one each in every corner of the design and one in the centre are placed. Beside the pots are placed a bowl of sacred ashes, a new cloth, camphor and plantains. A string is passed seven times round the four corner pots and tied to the central pot. The girl chosen to be a matangi has to observe fast for five days. She is dressed in a white sari and seats herself on the Saka, close to the central pot. A bamboo basket containing a pot bearing two footprints, an earthen or wooden receptacle and an iron lamp are placed on her head. The Asadi sings songs on Yellamma and the Vakkaliga priest throws rice over the girl's head, feet, knees and shoulders and ties two marriage badges (Yellamma's and Parasurama's badges). The basket containing the various articles listed is the symbol of a matangi. She carries some neem leaves with her. The basket, wrapped in a red or brown cloth, is hung up with a rope or kept in a niche in the wall.

The Matangi custom in the erstwhile Mysore state declined during the colonial period. This system was embedded in the religious practices of the outcaste communities in Andhra. The matangi's sacred function was to preside at all the purificatory ceremonies. She played a significant role in the religious life of the Madigas.

The custom of sacred prostitution was a relic of the primitive matriarchal society. Thus, it was within the strict patriarchal framework of the temple that such 'matriarchal' elements persisted. The matangi emerges as the supreme authority and as an intermediary between the divinities and the mortals in the sphere of her activity. Matangis receive offerings from her devotees for her ritual functions. Sometimes, inams were also offered to these women for their divine qualities and for the perpetuation of the tradition. The system is now slowly vanishing due to the efforts of the NGOs and the government.

On behalf of the RISE, women investigators visited all villages and developed rapport with the identified Matas and interviewed them. As already mentioned, Matas are living in a pathetic condition. They are unable to meet their basic needs. Most of them are residing with their parents or brothers. Talking to Matas about their sex life is a delicate task.

A workshop of Matas was organized and presided over by Karikala Valavan, the then joint collector of Chittoor district. Munivenkatappaiah, the principal secretary of the Social Welfare Department, was the chief guest at the workshop. Stri Sangathana Shakti took the responsibility of the rehabilitation of Matas.

Chittoor district consists of 66 revenue mandals. For administrative convenience, the district is divided into three revenue divisions: (i) Tirupati, (ii) Chittoor and (iii) Madanapalli. The Stri Sangathana Shakti identified 332 Matas in the district. There are matammas in 15 mandals of Tirupati division and four mandals in the Chittoor area. These Madiga families are very poor. The mandal-wise figures of the matammas are given in Table 5.8.

Table 5.8

Mandal-wise figures of the matammas

Name of the Mandal	*Number of Matammas*
Buchinaidu Kandrika	11
Chandragiri	06
K.V.B. Puram	20
Karveti Nagaram	02
Nagalalpuram	34
Nagari	17
Narayana Vanam	03
Picchatur	24
Puttur	10
Ramachandrapuram	03
Renigunta	08
Satyavedu	27
Srikalahasti	21
Tirupati (rural)	39
Tirupati (urban)	17
Vadamalapeta	18
Varadayapalem	06
Vijayapuram	41
Erpedu	25

In Chittoor district, the age of matammas ranges from Six months to 80 years. Table 5.9 shows the age-wise distribution of matammas in Chittoor.

This table shows that 15 per cent of the matammas are school-going children. In the 11–30 age group, the number of matammas is 235; these matammas require some training programmes as a rehabilitative measure. For the matammas in the 11–15 age group, compulsory education is required and for the 15–35 age group, some kind of training should be given. For those over 40 years, if some land or a petty shop is given, it will help them to become self-reliant. Pensions should be given to those over 55 years because women who led their whole life as sex workers cannot cope with any other profession.

Table 5.9

Age-wise distribution of matammas in Chitoor

Age group	*Number of Matammas*
0–05	10
06–10	45
11–15	50
16–30	91
21–25	59
26–35	35
36–40	15
40–45	17
46–50	05
50 and above	05
Total	**332**

Generally, matammas belong to the dalit community, especially the Madiga community. Their goddess is Matangi to whom they dedicate their girl children. But, Yellamma or Matangi are worshipped not only by Dalit communities but also by some backward castes. Table 5.10 shows the caste profile of matammas.

Table 5.10

Caste-wise profile of matammas in Chittoor

Caste	*Number of Matammas*
Madiga	234
Mala	73
Vadde	5
Golla	4
Mutharasi	3
Washermen	4
Yanadi	3
Pambala	3
Berisetti	3
Total	**332**

The highest number of matammas is from the Madiga community. Mala jogins are more in Telangana. The influence of these two communities must have prompted the other communities to dedicate their girl children to Goddess Matangi. It must be mentioned that no child from the upper caste is dedicated to the goddess. Apparently, this is a conspiracy of upper caste men to make use of these innocent girls for their carnal desires.

In spite of providing free education and residential facilities to the SC children, the dalit women are not in a position to send their girls to school. Table 5.11 shows how these children are deprived of their opportunity to study.

Table 5.11

Educational profile of matammas

Educational Status	*Number of Matammas*
Illiterates	239
5th Standard	68
6th–9th Standard	10
10th Standard	11
Intermediate	4

- Matammas' education is very low and the girls are not exposed to the outside world.
- Ill-treatment in the school is one of the reasons why they drop out.
- Even though they study hard, they do not get proper employment.
- Illiteracy, ignorance and the superstitious nature of the parents prevent the girl children from continuing their education.

Table 5.12

Employment profile of matammas

Occupation	*Number of Matammas*
Under age	105
Agricultural labour	93
Doing Kolupulu	90
Child labour	50
Physically handicapped	12
Sex-working	9
Sheep-rearing	3
Begging	2
Limestone workers	2

Girls, after their dedication to the goddess, live with their parents. Their main responsibility is to take care of the family. The

Matamma cult is prevalent more in rural areas where the matammas have no other occupation. If they work as agricultural labourers, they get a meagre amount which is not sufficient for their maintenance. As some members in the family expect money from them, they have to perform Kolupulu to earn more.

Stri Sangathana Shakti (SSS) and RISE tried to find out the reasons why girls are dedicated as matammas. Table 5.13 presents the different reasons.

Table 5.13

Reasons why girls are dedicated as matammas

Reason	*Number of girls dedicated*
Cold, cough and fever	56
Fits	46
Failed to open the eye	30
Dehydration	24
Smallpox and Chickenpox	22
Number of offspring for parents	20
Not able to suck the milk	19
Wounds	13
Polio	07
Illness of family members	07
Physically handicapped	06
Critical delivery	04
Deaf and Dumb	03
Accident	03
Jaundice	02
Abdominal pain	02

As most of the reasons relate to health, the dedication takes place when the girl children are between one month and five years old. Seventy per cent of the dedications took place below the age of one year. This reflects how superstitious and tradition-bound dalit women are. The lack of rational thinking in these women is exploited by the rich landlords.

The rural people regard the matammas as their common property. Hence, the entire community has a control over them. Though the matammas are allowed to have sexual relations with different people, they are not allowed to marry anyone. Table 5.14 shows the profile of matammas having sexual relationships.

Table 5.14

Profile of matammas having sexual relations with males

Sexual relations	*Number*
Children below 15 years	105
Without sexual relations	45
Relations with a single man	112
Relations with two men	24
Multiple relations	37
Professional sex workers among matangis	9

It should be understood that not every matamma is a sex worker. In fact, very few of them have selected sex for their sustenance. Thirty seven Matas have multiple professions. There is no constant relation with anybody and hence they maintain multiple sex relations. If a matamma has relation with a single man, she is treated as a kept woman. Table 5.15 shows the caste profile of males with whom matammas have relations.

Table 5.15

Caste profile of males with whom matammas have relations

Caste-wise males	*Number*
Mala	109
Madiga	205
Reddy	5
Washermen	2
Balija	3
Yadava	2
Raju	1
Tribal	1
Kamma	2
Modaliar	1
Vadde	1

Matammas have sex relations mainly with Mala or Madiga men and occasionally with men of other castes.

Table 5.16

Periodicity of matammas' relationships

Period	*Number*
Since 3 years	89
Since 5 years	10
Since 10 years	09
Since 15 years	07
Since 20 years	07
Since 25 years	09

It is ironical that when a girl is dedicated to the goddess, the villagers treat her as a representative of the goddess and later regard her as village property. As a child, she has to render service to Goddess Matamma and when she attains puberty she is expected to do Kolupulu in Matamma's festival.

The Madiga caste leader holds a meeting with four elders of the village to discuss the preparations for the Matamma festival. They then start collecting funds. The economic status of the villagers determines the level of the celebrations. Some villages celebrate it for nine days and some for five days. The festival ends with fire-walking. While doing this, they sacrifice animals as an oblation. Design-makers draw the rangoli of Matamma and the person who is going to do Kolupulu worships the goddess.

Notes

1. Edgar Thurston and Rangachari K., *Castes and Tribes of Southern India,* IV Volume. Seniormost Matangi of Madigawada is the Priestess of Matamma's temple. She is a non-Brahmin goddess. She enjoys the fruits of the bananas.
2. B. Rama Raju and Nayani Krishna Kumari have described about the power of Matamma in their book 'Janapada geyalu', The goddess, a Shakti and removed the bad people from the society. They are seven goddesses and whose brother is Potharaju. He is the guardian of his Seven Sisters.
3. Prataparudra of Kakatiya dynasty refused to worship Mathamma thinking that she was a woman goddess. He faced many hardships due to the anger of her and then he realised and prayed her. He pronounced the same and he was blessed by her .
4. Prataparudra, The Kakatiya ruler when he worshipped Matamma, she asked him to worshipped Yellamma. All these stanzas was about the prayer only. Yellamma was considered to be the Loka Mata.

CHAPTER 6

The Basvi System

The Basvi system is deeply entrenched in social customs and religious traditions. The custom of dedicating girls to temples prevailed in the third century. Devadasis were the custodians of music and dance and other arts and were treated with utmost reverence. They were regarded as eternal brides of the gods. Over the years, the system has degenerated into naked exploitation, the object being carnal pleasure. This is satisfying the extramarital sexual instinct of men. Basvis in the areas bordering Karnataka are dedicated to Yellamma or the Adi Shakti or Sarvamba. These are wedded to the goddesses Yellamma, Sunkalamma and Ulagamma or China Obulesu and they sleep with any man who seeks sexual gratification.

The goddess of the Basvi system is at the Soundatti temple, where thousands of young women are dedicated to the goddess every year. The destiny of these hapless victims is determined on the basis of blind religious beliefs. Exploitation of the lower caste people is an accepted social practice.

The factors responsible for the Basvi system are:

(a) **Superstitions, irrationality and blind beliefs in religious customs and traditions:** Members of the SC, because of the unhygienic conditions in which they live, contract certain diseases which if not cured are taken as being caused due to the wrath of Goddess Yellamma. Dedication, they believe, is the only way to appease the goddess. Generally, the eldest daughter is dedicated to the goddess. Another reason is the family tradition and practice to dedicate one girl in every generation to earn blessings for the family.

Plate 11 Basvi woman in Gulbarga.

(b) **Poverty:** The quagmire of poverty has forced the SCs to take shelter under the Basvi system. Propelled by hunger, they resort to this system to earn their livelihood. These women support their parents in their old age. A girl who is made a 'Basvi' is almost equal to a male earning member of any family.

(c) **Dowry system:** Most of the SCs prefer to make their girls basvis as they do not have the capacity to give dowry at the time of marriage. The exploitative system deprives them of social security. There is also the social stigma that these women are required to satisfy the sexual appetite of the rich and dominant groups in society.

(d) **Fear of transfer of ancestral property:** It is felt that through marriage system, one's ancestral property gets transferred to the bridegroom. If there is only one daughter in the family, she should be made a basvi and ancestral property remains intact. Sometimes, the parents resort to infanticide. When there is a male child in the family, they pray to the goddess to bless them with a female child so that they may make her a basvi.

It is surprising that the scientific advancement and modern planned development have made very little impact on the thinking process and belief system of the SCs who continue the Basvi system out of sheer necessity, a necessity which has sanctified itself with certain religious traditions and which is encouraged by the dominant sections of society. The sub-standard economic conditions pave the way for the continuance of the Basvi system. There are four tenets of the Basvi system, they are:

(1) Every Tuesday and Friday evening, the basvi has to offer puja to the goddess.
(2) She must attend the Yellamma festival.
(3) She must beg during Sankranti for at least three days.
(4) On Hutigamma festival, she must go round the temple, naked.

Thus, the basvis are trapped in the vicious circle of poverty and exploitation by high-caste people. The socio-cultural and economic causes are responsible for the perpetuation of the system which has come to be held in contempt as it has become a social institution devoid of religious background. It has degenerated to such an extent that the state governments concerned and NGOs have come forward to ameliorate the miserable conditions of the dedicated women.

Persistence of the Basvi System

At this stage, the author would like to pinpoint the factor for the persistence of the Basvi system and evaluate the impact of rehabilitative measures implemented by the state governments for the emancipation of the basvis from the shackles of servitude. Age-old beliefs, legends and myths play a pivotal role in perpetuating the system.

The Basvi system originated in the 12th century; prior to that, these women were called Sules (Sooleys in pronunciation) and they were dedicated to gods and goddesses. The system came into vogue due to the rise of Veerasaivism.

In Karnataka, devadasis are known by different names such as 'basvi', 'muttu kattikondavalu', 'gajjepuja', 'madisikondavalu', 'nagasani' and 'kasabi'. Even the devadasis used to purchase girls from backward class communities and dedicate them to the gods of upper castes.

In Karnataka, the word 'basvi' is used as a synonym of devadasi. 'Basvi' is the female gender of Basva or Nandi – the bull of Lord Siva. It means the female breeding bull. The Telugu equivalent is 'Achchu Vesina Amboteddu'. It is left free to move about. It is intended for public use. Likewise, girls dedicated to deities become public property. So, they are called 'village sluts'. The girl is taken to a temple and married *ex voto* the deity their in. She becomes a public 'cow'. However, she does not consort with anyone from a caste lower than her own. This type of prostitution is not frowned upon by her community; on the contrary, she is sought out to prepare the tali for a bride at the wedding of even a higher caste since she is like a devadasi, a nitya sumangali. However, with the passage of time, the idea of service to this goddess has dimmed and today these women live a life of dishonour.

The origin of the Basvi system is traced to the glorious conditions of Veerasaivism that prevailed in the 12th century. This system took its original form among the Vokkaliga and Komati castes and slowly spread to Vaishnavites. In those days, girls were dedicated only to gods, not goddesses. How did the custom come to the Mala and Madiga castes and a few backward class communities?

The dalit communities are denied entry into the temples of upper castes. The Malas and Madigas were not allowed to draw water from the wells used by the upper castes. They were driven to the outskirts of the villages. They wanted to imitate the upper castes by dedicating their girl children to the local deities. Abbe J.A. Dubois described basvis as women specially set apart, under the name of the 'wives of the goddess' for the service of one or the other of these deities.

Types of Basvis

Basvis can be classified into (1) Goodu-basvi, (2) Jati-basvi, (3) Balagada-basvi, (4) Ora-basvi, (5) Garudagambada-basvi, and (6) Linga-basvi.

1. **Goodu-basvi:** She is also known as Orabasvi, i.e., the wife of the principal deity of that village. Originally, a basvi was a virgin who maintained her chastity throughout her life. On retirement, she was supposed to nominate her niece as her successor to perform religious duties. When one of her brothers was blessed with a girl child, she was symbolically designated as a future 'basvi' of that village. She was then dedicated to the deity after performing the prescribed rituals. She was called 'Nitya sumangali' or 'Akhanda Soubhagyavati'
2. **Jati-basvi:** She is a caste basvi or Jati-basvi. It is not known whether she can have sex with men outside her caste. She can live with any man of her choice.

3. **Balagada-basvi:** Parents who do not have any male children dedicate one of their daughters as a basvi and she is required to propagate their progeny. The children of the basvi claim membership of the same family.
4. **Ora-basvi** is Basvi belonging to the village. Ora Panduga is also performed and Basvi is the 'priestess'.
5. **Garuda-basvi:** Those who consecrated to Vishnu as Garuda Basvis.
6. **Linga-basvi:** The priestess of Siva is Linga Basvi.

Apart from these basvis, there are other types of basvis such as Divatige Basvi, Yade Basvi, Hennu-Basvi, Bala Basvi and Batla Basvi. Divatige Basvi carries the sacred torch when the deity is taken out in a procession. Yade Basvi carries the Naivedyam to the deity and she has a share in that sacred food. Another type of basvi is Hennu-basvi. This type of basvi existed in the erstwhile state of Mysore. 'Hennu' means female. When she is dedicated to a village deity, she is called 'Hennu-basvi'.

A basvi belonging to the Mahar community is called Bala Basvi. Over the years, the significance of Bala Basvis has declined. However, the Bala Basvis are still found in some villages of North Karnataka. They get rewards from the temple as well as from the community.

The only difference between Bala Basvis and Batla Basvis is that the latter carry a concave metal vessel, which is their distinguishing symbol while that of the Bala Basvi is the tamburi (tanpura). The vessel is gifted by the Veerasaiva community, especially the merchant class. The Batla Basvi had an advantage – she was free to thrust the vessel into the heap of any food grains in any shop and get as much grain as the vessel could scoop out. Her brothers had no claim on her property. However, if there was any movable property, they were eligible for only one-fourth of it.

The basvis were dedicated to serve the Veerasaiva community, but members of this community were not supposed to have sexual relations with a basvi as this would deprive her of the vessel with which she used to collect grain for her livelihood. A basvi was expected to be faithful to the Veerasaivas to attain heavenly abode. This rule was included in the 64 rules of Veerasaivas.

Basvis usually live on concubinage. Sexual acts are sanctioned by wedlock, that is, they are dedicated to village gods and goddesses. Dedicating a daughter as basvi means perpetuation of the patrilineal link. In Karnataka, Madiga, Holeya, Beda, Kuruba, Golla, Dombar, Woddas, etc. are castes who dedicate their daughters as basvis. The girl stays in her father's house and is treated as a son and her son becomes a member of her father's family. She can have sexual relations with a man of equal or higher caste. Generally, a basvi lives as a concubine with one person who allows her a fixed weekly or monthly sum for her sustenance. Apparently, no stigma is attached to her or to her children. People say that she is equal to any woman in her community. But, in practice she is not equated with the wife of any man. She is believed to be immune from widowhood. She is a welcome guest at weddings and she is considered as a person who brings good luck. She prepares the tali with beads from her own chain.

The dedication ceremony includes the wedding of the girl to the idol of the presiding village god or goddess such as Hanuman, Virabhadra, Yellamma and Dyamavva or to inanimate objects like a dagger, a sword or a drum and bells. Some parents vow to dedicate their daughter as a basvi even before her birth. She is initiated into Basvihood by her maternal uncle. When she attains puberty, the consummation ceremony takes place. Three days later, a feast is organized for the community people. The girl is then free to have sexual relations with any man whose caste is not lower than her own. The man who receives her favours has to bear the expenses of her dedication as the basvi.

Initiation into Basvi System

The initiation of a girl as a basvi gives her the right to perpetuate the family. She has the same rights as those of a male member to perform the rites on the death of her parents. The institution of Basvi entitles the parents to control her sexuality for their own selfish ends as a security in their old age. A basvi inherits the family property as though she were a son. She takes care of the family's needs with the earnings she gets either by her concubinage or prostitution. If she has a son, he is treated as the son of her father and if she has a daughter, she takes the mother's path.

These cultural values have an economic base too. The basvis are mainly from the Madiga caste but some are from Mala and other backward class communities. The rich people, especially the landlords, control the land as well as money. If a landlord likes a good-looking girl, he bears the entire expenditure of her dedication and maintains a permanent bond with that girl. She also serves as a daily labourer on his land. In olden days, for a man to have extramarital relations with devadasis or basvis was considered a status symbol. For lower castes, it was not a status symbol but a means of livelihood. Moreover, they could maintain close relations with upper castes. Though a basvi was regarded as an untouchable woman, the upper caste men had no qualms in using her to satisfy their carnal desires.

Beliefs, legends and myths play a significant role in the perpetuation of the system. Natural calamities like floods and drought, diseases in the family and absence of a male issue – all these are attributed to the wrath of a god or goddess and the remedy lies in appeasing the deity by dedicating a girl from a particular family to the deity.

Another important reason for dedication in recent years is abject poverty in the drought-prone border districts of Karnataka and Maharashtra. Sometimes, a basvi is sold to a broker who pushes her into the flesh markets of major cities. It is no wonder that 50 per cent of the prostitutes in Mumbai are devadasis from North Karnataka.

Thus, the institution of Basvi or Devadasi has a definite place in the socio-religious and economic life of the people. The system has gradually lost its ritual role and has been reduced to the status of commercial prostitution. The priests are indirectly encouraging the system for their own personal gains.

Petitions to become Basvis

It is interesting to note that some girls who were about to become basvis had presented petitions to the European magistrates and superintendents of police. They were as follows:

1. Petition of .... wife of .... "I have got two daughters, aged 15 and 12 respectively. As I have no male issues, I have got to necessarily celebrate the ceremony in the temple in connection with the tying of the Goddess's tali to my two daughters under the orders of Guru, in accordance with the customs of my caste. I, therefore, submit this petition for fear that the authorities may raise any objection (under the Age of Consent Act). I, therefore, request that the Honourable Court may be pleased to give permission to the tying of tali to my daughters."
2. Petition of .... aged about 17 or 18 years. I have agreed to become a Basvi and get myself stamped by my guru (priest)

according to the custom of my caste. I request that my proper age which entitles me to be stamped may be personally ascertained and permission granted to be stamped.

'Stamping' refers to branding with the chank (conch) and chakram (wheel) emblems.

3. Petition of two girls, aged 17 to 19 years.

"Our father and mother are dead, now we wish to be like prostitutes as we are not willing to be married and thus establish our house name. Our mother was also of this profession. We now request permission to become prostitutes according to our religion".

The permission referred to in the above petitions refers to a decision of the High Court. The dedicated girls cannot have a legitimate marriage. The dedication of a minor girl was an offence under the then Indian Penal Code.

There are many reasons why the Basvi institution exists. Three important reasons are:

(1) The worship of village goddesses requires the services of women.
(2) To appease the goddesses, both males and females should be dedicated.
(3) The impact of feudal values and the patriarchal system.

In Karnataka, dedication takes place in the Soundatti temple or Kokatnur Yellamma temple. In Soundatti, 2,000 girls were about to be dedicated to Goddess Yellamma in 2004. Due to the timely intervention of the government, the temple authorities shifted the dedication ceremony to small Yellamma temples.

Analysis of the Basvi Institution

(a) The Basvi system belongs to pre-Aryan times.
(b) Dedication is not always voluntary.
(c) The purohits who perform the ceremony are Lingayats.
(d) All the basvis are very poor and they feel forced to take to this ignoble profession.
(e) Childless people adopt girls and dedicate them to the goddess.
(f) Wealthy people support the system as it enables them to indulge in extramarital flings.
(g) The system persists despite there being many laws to check it.
(h) Social reformation should go hand in hand with the economic rehabilitation of the basvis.

Some NGOs have shown a keen interest in rehabilitating the jogins of Andhra Pradesh and the basvis of Karnataka.

Controversial Ideas on Dedication

In the Bombay Presidency, a bill to prevent the dedication of women to Hindu temples was moved by Rao Bahadur S.K Bhole. In the bill, called Bill No. XXVII of 1933, Bhole said, "Once such girls are dedicated to these services, they must remain unmarried throughout their lives." These women or girls were made to undergo a kind of fictitious marriage ceremony after which they could not marry any human being. They were dedicated to the objects of worship and regarded as wives of the deity. Bhole said, "The dedicated girls are known as Devadasis, Bhavins, Basvis Jogtis and Muralis. As dedication entitles these women to do all sorts of services in temples, they vitiate the whole religious atmosphere." They first serve the priests and then the worshippers who frequent such temples. There is no doubt that in recent times, the practice has degenerated into a method of initiating young women to a life of immorality and prostitution, which in many cases becomes compulsory by reason of the cruel custom that a girl so dedicated cannot contract a valid marriage. Experience shows that the provisions of Sections 372 and 373 of the Indian Penal Code have been evaded. Consequently, a few provinces of British India like Madras and the United Provinces of Agra and Oudh brought in some legislative measures to eradicate this evil. Likewise, the Mysore government passed orders as early as 1909, directing the exclusion of devadasis from temple service. Similarly, the Maharani of Travancore state passed orders to prohibit devadasis from service in the temples of that state. In 1930, the Portuguese government of Goa passed an act making illegal the practice of dedicating women to temples in the Portuguese territory. With the same object, an act was passed in the Savantwadi state in 1931.

In some parts of the presidency, such as Karnataka, usually girls aged between 6 and 15 years are dedicated to a temple of Yellamma at Soundatti. This evil custom of dedication is responsible for creating a number of castes which subsist on the gains of prostitution. Thus, it has become a source of perennial supply of prostitutes who infest their own villages and every town they visit for carrying on their nefarious trade. In an amendment to the bill introduced by Bhole, Dr P.G. Solanki said, "The dedication of a woman to service in a temple is not dedication to a life of prostitution ...".[1] The assumption in the Bill was that a dedication for service in a temple is dedication to a life of prostitution. Dr Solanki agreed but his objection was to the dedication of virgin girls to the idols in a temple or outside a temple and denying them a legal marriage. He said the dedication of women and girls to temples was rampant in the Goa territory. His point was that this evil practice had crept into the untouchable communities, who had no access to temples and were ill-treated and humiliated by caste Hindus, especially Brahmins. Such people dedicated girls to the gods, but under a tree outside the temples for sometimes they built their own temples for dedication of girls. The well-known social scientist M.N. Srinivas described it is as sanskritization. In the course of time, it became a habit of the parents from among the untouchable classes to dedicate their girls to the object of worship and thereby lead them into prostitution. Dr Solanki's amendment sought to include in section 2 (a) a Hindu woman dedicated by any form of ceremony performed anywhere outside a Hindu temple to a life of prostitution such as basvis, jogtis, sules (soolays) or muralis among the untouchable classes.

The Basvi system is prevalent in Kurnool district of Andhra Pradesh. There are more than 2,000 basvis in Kurnool town, Tuggali, Maddikera, Chippagiri, Halaharvi, Hoigunda, Alur, Adoni, Kauthalam, Kosigi, Mantralayam, Nandavaram, Devarakonda, Aspari, Peddakadbur, Pattikonda and Yemmiganur revenue mandals.

About 80 per cent of the basvis belong to the Madiga caste and the rest are Malas (17.6%); Dommaras (1.6%); Boyas (0.4%) and Maladasaris (0.4%). In these communities, when there is no male heir in the family, it is customary to dedicate a female child as basvi to perpetuate the patrilinear line. Dr J. Sujana Mallika who studied the Basvi system in Kurnool district explained, in terms of percentage, why the system persists.

Reasons for Dedication

(i)	Absence of a male heir in the family	—	63.2%
(ii)	In fulfilment of a vow taken when there was serious illness or distress in the family	—	24.%
(iii)	Relief for their children	—	10.0%
(iv)	Longing for a male issue	—	16%
(v)	Children of any gender	—	0.4%
(vi)	Poverty of the parents	—	2.8%

According to Sujana Mallika's study, in the grandmother's generation, only 24 women were dedicated to the village deity as basvis. The number increased to 36 during the mother's generation and peaked to 73 in the younger generation. Poverty seems to be the main cause of this custom. The basvis belong to different age groups, the majority being in the 21–30 age group. Table 6.1 shows the details collected by Sujana Mallika.

Table 6.1

Age group of dedication

Frequency of age	*No. of Basvis*	*Percentage*
15–20	11	4.4
21–30	71	28.4
31–40	43	17.2
41–50	56	22.4
51–60	35	14
61–70	34	13.6
Total	**250**	**100**

The fact that there are only 11 basvis in the 15–20 age group as against 24 in the 21–30 age group indicates that awareness programmes have been effective and that the rehabilitation work is good. The small number of basvis in the 15–20 age group suggests that they were initiated into Basvihood a decade ago. All of them are uneducated. At present, some basvi children are going to school, some at the primary stage and the others at the secondary stage of education. A negligible number studied up to the High School and Intermediate levels. There may be one or two graduates.

Gods and Goddesses

In the case of basvis, the rite of dedication means the wedding of the girl at the tender age of 8 to 10 years to some deity such as Anjaneya, Lord Venkateswara, Mallayya, Muniswami, Rangaswami, Vrukonda Veeranna, Durgamma, Ellamma, Kolhapuramma, Mahalakshmi, Maremma, Tayamma, Tikka Lakshmamma and Uligamma.

Among the female deities, Yellamma and Uligamma are the most favoured deities. In Kurnool district, girls are not married to some inanimate object like a dagger, sword or a drum or a bell. The ceremony differs from one place to another and from one deity to another.

Dedication

The dedication ceremony requires elaborate preparation on the part of the parents who want to dedicate their daughter as basvi. The initiation rites are like a Hindu marriage ceremony. Friends and relatives are invited. The girl wraps her nude body with neem leaves and worships the deity. She sits in front of the deity and a necklace of black or white beads and gold mangalasutra is tied around her neck by the caste priest of Madigas or maternal uncle Bayannayana or Goravaiah, if she is a devotee of Lord Siva. The ceremony comes to an end with the priest being given a gift, followed by a non-vegetarian feast. A ram or a goat is sacrificed to the deity.

The girl who is dedicated as a basvi remains a concubine for some time or lifelong. If that man belongs to a caste which is lower than her own, the basvi is expected to visit the shrine where she was dedicated at least once in a year. She is required to take part in the jatara. The basvi has to undergo re-initiation ceremony before the wedding of her son to ward off a calamity. She has to circumambulate the shrine wearing neem leaves around her naked body. She has to arrange a non-vegetarian feast too.

The dedication rite at the shrines of male deities is not expensive, nor is any animal sacrifice required. The procedure is very simple. The prospective basvi wears a white dress and is decked up like a bride; rangavalli is drawn where she sits and the tali is tied by the priest or by the maternal uncle. Sometimes, the initiation is done in the basvi's home.

In the case of a basvi dedicated to God Mallanna, the procedure is quite different. It is not the priest or the maternal uncle but Goravaiah, a devotee of Mallanna, who ties the tali to the basvi girl. This takes place during the Mallanna Jatara in the main temple near Alur. Carrying the basvi on his shoulders, Goravaiah dances around the temple. This is done because the basvi is considered to be the consort of Lord Siva. If the girl is to be dedicated to Vrukunda Veeranna, the ceremony is performed on Monday. In the case of dedication to Anjaneya, Rangaswamy and Venkateswara, Saturday is considered the most auspicious day. For worshipping female deities, Tuesdays and Fridays are preferred.

Begging is a means of livelihood for basvis. They have to collect alms from at least five houses. During the Sankranti festival, they have to follow this tradition. In Gulbarga of Karnataka, the author saw some basvis collecting alms from people. When the basvis become old, as they cannot work as farm labourers or sex workers, begging is the only way left to them.

Rules and Regulations

A basvi's social status is quite different from a non-basvi's. The differences are:

- She cannot think of legal marriage to a human being.
- Her unmarried status is legal in customary terms.
- She cannot escape from economic activity, i.e., she has to take care of her parents in their old age.
- She need not go to anybody's house; customers will come to her house. She can say no in case she is sick or for any other reason.
- Her children have no legal father.
- The expenditure on the dedication is met by the man who desires to have her favours after she attains puberty.
- A basvi's dedication is a prestige symbol and maintaining her is considered a privilege.
- The children of a basvi have no legal claim on the ancestral property of their 'father' whom they cannot claim as their father.
- The basvis do not usually live on flesh trade.
- Sometimes, the maternal uncles can keep the basvis as 'kept women'.
- Generally, the basvis have paramours belonging to their caste only. Occasionally, they have contact with men from Boya, Uppara, Reddy, Wadde, Korava, Pinjari and Sale castes. A basvi's contact with a man from any of these castes is only temporary. A basvi who lives as a concubine gets weekly or monthly maintenance allowance from the so-called paramour. No stigma attaches to the basvis or to their children.
- A basvi is regarded as 'Akhanda Soubhagyavathi' or 'Nitya Sumangali'. She is a welcome guest on auspicious occasions. Even her death is considered auspicious.

- The basvis have to eke out their livelihood by working as casual labour or by begging.

Some basvis work in a ginning factory, but this is only seasonal work. Some of them bring firewood from forests and sell it to the people. Their paramours are mainly farm-hands but they also do petty trade, clerical work, driving, tailoring or some other work.

The basvis have become aware of their miserable life and the NGOs are helping them to come out of the rut and lead a normal life. They have resolved not to make their children basvis. Some live in thatched houses and others have government constructed pucca houses. The children of basvis are attending school.

The factors responsible for the perpetuation of the Basvi system are:

- The system is a pointer to the family strategy whereby a family with its patrilineal ideology uses its women to perpetuate it.
- It is a by-product of the cultural strategy. The caste has been a very important factor in its perpetuation. People of all castes who have dedicated their daughters to the deities are below the poverty line.
- The landlords and rich people use this system for their own selfish ends. That is why they bear the expenses of the dedication ceremony and, therefore, they always have an upper hand in dealing with the downtrodden communities.
- Legends and myths have played a major role in perpetuating the system. Absence of male issues in the family prompts the parents to dedicate their girl child as a basvi and she becomes their social security in their old age. The question of seeking her consent does not arise.

In order to get a comprehensive picture of the Basvi system and the continuity of the cult, an in-depth analysis is required. Case histories of basvis are an important source to construct the story of basvis. They provide an insight into the situation where the basvis are compelled to accept the tradition.

A few case studies with the family background of the basvis are given in the appendix. They provide empirical data and throw light on the factors responsible for the perpetuation of the cult. Table 6.2 shows the frequency distribution of basvis dedicated to various deities:

Table 6.2

Frequency distribution of basvis dedicated to various deities

Deities	*No. of Basvis dedicated*	*Percentage*
Male deities:		
Vrukunda Eranna	37	14.8
Anjaneya	56	22.4
Mallaiah	12	4.8
Munuswamy	2	0.8
Rangaswamy	3	1.2
Venkateswara	7	2.8
Basappa	1	0.4
Timmappa	2	0.8
Penna Obulesu	1	0.4
Narasappa	2	0.8
Avkantaiah	1	0.4
Female deities:		
Mahalakshmi	2	0.8
Yellamma	43	17.2
Tikka Lakshmamma	17	6.8
Uligamma	40	16.0
Maremma	12	4.8
Kolhapuramma	4	1.6
Ramulamma	1	0.4
Sunkalamma	1	0.4
Durgamma	4	1.6
Tayamma	2	0.8
Total	**250**	**100**

Source: Sujana Mallika's empirical data.

The highest percentage of dedication to Anjaneya is in Kurnool district. Anjaneya's devotion to Rama is considered unparalleled.

Swarna Vemayya, a former MLA and vice-president of the A.P. Agricultural Workers Union, Nellore, wrote a letter to the chief minister about the hardships of more than 400 basvis and requested the government to

- abolish the Basvi custom.
- rehabilitate the basvis.
- treat the children whose fathers were not accepted as their legitimate fathers on a par with other children.
- make laws to punish the anti-social elements in society.

- constitute a committee to go into the Basvi system and suggest measures to eradicate the custom, thereby emancipating the basvis.

Adoni, famous for its cotton ginning and spinning mills and oil mills, has a sizeable floating population. Earlier, it was a part of Karnataka where the Basvi system was prevalent. Adoni is now in Kurnool district of Andhra Pradesh.

Gods and Goddesses of Basvi System

The various goddesses worshipped by basvi women are Yellamma, Maremma, Sunkalamma, Thayamma, Bochulamma, Jambulamma, Kosigi Yellamma, Mallamma and Pedda Uligamma. The basvis also worship Hanuman and Parasuram.

Dedication Rites

A day before the dedication, the girl to be initiated is anointed all over with turmeric paste. On the day of dedication, she is given a bath and clad with bunches of neem leaves. She is taken in a procession to the temple along with 'Bhairavi', a priest. After the dedication ceremony, she is dressed in a white sari and a jakini (a kind of bangle) is slid onto her hands. Around her neck is tied a chain consisting of metal coins with the replica of Goddess Yellamma's feet on them. She is then given three baskets of different sizes to be used for begging. This custom is followed in Adoni even now.

Once dedicated, a basvi used to spend most of her life performing 'pujas' to the goddess. As time passed, the practice began to degenerate and did not entirely remain within the purview of religious duties, with the result the basvis were exploited for sexual satisfaction. Denial of marital rights to these women also contributed to the degeneration.

Location of Yellamma Temple

In Adoni, the Yellamma temple is located on a small hill. Only on full moon nights do the Harijan families visit the temple and offer prayers. 'Jangamaiah', the priest of the Madiga community, offers prayers to the goddess. He performs puja at temples and weddings. The Malas have their own priest called Dasari.

Girls are generally dedicated on Naga Panchami which falls in August. Relatives gather to witness the dedication and bless the young basvi, Dasari performs the puja and ties the ceremonial tali to the basvi and declares that she is wedded to the deity, and would thenceforth be known as basvi. The basvi has no legal protection or family identification.

A welcome development is that more and more basvis have realized that they must free themselves from this oppressive system.

Awareness of Basvi Women

Most of the basvis in Adoni are in the 19–50 age group. They live in eight scheduled caste bastis called 'ghers'. The basvis are looked down upon by the society. They have no security or legal protection and their children have no legitimacy. Poverty, chronic illness, diseases, desire for a male child – all these are considered reasons enough to offer their daughters to Yellamma. The basvis have to carry the entire burden on their shoulders throughout their life. Many basvi women tried to suppress the fact about the continuity of the evil practice. At a convention of women on 10 March 1983, Shekamma who organized the conference said, "We, the Basvi women, will organize protests demanding a relief programme from the Government for economic independence. In future, no woman will be allowed to be exploited in this way."[2] Another basvi, Laxmi, said, "We want justice. A man who participates in such a relationship is not socially deprived in any way. Why should the woman alone suffer so much?"[3]

Slowly, every woman started working towards emancipation. Each one tried to break out of her shell and come out. Finally, all of them unanimously decided to form an organization – the 'Basvi Mukti Sangham'. Basti committees with five members each were formed. Rangamma, a young basvi, said, "I declare that in future I shall never entertain any man."

So, economic independence is vital if this custom is to be wiped out. The government should take upon itself the task of eradicating the Basvi system and rehabilitate the basvis through legislation and social welfare measures. The Karnataka and Andhra Pradesh governments enacted laws in 1982 and 1988, respectively to abolish the dedication of women to goddesses. The government should come out with a similar law to end the practice in Maharashtra, Tamil Nadu and Goa.

A Brief Note on the Basvis of Chittoor District

Dedication of women to the service of a deity is mostly from two castes in Chittoor district; they are Madigas and Dommaras.

Differences between Madiga and Dommara Basvis

1. **Dommara basvis:** These people come under the backward classes 'A' group. Dommaras are acrobats by profession (Gavadi/Samuvidya) but they also rear pigs to earn their livelihood. The survey revealed that any one girl in the family is dedicated to the deity prompted by blind faith and superstition and in some cases due to poverty. After the girl attains the age of puberty, elders (Kula Peddalu) of the village perform a ceremony on an auspicious day to dedicate the girl to their deity called 'Gadimanu'. After dedication, the girl is not to marry any mortal. All Dommara basvis live in Pedda Panjani, Baireddypalle Kola village and Palamner mandals of Chittoor district.
2. **Madiga basvis:** All Madigawadas have a Matamma temple. It is not compulsory for each family to dedicate a girl of their family as basvi/matangi. If any child irrespective of its age before maturity falls seriously ill, its parents dedicate her to their goddess 'Matamma' only with the objective of curing her. When the girl becomes mature, the elders of the family and 'Guru', called Baineedlu, conduct a ceremony on an auspicious day and dedicate the girl to Matamma.

In 1986, in Chittoor district there were only 83 basvis/matammas. Now, the number has increased.

Basvis in Anantapur District

There were 556 basvis in Anantapur district, most of them over 30 years and belonged to the Madiga caste. They were not educated and at that time and they did not have any property. Their main occupation was agricultural labour. Their monthly average income was in the range of Rs 100 to Rs 200. They did not have skills to do any technical work and 550 basvis did not get any government help. About 375 basvis did not have pucca houses. The district administration drew up plans to build houses for them and formulated schemes to give them training in several crafts such as tailoring, embroidery and socks-making to enable them to earn in a decent way. The district administration tried to help the 95 basvis who had lands with irrigational facilities. Schools and hostels for the basvi children were included in the women's welfare programme. It was decided to admit the 39 basvis who were below 18 years to Women Welfare Service and Home for Formal Education.

Anantapur then had 63 mandals and basvis lived only in 22 mandals. The number of basvi families in the district was 556.

Age of the basvis

(a)	Below 18 years	39
(b)	Below 30 years	170
(c)	Below 50 years	204
(d)	Above 50 years	143
	Total	**556**

Of the 556 basvis, 53 belonged to the Mala caste, 409 to the Madiga caste and 94 to the other castes.

Age-wise classification of the children and dependants of the matammas/basvis

Dependants		*Boys*	*Girls*	*Other*
(a)	Below 5 years	130	71	—
(b)	Below 10 years	106	90	—
(c)	Below 15 years	77	62	—
(d)	Below 30 years	63	53	—
(d)	Above 30 years	—	—	—

Educational qualification of basvis

		Boys	*Girls*
(a)	No education	293	241
(b)	Below 5th standard	42	29
(c)	Below SSLC	8	5
(d)	Above SSLC	6	1

Accommodation of basvis

(a)	Huts	236
(b	Semi-permanent houses	62
(c)	Permanent houses	119
(d)	No houses	139

Number of basvis having landholdings		
(a)	No holding	461
(b)	Less than 2 acres	47
(c)	More than 2 acres	48

These figures indicate the poverty level of most of the basvis. Most of them did not have even one acre of land.

Occupation of basvis		
(a)	Agricultural labourers	472
(b)	Contract labourers	11
(c)	Other types of labourers	73

Average wages of basvis		
(a)	Upto Rs 100 per month	436
(b)	Upto Rs 200 per month	115
(c)	Upto Rs 300 per month	5
(d)	More than Rs 300 per month	Nil

How pathetic the economic condition of basvis was can be well imagined. One basvi was familiar with weaving. In 1986, when the survey was conducted by the district administration, no assistance was given to them. For want of sustenance, many of them suffered from malnutrition. Due to old age, 54 basvis had defective vision. Two basvis had sexually transmitted diseases (STDs). However, none of the basvis of Anantapur district was physically handicapped. All the 2671 basvis were rehabilitated by 2002–2003.

On the lines of an Act passed in Karnataka in 1982, Andhra Pradesh passed an Act in 1988 to award deterrent punishment to those who perform, promote or take part in the performance of any ceremony for dedicating girls to any deity. The offender is punishable by imprisonment for a minimum period of two years and a fine ranging from Rs 3,000 to Rs 5,000. As an incentive to marry a basvi's daughter, the Social Welfare Department offered Rs 10,000. However, not a single case of default is recorded and there is no vigorous implementation of the legal provisions protecting the dignity of women. Despite official claims, to the contrary, there have been some incidents of dedication at least in secrecy. It is reported that every year, at least 200 innocent girls voluntarily or forcibly accept this custom of dedication. In 1990, a few theogamous marriages took place in the Balkampet area of Hyderabad itself. Now and then, such incidents take place in the interior villages of Mahaboobnagar district of the Telangana region of Andhra Pradesh. How to put a stop to this custom of dedication is a big challenge.

In Kurnool and Anantapur districts, girls are dedicated to both male and female deities. The mode and details of dedication and worship differ depending upon the place and the deity to whom the girl child is dedicated. The tali is tied by the maternal uncle or Boyannaya or Dasaraiah or a senior basvi. It is a pity that no one seems to realize that in the name of religion, an innocent girl's future is sealed.

In 1992, when the author interviewed the basvis of Anantapur they said that the government had built pucca houses for them, but they had no money to send their children to school. "They accompany us to the workspot", they said. The basvis were then not interested in the long-term benefits; they were satisfied with short-term benefits. While at some places the government had given Rs 15,000 to each basvi, in some other places no such assistance was given.

When there is a famine, the basvis go to some other place leaving the old people to fend for themselves. They work as labourers at a distant place and come back in June.

There was a time when Malas used to become basvis but now they shun this custom. Their parents and grandparents were responsible for making them basvis. Though they perform the marriage of their daughters, their family is different. The basvis are stigmatized due to their parents' selfishness. To help them get rid of the stigma, (1) they should be educated, at least their children should be made to go to school; (2) the children born to them should be brought up in a different atmosphere.

The basvis have realized that they are the victims and they would not like their children to suffer the same fate. The author met more than 100 basvis in Guntakal, a place not mentioned in the government survey. The villagers call them 'Bajarudi' or 'public slut'. All the basvis are dedicated to Sunkalamma or Uligamma. Uligamma temple is in Munirabad of Karnataka.

In Anantapur, Boyas also dedicate their children to Uligamma. In Reketla, of the 25 basvis, 23 were Boya basvis and two were Madiga basvis. The upper caste people allow Boya basvis into their houses, but not Madiga basvis. The problem of untouchability persists in some of the villages.

Social Analysis of Basvi System based on their Songs

If we study the literature of basvis, we can understand the different stages of their life and how they suffered. All these factors are reflected in their songs and other forms of literature. Through this media, we can analyse the socio-economic, religious and cultural conditions of their lives.

Basvis play a significant role in rural society. Marriage is a very important occasion in any caste and the people observe certain customs and traditions. We have already discussed a basvi's marriage to an immortal being and why she is called 'Nitya Sumangali'. While deciding a marriage proposal, the parents of the bride invite a basvi and discuss things in her presence. There is a song in Kannada literature which goes:

> The in-laws have come, what is the matter
> what is the matter, please tell
> please give your daughter to our son,
> I will give, but we have to see the house first
> We will see the bridegroom and decide next ...

They elicit all the information and spend good time with them and fix the marriage. In ancient times, marriages in SC families used to be celebrated for five days as they thought that the number 5 was lucky for them. The first day was known as 'Nibbanam'. That day, the marriage pandal was prepared. They would receive the guests and the bridegroom and arrange for their stay. On the second day, 'Nalugu' or preparation for their bath would take place.

They would narrate how Sita was married to Rama. The people who assembled would sing a song, describing saris of different colours given to the bride. The married women would apply turmeric powder to the bride while tying the 'tali' or mangalasutra. The basvis would add the footprints of Yellamma and beads of their own necklace in the mangalasutra. They would make the bride sit in 'Saka' and give her Yellamma footprints. Then, one group of people would gather in a place and take their food separately behind the curtain. Physically handicapped persons and illegitimate children were not allowed to have their meal there. The basvi's presence at the feast was a must. In the evening, gifts would be given to the bride and the bridegroom. Next day, a non-vegetarian feast would be served to them. At night, the basvi would decorate the bride with kumkum and perform an arati. That night is considered to be very important. The following day 'Nagoli' would take place. The bride and the bridegroom change their dresses. The basvi would take them to an ant-hill and they both would perform puja. They were then expected to worship Gangamma. They remove the pandal and put out the country ovens. Previously, there used to be Basavi's Mudda, Basvi's pita and Basvi's kumkum. Such an influential person later became a beggar.

Before starting activities of the marriage, turmeric powder is prepared. The people assembled treat the bride as Janaki and sing a song. And they also treat her as Parvati. All the things needed for her new family are described in the song. The basvi is given a new sari and a blouse. The new bride is compared to 'Rambha', the celestial dancer. Then 'Saka' is arranged where both the bride and the bridegroom sit.

Though they are poor, they sing songs about diamonds and pearls. They also mention the names of deities like Narayana, Govinda, Siva, Sita and Rama. This indicates the sanskritization process.

There are no differences between their own deities and the deities of other castes. They worship their own deity in a song as follows:

"Friends! What have you brought for Yellamma?"

"We have brought leather feet and we have come here to take her to our house."

In the song, they also mention silver plate and gold feet.

The Basvi system is prevalent among Dommaras, a semi-nomadic community in the Telangana and Rayalaseema regions of Andhra Pradesh. The basvis participate in all activities. When a girl is made a basvi, the marriage badge is tied to an idol of the deity or a dagger. When the marriage is over, the girl is proclaimed a 'basvi'. A senior basvi teaches the new basvi what to do and what she is expected to do in jataras or other religious ceremonies. They also participate in the weddings of other castes.

In olden days, when medicines were unheard of, people used to think that epidemics were caused by village deities who were unhappy with them. They would attribute epidemics such as cholera, to the wrath of the village deities.

Cholera: It was called 'Maridamma', 'Mahammari', 'Maremma'. This contagious disease generally used to spread during jataras. Everyone knows that it comes due to unhealthy food and unhygienic conditions. If we analyse the situation, there is water scarcity both in

Telangana and Rayalaseema. It is natural that some diseases occur in those places. But, the superstitious people think that it is due to the wrath of the deity and that they must appease her. Otherwise, she will take the lives of the people. That is why she is called 'Maremma' or 'Maridamma'.

The people ask the village potter to make a small image of the deity and build a small temple to her on the outskirts of the village. Later, jataras take place there where goats, sheep and buffaloes are sacrificed. The upper castes do not participate in jataras. When a catastrophe comes, the whole village stands united. However, the upper caste people say the backward classes should take the customs and traditions seriously; otherwise, the village will be ruined. After the sacrifice, people cook there and eat together and name their children after 'Maremma'.

Measles or smallpox: This disease, the people believe, is caused by a village deity called Polamma. There is a story that Polamma and Posamma were sisters. One day Polamma, who had no children, went to Posamma along with their brother Potharaju to see Posamma's children. Posamma did not allow them. She hid her children. This angered Polamma and she cursed the village people that they would be affected with a disease. And so the whole village was affected by measles. People implored Polamma to save the village and safeguard them. All the same, they sing a song deriding her barrenness. The song has 58 lines.

All the villagers start their journey to the jatara along with potharaju and take as many eatables as possible. In the end, they pardon Posamma and she explains the remedy for the disease.

> Please take water ! Nagayalo Gobbillo
> use turmeric powder and bandaru, sister
> take neem leaves
> and use them for children ...

That Posamma is a fierce goddess is known through the children who are affected by smallpox and the worry it causes to their parents.

An ode to the goddess runs thus:

"Changalva flowers, lemon, white sari, yellow sari are required for the village deity. After seeing Polamma, the heart-beat will increase ..."

Thus, the goddess is depicted in different ways. Diseases are not caste-sensitive. They visit everybody regardless of the caste. The elders would not sleep. 'Wakefulness' is found everywhere. They sing a song on Polamma's entry as follows:

Polamma wanted to go to Madigawada
But she did not go there
She wanted to go, with drum-beats
Then Polamma went to affect them
But she did not go to Kapuwadalu
Polamma went to Yerukalawada
Kuravas wanted to go but did not go
Polamma went to Balijawadalu.

People of every caste remember their duty in order to prevent Polamma from entering their village. The only thing that they have to do is appease her with some animal sacrifice and offerings typical of their profession.

Neem garden is dear to Polamma. It is perhaps for this reason that neem leaves are important for curing measles. Neem leaves are boiled in water with which the patient is given a bath. 'Sukasaptati', a book in Telugu, says diseases such as smallpox were due to the devils.

Worshipping the 'God' is known as 'Devarlu'. All the elders of the village worship the village goddess known as Uligamma. In the Rayalaseema area, the eunuchs dress like females to indicate that they have transformed themselves as Uligammas. (This is narrated in the story, 'Bambeyyadu Ganda Jogammayyeda' written by Nagappa.) Uligammas are invited to pour water into an unburnt pot kept in a place called 'Bodrayer'. Basvis/Jogins worship the feet of Yellamma and decorate her. They stand there and do fortune-telling (Gadde). Several people ask questions and she answers them when she is in a trance. Patwaris, Reddis, Gouds, Patels, palegars do the things necessary to send her away from the village. Basvis/Jogins, Baineedlu, watchmen, Velpulollu, Mahendars and Yadavas all participate in this event.

This event takes place on the outskirts of the village. They use only a male doll and a female doll and Velpu woman takes 'Ranagumpati' (a pot with fire) in her hand. They go to the outskirts with a sari, a blouse piece, a new earthen pot, goat, sheep or cocks. They take everything to 'Kottam' (place where they keep cows or buffaloes). There they improvise an oven with some stones. Jogins and basvis prepare 'Rangam' and prayers are offered to the goddess and she is hailed as 'You are the first mother' and 'jaganmata'. She is beneficent to those who have faith in her and shows a dagger to those who opposed her. They recite the story of how Parasurama came into this world.

Interestingly, some basvis take part in dramas. Some of them joined the famous drama troupe Surabhi which used to go from one place to another to stage plays such as Satya Harishchandra and Ramayanam. During their stay in a village, they would solicit customers to earn money. They toured throughout the year and returned to their village when there was a festival. According to Surendra Reddy, incharge of the Telangana Dramatic Association, the devadasis act as heroines in dramas.

The basvis mainly worship village deities. The deities of Aryans are male whereas Dravidian deities are female. While the Aryan deities are concerned with war, Dravidian deities guard agriculture. Mentioning these deities in his book *The Village Gods of South India*, Whitehead says that the normal function of the village deity is the guardianship of the village but many of them are believed to have other powers, especially in relation to disease and calamity. The Dravidian culture belongs to the pre-Aryan period, i.e., the period of Indus valley civilization. The Brahmanical tradition must have influenced the Dravidian culture and modernism has seeped into this culture. Otherwise, its culture represents totemism. The various village deities are only different manifestations of the same goddess.

Each deity is connected with a disease. For instance, Maremma is connected with cholera, Sankulamma with smallpox and Peddamma with measles. Poleramma is a border deity and Pochamma is the custodian of the life of the people. She protects the agricultural products and wealth of society.

There are seven deities or matrikas who have a brother called Potharaju. The seven names vary from region to region. There is a song:

Karremma, Kanchemma Uyyalo Vallakka Sellela Uyyalo
Yellamma, Jimulamma Uyyalo Vallakka Sellela Uyyalo
Polamma, Posamma Uyyalo Vallakka Sellela Uyyalo
Dhanalachmi, Bhulachi Uyyalo Vallakka Sellela Uyyalo.

Goddess Yellamma is famous in almost all the villages of Telangana and Rayalaseema and of course in Karnataka. People of many castes worship her. They believe she protects them from famine and diseases and they sacrifice sheep and he-buffaloes to her. Madigas say that Yellamma is as old as the earth and she has been their goddess from the beginning. Gouds also worship Yellamma. There is a Yellamma temple in Mahuram. Upper caste people call her Renuka. During the Kakatiya period, Madiga women and Baineedlu used to narrate the story of Yellamma. In 'Kridabhiramam' of Vallabhamatya, there is a poem which mentions 'Kakathammaku Saidhodu Yekavira'. Yekavira is the mother of Parasurama.

Yellamma of Orugallu (Warangal) is a famous deity. In Orugallu, there is Yellamma Bazar. Yellamma is also known as 'Jogulamba' which means she is definitely a Jain goddess. A naked idol in Alampur Brahmeswara temple is identified as that of Yellamma or Renuka.

The basvis also used to recite the story of Yellamma along with Baineedlu who are professional artistes. The story of Renuka Yellamma is told by Prof. B. Rama Raju in his Telugu folk poetry. Laxmikantha Mohan also published 'Yellamma story' in his folk poetry. "Oggu katha" artistes like Chukka Sattayya and others recite the story of Yellamma.

Yellamma was the daughter of Siva. She married the sage Jamadagni, the son of Gautama. He did penance to rid himself of the sins of his father. Renuka became his wife after undergoing several rigorous tests. She was asked to prepare a pot to bring water to Jamadagni. Ranuka's chastity and greatness proved her to be a great deity. Baineedllu sing songs of Yellamma and every aspect of her life. A song goes as follows:

> Your father is Muni Raju, Yellamma
> He prepared a pearl pandal, Yellamma
> In that pearl pandal he arranged diamonds 'Saka', Yellamma.

In the stanza, there is a mention of a chain of shells. The song describes the details of her marriage. The same tradition is followed in basvi's marriage to the deity. The same song is sung by basvis at marriages. Wherever there is Yellamma, there are neem leaves, Ganda Jyotulu (lights), chain of shells, toddy pots, silver plates and gold plates.

In another story, Jamadagni produced three children by Yellamma to test her. They asked for the food which she was taking to Jamadagni. Jamadagni had cooked some rice and it was missing.

He told Yellamma to feed the children. The three children asked her to give them food without wearing anything. There is another version of the story. Yellamma saw a king and a queen and for sometime, she imagined herself as the queen. Jamadagni saw this with his third eye and asked his sons what to do with their mother. All the three children said that she should be condoned, but the last son Parasurama said she should be beheaded.

Parasurama beheaded his mother but later prayed to god for a boon with which he could bring his mother back to life. The story was described as follows:

> Mother, Yellamma, please come Mahurala,
> Your son is Parasuramudu
> Don't create any trouble for me
> Don't create any trouble for me
> I will become a date tree
> If you become a date tree
> I will become an Ediga person
> If you give trouble, I will become black earth
> If you become black earth and I will plough the land, my mother
> If I become a black round stone, Ramudu
> If you become a black round stone, I will become an Oddera.

It is part of the sanskritization process that SCs are worshipping these deities. The dalits have had a relationship with Yellamma for a long time. They do not maintain this kind of relationship with other gods. The upper castes know that dalits worship some of the gods the upper castes worship. Anjaneya Swami (Hanuman) is very important among the gods the dalits worship. The reason why dalits worship Anjaneya Swami is that Anjaneya had gone to Lanka and given Rama's ring to Sita and he had helped Rama in the war against Ravana.

Here we can say that Dravidians since time immemorial used to worship trees, stones, sun, moon, etc. The same habits are seen even in rural folk and especially among the dalits. In some places, there are 'Landelu' beside the temples. Nowadays, in the temples of the village folk deities we see 'Om' or 'Swastik' mark. That is definitely an impact of the culture of neighbouring places.

There is no intermediary element between the village deity and its devotees. The deity is not worshipped daily, but only during festival days and on the 'kolupulu' day. They break a coconut, burn incense and light 'Agarbatti' and use kumkum and turmeric powder. They tell the deity about their joys and sorrows as if they were talking to a human being. How they perform Yellamma Puja and what they offer to the deity is described in a song. The song also mentions the number of animals that are to be sacrificed to the deity.

The basvis believe that if they do not worship the goddess every week, she will get angry. They also believe that if she is not satisfied with the worship, she will become a spirit. Previously, basvis worked as pujaris. Now, new basvis are temporary pujaris and are treated as 'elderly' persons as far as the temple is concerned.

Socio-economic conditions: Previously, the basvis used to live in temples. During the day, they used to go to 'Jogi' and spend the night in the temple.

In villages, they live in thatched houses amidst the people of their own caste. The Government of Andhra Pradesh has built pucca houses for them and now they have their own colonies. This rehabilitative programme, however, is not complete in all places. Whether they live in thatched huts or pucca houses, the basvis maintain sexual relations with others. A basvi's sex partner promises that he will do something substantial to her. The basvi asks him:

> Where have you constructed the house, you are not a useful person.
> I will do day after tomorrow,
> You have not sold the sheep and the walls are not constructed by you,
> Husband, I cannot live among the sheep,
> You have sold goats, you have not constructed a pucca house.
> I cannot lead my life with goats ...

The basvi has to take her entire family to the paramour's house. The basvi's staple diet differs from place to place. In Telangana and Rayalaseema, the basvis eat maize, sajjalu and korralu which they produce. They cook rice only on some occasions or whenever they have a guest.

They have eatables and Bonalu, without which they cannot perform the puja. For two days they neither drink toddy nor eat meat. Some people think that Yellamma likes toddy and so they drink it. Whenever a death occurs in anybody's house, they do not eat until the cremation of the body is over. Tuesdays and Fridays are meant for Yellamma. On Sundays and Wednesdays, they worship some other gods and they observe fast. On some occasions like marriage and kolupulu, they neither eat any food nor drink any water.

In any girl's life, puberty is an important development as it is followed by physiological and psychological changes. She attracts the attention of her close relatives and later of other people. If the girl happens to be the daughter of a basvi, then all the villagers wait for an opportunity to notice the physiological changes in her body. Every basvi thinks that her daughter should not become a basvi. She would like to perform her marriage immediately after she attains puberty so that her daughter should lead a happy married life. She should bear children who will get the benefit of both the parents. She realizes through her experience that she should have the company of some male person. She thinks:

Chandanam Lanti Kuturini
Sirimanthudi Kodukkivvali.

She hopes her daughter would be very beautiful and be married into a rich family so that she will have a bright future. But who will come forward to marry the daughter of a basvi? She dreams about her daughter's marriage. In rural areas, a girl going to her in-laws means that she will be an economic asset to the family. She works in the kitchen as well as in the field. In fact, every woman be it in villages or cities contributes to the family, though the significance of her contribution is generally not recognized.

When a girl attains puberty, her maternal uncle buys the upper garments for her. And if she does not have any maternal uncle, then her mother buys her the garments on behalf of her brother. There is a song that says:

Your bangles are gold, your hair is beautiful
Why are you sad? Has anybody scolded you?"
"Nobody has scolded me
They've brought a sari not of my liking.

At puberty time, the mother gives her nutritious food consisting of black gram, rice, kudumulu (prepared with rice flour and sugar). The neighbours also bring her some eatables. On the fourth day, the girl is given a purificatory bath. This is the time when the mother realizes that after marriage, her daughter will be separated from her. The father makes her child a basvi because he is a drunkard.

The basvis have had no problem as far as the marriage of their children was concerned. However because of the degradation of the status of the basvis, their daughters came to be called basvis. This is the main reason why a basvi's children are also made basvis.

As regards a basvi's funeral, it used to be performed according to the tradition of the temple. Previously when a devadasi died, no puja was conducted in the temple. When the funeral procession arrived at the temple, a garland used to be taken from the deity to decorate the corpse. It was an honour observed meticulously. After the cremation of the devadasi, the temple was purified and a bitter vegetable curry was offered to the god. This was in regard to a temple dancer. In the case of a basvi, a new 'tali' would be prepared, new clothes, bhandaru, kumkum, and bangles would be bought. A senior basvi or Dasaraiah or the pujari would remove the old tali and tie a new 'tali'. They would adorn the corpse as if it were a bride, prepare a new pandal and then take the body for cremation. When the father of a basvi died, the basvi would act as a man and perform all rituals. Whenever anyone died in the village, the basvi would observe a fast.

Festivals, special occasions and jataras: The basvis celebrate the festivals like the other people in society. They compulsorily do 'Jogu' these days. Every Friday, Tuesday, full moon day and Amavasya, they give a bath to Yellamma and observe fast.

Attending jataras is mandatory for the basvis. Jataras are held every year in the month of Magh in Rayadurg, Tirumalapuram near Amrabad, Rangapuram (Kalwakurti taluka) and Chekkarapalli (Narva mandal). In Chandragutti of Shimoga district, the basvis go to the temple naked.

The basvis used to have lands allotted by the landlords and other village elders. The lands would remain in their possession as long as they performed the duties of basvis. They have no permanent claim on the land. Lands are no longer allotted to the basvis. The government is doling out meagre amounts to the basvis as a rehabilitative measure. This could be one of the reasons why prostitution in this community has increased.

In today's circumstances, a basvi is not patronized by the village. It is not a problem when the basvi is young as her maternal uncle or someone else would keep her temporarily or permanently. However, she cannot demand anything from him on the ground that he has fathered all her children. If no one is willing to look after her, she has to do Jogu and earn something to maintain herself, her children and her parents too. She is caught in a vicious circle.

Sometimes, a basvi who has spent the prime of her life in prostitution is forced to become an agricultural labourer or a vegetable vendor. She knows that she cannot take seriously her customer's promises. He says:

> your anklets belong to both of us, Sathemma.
> I am not going to give, Dakutari Sinnoda
> There is a gold piece in your neck, that belongs to both of us, Sathemma,
> I am not going to give, Dakutari Sinnoda.

In the harvest season, the basvis get more paddy than at other times. Telangana basvis think that they have a claim. In Rayalaseema, people ask a basvi "why don't you work? The government is giving you money, house and other things." Many basvis stopped doing Jogu in view of the criticism they have to face in the day-to-day life. In urban areas, they go and beg in the streets or sing songs at weddings and earn money.

When no alternative is available, the basvis think of prostitution for which they go to the red light areas and earn money. They send it to their family for their sustenance. The government and NGOs are conducting awareness programmes, giving them financial assistance and providing training programmes with a view to eradicating the Basvi/Jogin/Matangi system.

The basvis have their own myths, beliefs and philosophical ideas which are described in their songs. They perform Kolupulu whenever a calamity befalls the village or an individual. Basvis sing devotional songs on Tuesdays and Fridays when they perform puja.

Beliefs of Basvis

The basvis believe that gods and goddesses are their saviours. They are afraid for their life. Fear comes out of ignorance. They think that anything bad happening in the village is the result of their failure to worship the deity or fulfil their vows to the deity.

This thought is conveyed by the song:

> Polamma has come and has gone to Madigawada
> The drums are beaten and she wants to go somewhere but she did not go.
> Polamma has come and gone to Kapuwada

I am going/I am going/she did not go because of her passion
Polamma has come and gone into the area of Yerukalas.

All major castes are included in this song. Every caste has its functions but it has to worship Polamma. If they neglect their duties, they cannot escape the wrath of the Goddess. Though Polamma looks frightening, she protects the village. Wadderas, weavers and other castes worship this deity to stave off smallpox and other diseases.

They feel that Goddess Yellamma is inseparable from them. They sing a song describing how the goddess is a personification of chastity.

Your father is Muni Raju
Pearl pandal is ready for you
Beneath this pearl pandal
The purohit prepared saka, Yellamma.

This saka is prepared with diamonds. A situation similar to the one in which a basvi is initiated into Basvihood is created for Yellamma. In the song "Yellamma Uyyalo, Lingampallilo Uyyalo", the Yellamma Jatara of Lingampalli is described. Regardless of the number of colourful saris offered to her, Yellamma likes the sari with neem leaves. While the well-to-do devotees offer her animal sacrifices, some others take eatables to Yellamma and some others bring Bonalu Buttalu, drums and Jankelu. In another song, they describe the beauty of Yellamma in coloured saris.

"Vallava Neredallo Putta putta lella
putta lella, Vallava Neredallo ..."

Whatever is offered to Yellamma is mentioned in the song which also describes basvi and her dance during the jatara.

In Andhra Pradesh, basvis are present in Kurnool and Anantapur districts. They mostly belong to the Madiga caste. The author found that only in a place called Reketla, the basvis belonged to the Boya community. There are 23 Boya basvis and 2 Madiga basvis in that village.

Usually, SC families which do not possess even a small bit of land and who have no means to do any business are the ones who dedicate their children to the goddesses. Sometimes, widows and girls deserted by their husbands become basvis. Their main occupation is serving the goddess and they live by begging. The dedicated girls are expected to observe physical chastity.

The author interviewed basvis of more than twenty villages in Anantapur district and three villages in Kurnool district and found that none of the basvis interviewed was willing to dedicate her daughter. They were all keen on educating their children. Also, most of the basvis felt that married life would be more meaningful than the lives they were leading. They felt that they were risking their health due to sexual exploitation. Among the children of basvis, we found only one boy who had studied upto the university level. Now, many students are from basvis' families.

Despite enactment of progressive laws and provision of liberal financial assistance and anti-dedication programmes by NGOs, there are thousands of basvis even today. Several socio-cultural and economic factors have contributed to the continuance of this system. Many basvis have migrated to urban brothels.

Only in Andhra Pradesh we have three different names in three different regions. There are subtle differences between one system and the other. Even sometimes there is caste difference is also found. In Matangi system, 98 per cent are Madigas only. Among the Jogins Malas, Madegas and a few other backward classes are included. Among the Basvi system Madigas and Boyas are there. There are subtle differences between the worshipping of the deity. These differences are not found either in Karnataka, Tamil Nadu or Maharashtra. These differences are not mentioned and I have drawn this comparison after doing fieldwork in all these places.

Comparison across Jogins, Matangis and Basvi Traditions

S.No.	*Jogin*	*Matangi*	*Basvi*
1.	Girls from Mala, Madiga, fishermen community are dedicated	Only Madiga community	Madiga and Boya (Valmiki) communities
2.	Funeral dances are in vogue	Kolupulu or Jataras	Worship of the goddesses
3.	Yellamma, Matamma, Maisamma, Renuka	Matangi	Yellamma, Renuka, Matamma, Sunkalamma, Uligamma, China Obulesu

Cont'd...

Cont'd...

4.	Potharaju ties the knot to jogin	Pedda Madiga or maternal uncle	
5.	Jogin Parvati in Telangana	Matangi	Basvi, Renuka, Matangi, Sule (pronounced soolay) (in Karnataka)
6.	Virgin girls are dedicated	Only virgins are dedicated	Virgins and widows are dedicated
7.	Participate in rituals	Participate in rituals	Not allowed to enter the sanctum sanctorum
8.	Cowry shells	Cowry shells	Cowry shells
9.	Leather tali and black beads	Leather tali and black beads	Leather tali and black beads
10.	Age between 5 and 12	Even a 6-month baby	5–6 years
11.	Nose-ring and dressing pattern are different	Ordinary sari and blouse	Nose-ring is not used
12.	Nitya Sumangali	Nitya Sumangali	Nitya Sumangali
13.	Yellamma came out of an ant-hill	The origin of the supremacy of the Matangi is shrouded in legends. She also came out of an ant-hill.	Ant-hill
14.	All the religious symbols and rituals indicate the Shakti cult. Yellamma is a fertility goddess		
15.	The Basvis use their father's surname as their surname. Their children inherit the same surname and they have a share in the property of their parents.		
16.	Dedicated girls in all traditions discharge the responsibility to their parents in their old age.		
17.	Animal sacrifice is quite common in all the traditions. Thus, there are many affinities and few differences between these traditions in Andhra Pradesh.		

Conclusions and Suggestions

From the above description, the author believed that it is extremely difficult to establish that the women in these traditions are prostitutes. The attempts to brand these women as prostitutes might still influence the present understanding of these traditions; but from our own research, we find it hard to arrive at such a conclusion. These traditions have been imbued with multiple cultural meanings as discussed above. For instance, the women involved are also perceived to be goddesses, who are believed to be guardians of communities against calamities and personal tragedies.

However, the aspect of control of sexuality can be ascertained from these studies. Two observations are crucial to establish this point. First, women's involvement has not been taken into consideration. Second, the perpetuation seems to flow from the involvement of the upper caste groups and landlords who seem to have an explicit interest in creating these spaces for extra-domestic sexual gratification.

The present condition of these women seems to be mired in economic misery and what is perceived as a morally degraded position. While the degradation may not be perceived as such by the caste groups of which these women become goddesses, there seems to be an evaluation of that kind that stems out of the general society. In this sense, certain rehabilitation programmes that take into account the cultural complexity of these traditions should be encouraged so that these women can stand up independently and lead a respectable life.

We will end this essay by highlighting one such attempt at rehabilitation: In Nizamabad, 'Chelli Nilayam' has undertaken the rehabilitation of the jogins on a large scale, the ultimate aim being eradication of this system. To eradicate these traditions in the three different regions of Andhra Pradesh it is recommended that:

(a) The socio-economic rehabilitation of women who have been the victims of these traditions has to be launched uniformly in the whole state. For middle-aged people, skills should be imparted and loans for income generation should be given.

(b) Social awareness camps should be started in the areas where these traditions prevail. The basvis should be organized into self-help groups so that they may discuss the bad impact of the system on young minds and how they can overcome the evil effects of the system.

(c) The government, NGOs, social workers and women's groups should protest against the dedications and stop the 'Kolupulu', funeral dances, begging and other activities.

(d) The old women should be given compulsory pensionary benefits.

(e) The district administration should look into the matter concerning the education of jogins', matangis' and basvis' children. All eligible children should be admitted to school and provided with hostel facility on a priority basis. To motivate the children of basvis, matangis and jogins, stipends should be provided. Non-formal education centres for those who cannot attend schools and adult education centres for the middle-aged should be started. The curriculum should be drawn up at a meeting with teachers who are expected to monitor the progress of the learners.

Notes

1. P.G. Solanki differed with Bhole. In his opinion that dedication of a woman to service in a temple is not dedication to a life of prostitution. If that is the case the girl's marriages should not be prohibited on any ground.
2. Shekamma, a basvi, who organised the conference said that the basvi women wanted to protest against the government for their economic independence. She says no woman hereafter is sacrificed or exploited in the society. This is a concerns about women's dignity and self-respect.
3. Another basvi woman by name Laxmi, expressed her opinion that woman should not be deprived of her right and she questioned that why should there be distinction between a woman and man?

CHAPTER 7

Identical Cults in Other States

The prevalence of religious prostitution has been noticed in all South Indian states except Kerala. While the names may vary from district to district and state to state, the basic features of the system are the same. The root cause of the dedication of girl children is poverty. The other reasons for dedication are illness of family members, death of children in the family and desertation by husband.

This system has been imposed by the feudal lords on the poor, innocent girls of dalit and backward class communities. It revolves

South India

around the religious customs and traditions of that particular society in which women are caught in the cobweb. For generations together, women have been exploited in the name of tradition.

In this study, we discuss how these poor people are exploited socially and economically. In spite of many obstacles and humiliations, these women have moved forward to achieve their goal. The dedication system is known as 'Nats' in Assam, 'Murali' in Maharashtra, 'Mariamma' or Thayamma in Tamil Nadu and Basvi or Devadasi system in Karnataka. We will briefly analyse the various systems of our neighbouring states.

Devadasi System in Karnataka

In Karnataka, we have the Basvi or Devadasi system. There are many theories about the custom of dedicating girls to temples. Some of these are as follows:

- The custom of dedicating girls emerged as a substitute for human sacrifice to appease gods and goddesses.
- It is considered to be fertility cult, that is, to increase the population of both human beings and animals.
- It is a part of phallic worship.
- It is called sacred prostitution which has its origin in the custom of providing sexual hospitality to strangers.
- This licentious worship was offered to the priestly class by the subservient womenfolk.
- The feudal lords were primarily responsible for this cult coming into existence under the cover of religion so that they could satisfy their carnal desires.

In this system, lower caste women are dedicated to a deity called Amman, Yellamma, Kanchamma, Dayavamma and Marigamma. All these deities are worshipped in many areas of Karnataka. These dedicated women are called 'Basvis' or 'Jogitis' in Karnataka. Sometimes, men are also dedicated to the above deities. They are called Jogappas. The services of the dedicated women, in the course of time, shifted to the earthly gods like priests, kings, feudal lords and rich men. Though the mistake is made by both women and men equally, only women are blamed, victimized and stigmatized. This only shows the general tendency of passing on the blame to the weaker sex.

This victimization is termed 'sacred prostitution' or 'religious prostitution'. As already mentioned, the Devadasi system was prevalent in upper castes also and they had their own advantages such as:

- The upper caste devadasis were licensed to carry on their profession in the name of religion. They were great artists proficient in music, dance and literature. Hence, they enjoyed respect in society.
- The so-called untouchables were not allowed entry into temples and so they built their own temples and dedicated their own daughters to those temples.
- This system is the creation of the rich people for their sexual enjoyment. Upper caste people are hypocrites in as much as they talk of untouchability but have no compunction in cohabiting with the 'untouchable' women.
- The system destroyed the dignity and self-respect of women in general and women belonging to SCs and backward classes in particular.
- Like the upper caste devadasis, the lower caste women also have their own pattern of music and dance. As Nataraja Ramakrishna said in an interview, "the jogins, especially those at Armoor in Nizamabad district, are good at dancing". He visited that place and appreciated the dance by the jogins there. Similarly, in Karnataka the jogitas have their own dance form.
- There were no funeral dances in Karnataka but nude dances were prevalent in Chandragutti village of Shimoga district. Although the government banned the nude dances, these continue to be performed in some villages surrounding that area. Wherever this cult exists in Karnataka, the devadasis beg. The author saw some jogavvas beg in a Gulbarga temple. They are required to beg at least at five houses on particular days. People believe that it is both mandatory and auspicious for them to supply whatever the jogavvas need. As written documents are not available, we have to depend upon the oral tradition and case studies in order to know the present position of the devadasis.
- The system is accepted as a social norm and so it is not stigmatized.

- In the absence of male issues, girl children who are dedicated to gods and goddesses serve as social security for their parents and guardians in their old age.

These explanations are not sufficient to understand the real significance of the Devadasi cult. So, we have to compare the systems prevalent all over the world and then come to certain conclusions. There may be affinities and contrasts between one system and another.

Belgaum, Gulbarga and the border districts of Karnataka have their own mosaic of linguistic composition. The major religions in these areas are Hinduism and Islam. Hindu goddesses like Karavva, Kahai, Janai and Masayi are considered to be the mother goddesses. These goddesses are malevolent and cause harm to the people if they are not properly propitiated. Among them, Goddess Yellamma of Soundatti is a famous deity to whom dalit girls are dedicated. Men and women who dedicate themselves to her service are called 'Jogayya' and 'Jogati', respectively.

Among the untouchable communities in Karnataka, there are Samagars, Holers and Madigas. Samagars used to dedicate their women to Yellamma and Khandoba.

Holeru is another community whose family deity is also Yellamma. They offer nude worship to her. Yellamma is said to be the same as Renuka, the wife of Sage Jamadagni and the mother of Parasurama.

Goddess Lakshmi at Badakundri in Hikeri taluka is called Holemma. The Kalika devi temple at Sirasangi is another centre of Shakti worship. Goddess Dyamavva and Durgavva are worshipped by the people of Belgaum district. Gullavva is another female deity whom rural women worship in the month of Ashadha.

The girl to be dedicated to Yellamma is supposed to be a virgin and she is dedicated before she attains puberty. The dedication ceremony is called 'Muttu Kattuvadu' (tying the beads) or 'Devarige Biduvadu', dedicating to the deity. Generally, full moon days in March, April, November and December are considered auspicious for dedication. Once, these ceremonies were conducted on a massive scale in the Yellamma temple in Soundatti and the Yellamma temple at Kokatnur. These days the ceremonies are conducted secretly in small temples of Yellamma or in their homes. Sometimes, 'Gharwalis' (mistresses of urban brothels) sponsor these dedication ceremonies to make sure that these girls join them in future. Parents, relatives and local senior devadasis attend this marriage ceremony and enjoy the feast. The following items are required for the ceremony: kumkum and bhandar, black powder, rangoli powder of different colours, plantains, betel leaves, cotton thread, dry fruits, vibhooti, sandal paste, a few coins, kalasam, jaggery and muttu or mangalasutra.

The place of worship is washed and purified by a coating of cowdung paste and artistic patterns are drawn using rangoli powders. This is known as 'Jogatipatta'. Four pattas are drawn in four corners and a decorated kalasa is placed in each corner. Lamps are lit. The girl is asked to sit in the middle of 'Jogatipatta'. On all four sides, senior devadasis hold the thread in their right hand and sing songs extolling Yellamma's qualities. The singing is accompanied by instrumental music. The same procedure is followed in the preparation of mangalasutra. The purohit brings a necklace of white and red beads. When the girl is dedicated to Yellamma, it means that

- she will not marry any mortal man.
- she is considered to be a member of her parents' family and has a right to property.
- her son or daughter will have the same surname.
- she has to fast on Tuesdays and Fridays because both days are auspicious for Goddess Yellamma.
- in a week, she has to visit at least five houses and beg.
- she has to follow certain rules and regulations.
- she has to offer shelter to shelterless strangers.
- she should not retaliate when abused.
- she should not eat anyone's leftover food.
- she should chant 'Udho Yellamma' all the time.

In any Yellamma temple, the puja is performed by non-Brahmins, especially Lingayats. The deity is worshipped once in the morning and again in the evening. Each time, the priest removes the clothings and flowers offered to the deity during the previous worship. Using holy water, the priest bathes the deity. Devotees offer flowers, vermilion and turmeric powder to the goddess. A member of the priest's family offers her cooked food. No special day is prescribed for the devotees to visit the temple because every day is considered holy and auspicious. However, most devotees like to visit Yellamma temples on Tuesdays and Fridays and on all days between November and February. The temple ritual starts from the full moon day in October–November.

In Soundatti, the pujaris consider themselves to be the brothers of Yellamma and perform dual role – worshipping her and managing the temple. Today, there are 127 priestly families belonging to the Yellamma clan and they claim to be the descendants of the original priest. There are four groups claiming Yellamma as their family deity.

Soundatti town is famous for the Yellamma temple. The goddess is known by different names such as Renuka, Maya and Mayakarti. Near the temple there are three tanks known as Yenuhonda (tank of oil), Arisina Honda (turmeric tank) and Kumkuma Honda (tank of kumkum). Water collected from these three tanks is used for Yellamma's ritual bath. The tanks are named after the three things essential for her bath – oil, turmeric and kumkum.

Close to the temple, there is a shrine of Ravana Siddheswara (a Veerasaiva saint). Right opposite the shrine is the temple of Parasurama, the son of Renuka. Another nearby temple is that of Matangi, a disciple of Renuka. On the hillock, there are the footprints of Ekkayya and Jogaiah. In the vicinity of Renuka temple, there is Kalabhairava and there is a temple of Renuka's husband Jamadagni.

At the foot of the hill, there is a well called Jogulabavi. Next to it is the temple of Satyavva or Satyadevata. She had helped in the delivery of Parasurama and brought him up. Jogulabavi is the place where Yellamma took her bath on the advice of Ekkayya and Jogayya when she was afflicted with leprosy. The bath cured her of the disease. Today, devotees suffering from skin diseases take a bath in this well, wear neem leaves for their dress and have a darshan of Yellamma. They also worship Satyavva, Ekkayya and Jogayya on their way to the Yellamma temple. When the author went to Soundatti, she visited all these temples including the Satyavva temple. The Yellamma story is found in Vishnupuranam and Sivapuranam and the Mahabharata.

'Jogappa' derives from the Sanskrit word Yoga. Jogi and Jogiti are disciples of Yellamma and they are expected to lead a pure life praising the greatness of Yellamma. Jogappas are men who wear a sari and blouse and grow the hair long. They wear an anklet, a necklace of cowries and apply bhandar on their forehead and dance and sing in praise of Yellamma. Womenfolk provide background instrumental music. They wear white saris and a necklace of cowries and a small shoulder bag containing bhandar.

A jogappa carries on his head a copper or a brass pot containing Devi's prasadam. A small idol of Devi is tied to the pot. Some carry the idol of Devi in a basket while going for bhiksha. Jogavva carries a cowry. There is no age limit to become a Jogappa or Jogavva. As has been already mentioned, the people who have taken deeksha have no marital relations. Some people who are disgusted with their married life embrace this life. Even criminals and sex workers also opt for this life. The disciples of Yellamma offer them bhiksha and regard them as representatives of Devi. Jataras take place at Soundatti on Bharata Poornima day. People from far off places visit Soundatti with Jogappas and Jogavvas. The author interviewed some of the Jogavvas who had matted hair. They are required to visit the temple on Tuesdays and Fridays. The Jogubavi is an auspicious tank and people from Maharashtra and Madhya Pradesh and other parts of India gather here and take a dip in this tank and worship Goddess Yellamma.

Thus, the Soundatti Yellamma has devotees throughout Karnataka and in the neighbouring states of Maharashtra, Andhra Pradesh and Goa. The devotees are classified into two categories – Okkalu and Bhakta. Those whose family deity is Yellamma are called Okkalu and those whose favourite deity is Yellamma are called bhaktas. The vows taken by the devotees of Yellamma can be grouped as (i) personal, (ii) family, and (iii) village vows.

To overcome their problems, the devotees who visit the shrine take a vow to dedicate a daughter to the deity. People of lower strata of society dedicate their girls to Yellamma. They perform the initiation rites to make the girl a divine prostitute. Some parents take a vow to dedicate their daughter even when she is too young or even before she is born. The family will be ready with the money for the initiation ceremony. Sometimes, the man who wants to have her as his sex-mate bears the expenditure of the initiation ceremony. The girl has to have her bath at the Jogulabavi, the body covered either with neem leaves or a new sari. First, she is taken in a procession to the house of the Sthanika to get his approval. She is then taken to the temple and asked to go round it three times. The agent worships the deity and then ties the sacred necklace of beads (soolay muttu) around the girl's neck. If she has already attained puberty, then consummation of the marriage follows. It is known as 'Hennumaduvude'. The family chooses an auspicious day for the ceremony. In the evening, the girl takes a ritual bath and wears the new sari brought by them and like a bride she is taken in a procession to a well. Reminiscent of Renuka taking water to her husband Jamadagni, the girl takes a pot of water to the man who is supposed to have her. There is a belief that from that day onwards, the deity showers prosperity on her.

How long the two will have sex relation depends on her charm and his willingness to keep her as a concubine. Sometimes, she lives like a second wife to the man concerned or the next day she becomes 'a public woman'.

The devadasi woman is required to visit the shrine on all full moon days in a year. Girls in large numbers are initiated as divine prostitutes on this occasion.

The sacred prostitute is identified on the basis of the necklace of beads she wears – Garati Muttu, Soolay Muttu and Jogati Muttu. As good devotees, all devadasis vow to go through the three stages.

Another type of classification is on the basis of sexual functionary of the divine prostitute. In the third type, there are two stages of the divine prostitute – sexually active and retired.

Jogatis are those who are religious mendicants and wear Jogati Muttu. The jogatis carry three ritual objects with them: (i) paradi, (ii) joga, and (iii) koda. Paradi is a basket made of bamboo in which they carry Parasurama, the son of Renuka, and a bowl of vermilion powder. The devadasi from the soolay background collects alms from the people. 'Joga' means 'Jagat', i.e., belonging to the world. The other type of jogati is the one that carries koda, a metal pot. She is known as Kodada Jogati. These are divine prostitutes who have dedicated their virginity to Yellamma.

Thus, thousands and thousands of girls are dedicated to various deities. These cults are prevalent in backward regions. For example, parts of Belgaum, Gulbarga and Bijapur are more prone to failure of crops due to poor and irregular rainfall. Dedication as divine prostitute helps commercial prostitution. The poor Harijan families of Bijapur consider it their sacred duty to dedicate themselves to their family deity. Ignorance combined with poverty comes in the way of abolition of this custom.

On February 9, 1990, on Magh Poornima, over 2,000 young girls were dedicated to Goddess Yellamma at Soundatti. Some of them were sold in the sex bazaars of Mumbai. Among the prostitutes of Mumbai are devadasis, unwanted daughters, rape victims, kidnap victims and women from extremely poor families or from the families of landless agricultural labourers of perennially drought-affected areas.

The sacred prostitutes, basvis or jogatis, were numerous in rural areas. They discharged functions connected with deities and the marriages of the lower caste people. One of the rituals performed by the jogatis or basvis was 'Bettela Seva' (nude worship). This ritual is an indicator of the fertility cult prevalent in some areas. We can trace this cult from the Indus valley civilization. During their pilgrimage, both men and women would rub themselves with huttigi (sandal paste) in the name of Yellamma. The women devotees would strip themselves of their clothes, massage their body with oil, smear the whole body with sandal paste and cover it with neem leaves from head to foot. They would then go into the temple of Yellamma, bow before the goddess and offer her dress and food and then return home. Throughout they would chant 'Udho, Udho Yellamma'. The nude worship can be attributed to the poor economic condition caused by drought. Nude worship existed in Chandragutti village in Shimoga district until 1928, when it was officially banned. But, some people in Chandragutti whom this author interviewed said the practice was in vogue even until 1986 when a dispute between the caste Hindus and dalits resulted in a general boycott of the rural practice. Some people said that the practice was discontinued only in Chandragutti, and that it persists in the surrounding villages.

Chandragutti is on the banks of the Varada river. It is believed that in Kaliyuga, Renuka settled in this village. In the main temple at Chandragutti we find the statues of Saradamba and Renukamba. Opposite the temple there are idols of Naga and Vishnu and padukas of Renuka. Nearby is a small temple of Parasurama and a Matangi temple.

On the way to the Renukamba temple, on the hill is a Kalabhairava temple. Also there is a temple of Shoolada Beerappa and its priests belongs to Kuruba community. The Kurubas are called Oggus. Beerappa was the God of this community and he was a disciple of Parasurama. Parasurama was in meditation, Beerappa became a womanizer. Parasurama's mother Renuka and Matangi complained to Parasurama about his misconduct where upon Parasurama killed Beerappa with his trishul (trident). The devotees perform naked worship and dance wearing neem leaves. This is known as bebudige seva.

Every year, a Rathotsava (cart festival) used to be held at Chandragutti on the first navami after Sivaratri (February–March). On the fourth day of the five-day festival, nude worship used to take place. The Karnataka government banned this practice in 1986.

M.K. Dhavalikar, a historian of Deccan College, Pune, wrote about Goddess Sakambari, the presiding deity of Mahakut where the sculpture of the nude headless goddess, who is associated with vegetable fertility, was found. An interesting description of this goddess is given in Devi Mahatmyam, which is a part of Markandeya Purana. The female nude torso can be identified as that of Sakambari. Unfortunately, the portion below the waist is broken. One comes across this type of nude images at Siddankote in Karnataka, Ter and Mahurjhari in Maharashtra and Nagarjunakonda and Alampur in Andhra Pradesh. H.D. Sankalia, the great historian, branded her as 'the shameless woman'. Carol Elizabeth Radcliffe, a historian, also identified these images as the representations of Aditi worshipped by barren women for begetting children.

There are three nude torsos at Alampur of which two are Chalukyan, datable to seventh century. The third one, which belongs to a slightly later period, is installed in the site museum. This image, now being worshipped by barren women, is believed to represent Lajja Gauri and Renuka.

When Parasurama's father Jamadagni became suspicious about the chastity of his wife Renuka and his son Parasurama beheaded her at his behest, the latter was granted a boon. He wanted his mother's life to be restored. While cutting off the head of his mother, Parasurama had also cut the head of a Matangi, a pariah woman. While bringing his mother back to life, he interchanged the heads. That means, he put the head of the Matangi on his mother's body and that of his mother on the Matangi's body. And then both came to be worshipped, that with the Brahmin head as Mariamma and the other as Yellamma. Whitehead rightly observes, "... probably describes the fusion of the Aryan and Dravidian cults in the days when the Aryans first found their way into South India. A pariah body with a Brahmin head is an apt description of the cult of Siva, while a pariah head with a Brahmin body might well describe some of the cults of the ancient Dravidian deities, modified by Brahman ideas and influence."[1]

The dedication ceremony has become as important as securing a passport and visa to go to the Gulf countries. All rituals related to dedication are performed in a hurry and perfunctorily and in secrecy. The Karnataka government probably thought that the mere passing of legislation would immediately put an end to sexual exploitation based on a deep-rooted religious belief. In the wake of the government action, many newspapers reported that thousands of girls had been dedicated as devadasis. The General Secretary of the Indian Health Organization, Dr I.S. Gilda revealed that about 20 priests staying at the Yellamma temple conducted the dedication ceremonies in their houses in violation of the law and that the police remained 'silent spectators' at these events.

Though the Karnataka government started the socio-economic rehabilitation of the devadasis in Belgaum, it was not successful for want of officials with commitment. It is, therefore, hardly surprising that the evil system persists.

Muralis of Maharashtra

The girl who was married to a dagger was known as Murali. The sword or dagger belonged to God Khandoba. It was a custom among

Plate 12 Khandoba.

Plate 13 Jejuri – its surroundings.

the lower castes, mainly untouchables, to marry their daughters to Khandoba. On attaining puberty, the girls had to lead a life of shame supporting their parents with their earnings.

Khandoba is popularly believed to be an incarnation of Siva. The Khandoba temple at Jejuri in Pune district, Pali in Satara district and Agalgoan, where one of Khandoba's consorts lived are famous.

Jejuri is situated at the foot of a small hill. Atop the hill is the Khandoba temple. During her visit to Jejuri, the author learnt that the shepherds of the Maratha country are regarded as favourites of Khandoba because one of his consorts belonged to the shepherd community. She was his sister-in-law brought from her house to his home at Jejuri on horseback. A small temple was built for Banai, his shepherd wife. In the courtyard facing the inner temple stands a big image of a demon called Bali Malla whom Lord Siva killed with a dagger.

It is said that the now famous temple at Jejuri is not the original temple. The present one was built by Ahalya Bai, the queen of Indore. Outside the main entrance to the temple, against the wall on the left side, stands a stone column. The column is called by the name of Yeshwantrao, who according to the superstitious beliefs gives pilgrims all they want and children to issueless women.

It is to this image that the poor deluded women promise to sacrifice their first-born daughters, if Khandoba is willing to give them more children. The first-born girl child is offered to Khandoba by tying a necklace of seven cowries around the child's neck. When she attains puberty, she is formally married to Khandoba. She becomes 'Nitya Sumangali' and is forbidden to marry a mortal man. She can then earn her livelihood by prostitution. While some have to become wandering muralis, some stay at home and become public women and some others prefer to stay with one man as a concubine.

The parents or the guardians of such girls do not feel ashamed to live on the girls' earnings, as they think that it all belongs to Khandoba. Kunbis, Mahars, Mangs and other low castes comprise Muralis. Upper caste people also visit Jejuri but they do not dedicate their children to Khandoba. The reason for the SCs dedicating their children to Khandoba is mainly sickness of children. On an auspicious occasion, the parents go to Jejuri and the formal marriage takes place. If the parents are not in a position to go to Jejuri, they perform the ceremony at home.

Muralis are expected to sing obscene songs about Khandoba and they get paid for it! The service rendered by them is known as Jagaran or night-long vigil. Even their parents invite them to hold the Jagaran in their house.

In Jejuri itself, there are hundreds of muralis. Recently, the police registered more than 280 muralis. Marcus B. Fuller, the author of *Wrongs of Womanhood* says that this custom is a blot on society and shame on women and, therefore, should be abolished. Another feminist leader said, "I have felt sick at heart as I have thought of the thousands of muralis whose blood has been shed on the altar of the leader of seventy million devils. Khandoba is the Beelzebub of the Maratha country. One should rescue us from the cruel and filthy customs of the land."

A girl is made a murali at the age of five years and once left in the Khandoba temple, she does not have any relationship with her parents. For example, Chhaya Mallavi Bhandarkar who lives in a small house said that the government had not provided her with anything. However, things have changed consequent to the government ban on the Murali system. Parents have started sending their children to school.

Muralis can now stay with their parents and serve them in their old age. If there are no male children, the parents depend upon their daughters, especially muralis. That is because muralis are not married to any mortal person and, therefore, they have to depend upon their parents. Security is an important factor for them. The children are not aware of who their father is. They are admitted to school in the name of Khandoba. Earlier, Muralis had a tradition of dedicating their first child to Khandoba. Attestation of the school certificate is done in the name of the father, that is, Khandoba before the deity.

There is no certainty that a vaghoba will stay with one murali. Murali is always considered to be a 'Nitya Sumangali'. If a murali has a daughter, she will make her a murali and if she has a boy, he is called vaghya. Sometimes, not only the first child but other children are also dedicated to god. Murali in Marathi denotes impurity. Even though a murali is dedicated to Khandoba, she is not considered a chaste woman.

The Murali system is a blot on society and an insult to womanhood. The most reprehensible thing about this custom is that thousands of girls are placed in a position that compels them to become moral and physical wrecks. In one district where Christian missionaries were at work, the custom had almost disappeared.

Animals are sacrificed in the name of god. The vaghyas and muralis perform for their patrons Jagaran, a night-long vigil during which both of them dance. Other vaghyas accompany them with instruments and sing the padam of Khandoba.

The devotion of muralis and vaghyas to Khandoba is reflected in a folk festival called 'Somvati Amavasya' festival. The padams sung at Jagarans are in fulfilment of a vow. This festival occurs twice or thrice a year depending on the conjunction of the sun and the moon on a Monday. It attracts devotees from all over Maharashtra. The whole day, before the procession arrives at the river, the Dhangars (shepherds) break a heavy chain fixed to a stone pillar near the shrine of Rambha on the river bank. A pinch of bhandar is thrown on the chain and, invoking the god, the devotees break it at one go. If the chain breaks, the closeness of the lord is confirmed. And if it does not break in the second or third attempt, it signifies the inauspiciousness of the event.

Dance Pattern of Muralis

The Vaghya-Murali dance and the dance of the jogins have a linkage with similar performances in the adjoining regions of Karnataka. These traditional dances continued to be performed against heavy odds like foreign invasions and social distaste. Muralis are the dancing girls who have contributed to the tradition of non-classical dancing practices of Maharashtra. These girls take part in the ritual dance-drama called Jagaran where they offer their prayers through dances. Usually, muralis are clad in a nine-yard sari and wear a blouse made with nine pieces. They have two ghantis (small bells) in their right hand which holds the end of their saris, and with the left hand, they make hastas. They do baithak (sitting) in the *drut laya*. There are no ghunghroos tied to the feet. This is an entirely ritual dance.

Muralis and Vaghyas go together. Vaghya means tiger's skin. They are the special devotees of Khandoba. In Karnataka we have 'Vaghayya'. Vaghayyas imitate dogs. They carry a bag made of tigerskin in which they keep bhandar (turmeric powder). These vaghayyas behave, bark and eat like dogs. They pick up coins thrown at them with their mouth. During the jatara of 'Mailar' and on the special request of the devotees, they perform a circular dance accompanied by drums and chants. Even a Brahmin can become a vaghayya. The vaghayyas come from the Kuruba community (shepherds). Kurubas dedicate one or more children from their family to serve Mailar. Vaghayyas in Devaragadda maintain their traditional link with tribals. Some of the vaghayyas beg in the name of Mailar for their whole life on account of a vow taken by their parents. They have a peculiar long black woollen overcoat. On the back of the coat, images of the sun and the moon are stitched in colourful designs. The vaghayyas carry a trishula or a sula and wear a cowry necklace. Among the other things, they carry are a begging bowl, a scarf, tiger or bear-skin and a bell. They go on a begging expedition within Maharashtra, Andhra Pradesh and Karnataka. Their major centres are Devaragadda Mailar, Mangruli near Alni, Belgaum district, Mailar and Jejuri. Some of them also practise black magic.

During the festivals of Mailar-Khandoba, the vaghyas perform the feat of breaking a chain in fulfilment of a vow given in writing for domestic harmony and prosperity in agriculture. Newly-wed couples watch the event in the belief that god is present there. But the breaking depends on the purity and behaviour of the persons concerned. It is believed that if they have not kept their promises to god, the chain will not break. The chain-breaking ritual offers immediate relief and joy as it symbolizes freedom from bondage.

Bhavins of Goa

Bhavins and Deviles, also known as Nayakins and Nayaks respectively, numbered 975 in 1901 and 6,519 males, 6,460 females (R.E. Enthoven, *The Tribes and Castes of Bombay*, Vol. I, 1920, Bombay) in Ratnagiri and Kanara district and the Savantvadi state. They are said to be descended from the female servants of Savantvadi or Malvan chiefs to whom the chiefs presented land after dedicating them to the service of village gods. Their number increased with the addition of female servants of these chiefs.

Women from certain Sudra castes are allowed to become Bhavins after oil from a temple lamp is poured on their head. When a bhavin girl attains puberty, she has to undergo a form of marriage known as Shesh. On an auspicious day, Ganapati is worshipped and the ceremony of Punya Vachanam (holy day blessings) is performed both at the girl's house and in a temple. The Gurav pujari and the other servants of the temple go to the girl's house in a procession. A dagger is considered to be the mark of god. The ceremony ends with a feast for those assembled. The young girl dressed in her best attire goes to the temple to the beating of drums accompanied by a party of bhavins and temple servants. With a coconut and a packet of sugar in her hands, she bows to the god and the Gurav and other temple servants then invoke the blessings of god for her. With that, the ceremony comes to an end.

The bhavin practises prostitution but it is different from general prostitution. From among her children, she chooses two or three to succeed her as temple servants. In the social scale, her rank is below that of the Kalavantins and she is allowed to sing or dance in public. They speak Konkani.

Bhavins are Hindus and worship the local deities such as Mhalsa, Venkatarama, Ramnath, Ravalnath, Mahohi, Mallikarjuna, Nirakar and all Shaktis. They observe all Hindu holidays and offer goats and fowl to the village gods and Shaktis.

Their religious teacher is in a Sringeri monastery. They have great faith in soothsaying, witchcraft, evil spirits and omens. Bhavins are employed in temples to sweep and cover the floor with cowdung and wave the fly-whisk before the god. The men blow the temple horns and trumpets morning and evening and are paid partly in cash and partly from the offerings received by the temple. They also blow the horn at weddings. Some of them work as labourers holding land on permanent lease.

Their staple food is rice, pulses and vegetables. They eat fish, the meat of fowls and other food items consumed by the Marathas. Bhavins and deviles eat food cooked by Marathas. They do not eat food cooked by Sonars, Sutars, Jingars, Thakars and other low caste people. Some Marathas eat food cooked by bhavins, deviles and kumbins.

The bhavins, muralis and jogins seem to be considered as belonging to a lower order than that of the devadasis or the nautch girls, whatever be their name and whatever be the difference in their customs the principle is the same in all, immorality under the cover of religion and custom.

How are these people different from the bailadeiras or devadasis? The bailadeiras were Hindu dancing girls who belonged to a class known in Goa as Kalavantins. They were dedicated to god. The Portuguese called them bailadeiras. They sing and dance in the temples. On festive occasions, they would dance in public and in the houses of well-known people, including Portuguese officials. They were expected to dance first in the house of the most important Goans near the village.

Four groups of women performed several duties at the temple. They were Kalavants, Chedvas, Reulinas and Bandens. In Goan society, the generic name for such women was Naiquins. They were initiated in the profession through a ceremony known as Xens. The girls were presented for the ceremony by an important person of the village. This man had the right to have sex with any girl when she attained puberty.

The Xens ceremony was slightly different from a marriage. In this ceremony, there is an act called caressing or touching with hands. This act was banned by the state through legislation effective from 31 July, 1930.

Widows of the upper castes and divorced or abandoned women also joined this profession. Bailadeiras wore colourful saris when they performed a dance. Silk saris were imported from Belgaum and Nagpur. In Peshwa dances, they wore long dresses embroidered with sequins and loose pants. Jewellery was profusely used on hair, neck, arms, nose and anklets. Anklets toe-rings and nose-rings were their distinctive trademarks. Bailadeiras contributed to the upkeep of the temple. Their status was different from that of other prostitutes. Sometimes, the illegitimate daughters of Brahmins were handed over to these women to be initiated into the profession.

A majority of bailadeiras lived in New Conquests, where many great temples are situated. At the turn of the 19th century, bailadeiras began to migrate to British India to improve their standards of living. Most of them settled in Bombay where they accumulated wealth. Some of them established permanent contacts with rich traders, Nawabs, Rajas and high-ranking British officials. They remained their mistresses and had children by them.

According to the census of 1910, there were 852 bailadeiras in Goa. Most of them were found at Ponda, followed by Pernew taluka. The 1921 census showed that Goa had 405 bailadeiras.

When the Xens ceremony was officially abolished, a number of bailadeiras left Goa. Most of these women were pretty and hospitable. They used to smoke. At that time, women who danced in public were looked down by the society. Men were unwilling to marry such women. The daughters of bailadeiras followed in their mother's footsteps.

Reulinas, Chedvans and Bander could not dance in the temples. Reulinas usually lived on the outskirts of the village where they carried on their trade.

In 1700, the ban on bailadeiras was reimposed. The inhabitants of Goa were banned from having bailadeiras in their homes, palm groves or in other places. Despite imposing heavy penalty, the government found it difficult to enforce the ban.

The devadasis were to God what the upadasis were to men. Now there are no more devadasis in the precincts of the temples. The upadasis are trained as trade union members to fight for their rights. The devadasis succumbed first to the temple priests and later to the pilgrims.

The Kalavants were proficient in dance and music. Abdur Razaak described the kalavants as courtesans who had ceased to be the handmaidens of the gods. The presence of devadasis at weddings was considered auspicious but the symbolism was wicked and hypocritical. The society devised the system known as Sesha by which devadasi girls were dedicated to the temple even before they attained puberty.

The ceremony consisted of an offering by a 'Goakar', of a coconut and a supari pierced with a sword or a dagger. The pierced supari was the symbol of defloration of the girl. The Goakar who offered it had the right to spend the first night with that girl. An older devadasi used to act like a male and performed the wedding rituals. Her name was entered in the temple records as the 'husband'.

Another important feature is Garbhadana known as 'bot lavine' (pronounced 'boat laavinay') meaning the first touching of her body by a male hand. It is described as 'carnal knowledge of a woman'. They lived their fated roles till death. In Rajaram Painginkar's autobiographical novel *Mekhon,* the son describes the fate of his mother and the trauma he underwent during his childhood. What emerges from *Mekhon* is the practice of a vice as if it were a virtue. Painginkar along with others launched a crusade to redeem the clan.

The Saraswat Hindu mentors convinced these women that Dhavina was no basvi and she would become one the moment she left the temple periphery and settled as a prostitute. Until devadasis married their own community men legally, males played an insignificant role in their families. Devadasis belonged to a matriarchal family set-up where the daughters enjoy property rights. When the girls became prostitutes, the boys became pimps in their community.

There are good reasons for these women to practise birth control. Even in the early stages of their pregnancy, they used to have sex relations. It was not uncommon to dispose off male children by either abandoning them or giving them away for adoption. For example, Anjani Bai Malrekar was "a woman of rare beauty which set the hearts of many Rajas throbbing." The kalavants from Goa, according to Malbarao, were prominent in the Jaipur Gharana.

There are no kalavants in Goa anymore. The author interviewed only one woman who is a keep of a Saraswat Brahmin who is a temple purohit. The Gomantak Society is taking care of these women. The president of the Society said that marriages between bhavins' children and the kalavants are taking place.

Mariamma

Mariamma is the goddess of smallpox in South India. As a Hindu village goddess, she has female power or Shakti. She is the mother goddess whose generative powers are the foundation of life. She is known by different names. The Shakti or power of the goddess flows to human beings, especially to women. Mariamma's devotees nourish her through their worship and offerings, and in return she showers her grace on them.

Mariamma is a model of female sacrifice, female power and she has chosen to come down to earth to be close to her devotees.

The procreative power of Mariamma ensures the continuance of life. The ant-hill that Mariamma emerges from is associated with Siva's linga, symbolizing both creation and destruction.

The vast number of Mariamma temples in Tamil Nadu testifies to the popular belief that as a female Shakti, Mariamma sustains the universe. She is also called Bhavaniamma which means 'mother' or 'woman' or 'goddess'. She is the goddess of the lowest castes. As in Balaji temples, devotees offer their hair in Mariamma temples. Women are considered to be the special devotees of Mariamma.

The author had chosen Tiruvelkad, Tiruvallur, Trichy and Tanjore for her study of Mariamma temples. At Tiruvelkad, the author met a 100-year-old man who said that Mariamma is a goddess of the Brahmanical tradition. She then met a Tamil professor in Tanjore who read out a passage from an old Tamil book which says that Mariamma is the goddess of the downtrodden and women of the lower castes dedicated their first-born child to her.

Nowadays, Mariamma is regarded as a goddess of the Brahmanical tradition in the sense that a Brahmin purohit is appointed to worship her and prasadam is offered to the devotees. The worship is similar to that in Tirupati or other Vishnu and Siva temples. Besides, there is no animal sacrifice.

On the advice of some people, the author visited a small temple 20 km from Tanjore and found that girl children of Harijan families are dedicated to the goddess of Little Tradition. In Tiruvelkad, the purohits of Mariamma temple directed the author to another place, 1 km from the main shrine of Mariamma.

There the author found a middle-aged woman who said her name was Mariamma. Her family members were all devotees of Mariamma. Sometimes, she would go into a trance and tell about the future of the village, human beings and animals. People consider her to be the goddess and visit that place.

Plate 14 Mariamma of Tamil Nadu.

The author learnt that nagna puja (nude worship) exists in some parts of Tamil Nadu. This indicates that the practice of dedicating girls to goddesses is still prevalent.

Another interesting feature in Tamil Nadu is the Tayamma worship. As a matter of fact, it is prevalent on the borders of Tamil Nadu and Andhra Pradesh. One can see the traces of this kind of worship at Raya Vellore, Tiruttani and other places.

The dedication of girls to Matamma or Tayamma or even Mariamma is rare in Tamil Nadu. The reason for this could be the non-Brahmin movement that spread long ago and all the backward classes are grouped under the category 'Chakkiliyar'. Anna Dorai and other non-Brahmin leaders strived for the eradication of the Tayamma system in Tamil Nadu. They awakened the people to discard superstitions. Thus in all South Indian states, albeit slowly, the system is disappearing.

Notes

1. Henry, Whitehead, *The Village Gods of South India*, Calcutta: OUP, 1921.

CHAPTER 8

Reformation and Rehabilitation

Samskar Organization

The entire process of reform and rehabilitation of jogins involves the building up of their image as women like other women in society. It means making them aware of the ways in which tradition and religion have subordinated them. An atmosphere needs to be created in which these women can explore new ways of looking at themselves and their lives. What is needed is creation of a place as a focal point where they can discuss their problems and find solutions. In other words, it should be a place where they can meet the challenges of life. It should work at following levels:

- Counselling
- Health security
- Family life; marriage
- Reform and rehabilitation
- Building literacy skills continuing
- Livelihood; security
- Education of children vocational training

Counselling

Counselling on a wide range of subjects in an unstructured manner was held at Chelli Nilayam rehabilitation centre. The following are some of the points that were mentioned:

(a) The jogins must understand the vicious circle of oppression and subordination embedded in the system.

(b) The status of 'Nityasumangali' bestowed on them is illusory and they should understand the hard realities of life.

(c) Dancing at funerals, begging during the harvest season and other rituals are inhuman practices which are not going to give the jogin self-respect and dignity. Moreover, they must take care of their health as otherwise the evil system can ruin it. Marriage will give them security in life. A healthy environment should be created for the future of their children. Otherwise, the children will have to carry the burden of victimhood into their lives too.

(d) The jogins should be encouraged to explore alternative possibilities of livelihood such as agriculture or training in some craft or skill.

In Andhra Pradesh, whenever the subject of jogins is mentioned, 'Samskar' immediately comes to mind. The idea of 'Samskar', a non-profit service organization devoted to reformation, rehabilitation and upliftment of marginal groups, was conceived by Lavanam and Hemalatha Lavanam, two well-known social reformers of Andhra Pradesh. The word 'Samskar' itself signifies reform and improvement.

Feeling the need to work for social change, Hemalatha Lavanam went with Vinoba Bhave on his Chambal valley journey to bring about a change of heart among the dacoits. The padayatra inspired Hemalatha to work for the upliftment of the criminal tribes in Andhra Pradesh. She started 'Samskar' to reform the criminal tribes and help them lead a life of dignity. She proved herself as a relentless crusader for a real change in their life. Her success in this field prompted her to work for the amelioration of the jogins' lot. Samskar's fight against superstition resulted in the eradication of the Jogin system in Nizamabad district. No other pro-women organization in the five states of South India has been so successful.

Jogins constitute one of the marginalized groups among the weaker sections. These women are not allowed to marry, nor are they allowed to work for wages. They are forced to depend on other's mercy. The Jogin system is a product of the state and society. A Jogin sister says, "We were puppets in the hands of village elders. We were made to dance in front of dead bodies and beg throughout life." In spite of the Act that came into existence in 1988, even today there are cases where girls are inducted into Joginhood and later, they become public women. Eight-year-old Anjamma was made a jogin on 13 February 2006 at Vikarabad of Ranga Reddy district. The parents were responsible for this act. The president of a mandal, a political leader, was responsible for making her a jogin. The police were unmindful of this event. The president of the Dharur mandal said that the girl was going to get two acres of land and a house. She lost not only her childhood but virtually her life. Despite her grandmother opposing this idea, Anjamma became a 'jogin', the future sex worker of Dharur mandal. Thus, her life was exploited in the name of beliefs and customs.

The untiring and selfless efforts of Samskar have made the social life of the jogins of Nizamabad district respectable. The changed life of jogins has helped them to forget their agony and pain. The patta land gave them self-respect and improved their economic life considerably. Arranged marriages have brought back their family life. Let us see how Samskar is looking at the changed life of the jogin sisters.

Andhra Pradesh Time Line of Samskar Activities

Hemalatha Lavanam and Lavanam started the organization 'Chelli Nilayam' at Varni. The organization established contacts with jogins calling them 'Sisters'. The then Governor of Andhra Pradesh, Kumudben Joshi, who started the National Institute of Social Action (NISA), asked Hemalatha Lavanam to take the initiative in the rehabilitation work. Since then, the latter has been engaged in this activity with the financial support of the government, organizations like Helpage India and Oxfam.

Organization Chart

Headquarters at Varni

Programme Manager Documentation Officer/Administrator – Support Staff

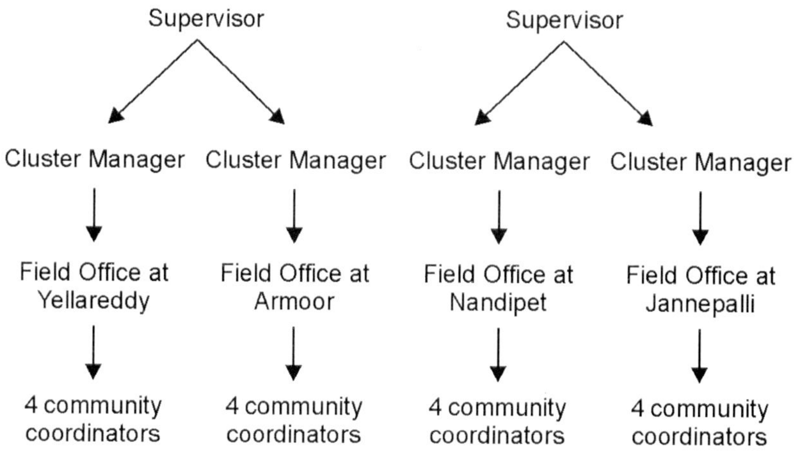

Organizational Objectives

The organization was registered in July 1983. Its main objectives are:

- To impart and promote responsible social behaviour among the abandoned and to make them better citizens by helping them, through various educational processes, realize their responsibilities and discharge their duties to society.
- To reform ex-criminals and their families by persuading them to change their ways of life and by providing suitable economic, social and cultural opportunities for rehabilitation. (From 1983 itself, the scope of this objective was expanded to include the reform and rehabilitation of jogins.)
- To promote and implement peaceful, non-violent and constructive activities for social change.

Time Line of Samskar Activities

1986	Efforts by District Collector, Asha Murthy IAS to start rehabilitation of jogins in colonies exclusively built for them. Relocation of jogins outside the village community was a failure. Samskar invited to come to Nizamabad to work out strategies to address the jogins' issue. Baseline survey conducted. Samskar starts work in the five mandals of Varni, Kotagiri, Birkur, Bodhan and Yedapalli.
1987	Establishment of Chelli Nilayam at Varni on land donated by R.K. Marni. Start of awareness programmes at the community level and initial direct contact with jogins. In partnership with the National Institute of Social Action, Samskar conferences at state and national level on the issue of jogins. First jogin marriage under the auspices of the Governor at Raj Bhavan.
1988	Advocacy with government to enact a law prohibiting the creation of jogins. Addressing old-age security through "Adopt a granny scheme" with support from Helpage India. Thirty old jogins from 10 villages adopted. Passage of Jogin Abolition Act.
1990	With Oxfam support, a massive campaign on the issue of "no new jogin. Propagation of the 1988 Act across the district. Large-scale social and youth mobilization in preventing initiations.
1991	Proposals sent to the government for assignment of land for jogins. Oxfam support for agricultural activities, tractors, seed.

Cont'd...

Cont'd...

1992	Ensuring a life of dignity for children of jogins. Integrated residential school for children of jogins and other children jogins from the community, the Samskar Ashram Vidyalaya started with assistance from NISA for the school's land and buildings and assistance from HAMU, The Netherlands, for meeting teachers and other costs.
1993–1995	Livelihood extended through fixed deposits for jogins not given land in the five focus mandals.
1996	Expansion of Samskar's work. Focus on child-centred community development through PLAN support.
1997–1998	Residential school for tribal children set up at Gandhari Mandal funded by government and HAMU, The Netherlands. Purchase of livestock and start of small enterprises.
1999	Under Plan Grant support for the Jogin project, reaching out to the whole district through advocacy campaign and livelihoods for all the 2,167 jogin sisters in the district.
2000	Expansion of the plan to Medak district with government support.

The Jogin system in the Telangana region of Andhra Pradesh is similar to the Matangi system of coastal Andhra and the Basvi system of Rayalaseema.

Earlier, there was some social security for the jogins, in the sense that they used to be paid with grain for the dances they performed at funerals and marriages. Especially after the harvest period, jogins and potharaju would beg for alms in the village. This was an accepted custom as there is a general belief that giving of alms helps in one's salvation.

Common Explanations for Making a Girl a Jogin

- As deliverance from disease and pestilence for the individual family or the community.
- Deliverance from failure of rains and destruction of crops due to insects.
- As old-age security for poor families who have no son.
- To carry on the traditional and customary role of jogins at times in various rituals, especially at the time of death.
- To continue hereditary practice, jogins dedicate their own girls.
    (i) Gaini Chinna Laxmi was made a jogin as her parents had vowed that they would dedicate their first born child to Goddess Lakshmamma.

(ii) Gunta Pochamma lost her eyesight five months after she was born, and was dedicated to the deity when she was 10 years old.

(iii) Jagadamba, daughter of a potharaju and his wife Saraswati, was dedicated at the age of 4. Today, she is a confident trained nurse.

(iv) For Neeruri Lakshmi, a death in the family and the loss of livestock decided her fate, and she was dedicated at the age of 9.

It is a good feature in the Jogin system that the jogin is not ostracized by society. It is unfortunate that 10 to 15 per cent of the jogins are pushed into prostitution. Of course, there are no middlemen in the whole system.

Efforts to set up separate housing colonies for jogins failed not only in Nizamabad district but also in Sangareddy in Medak district and in Basar in Adilabad district.

Rehabilitation of jogins is bound to fail if they are not provided with economic security. To bring about a change, the problem should be tackled at three levels – individual, social and government level. Though the dominant castes and cultures were responsible for the perpetuation of the Jogin system, the lower castes realized that they had also played a role in perpetuating the system. Protective legislation served as a deterrent, rather than a real tool for punishment.

Samskar's efforts were based on the following premises:

- Change is an integral part of awareness building and even a small step in this direction could lead to complete transformation.
- Sensitizing of various types of people who uphold the Jogin system, i.e., the parents, the priests, the community, state-level system and finally individual women.
- Visualizing the roles of various people to bring about the required change.
- Utilization of various media to reach the hearts and minds of the people.
- Focussing attention on the pathetic situation of jogins.
- The district collector and mandal officers are authorized to mete out punishments to the violators of the Act such as:
- Any person who dedicates girls to goddesses Yellamma and Pochamma or encourages or participates in any function or has any role to play in such dedication is liable to be punished with three years imprisonment and a fine of Rs 3,000.

- Those who publicly favour the Jogin/Devadasi system will get three years imprisonment and a fine of Rs 5,000.
- If the parents, guardians or relatives of a girl take an active part in making her a jogin, they are liable to five years imprisonment and a fine of Rs 5,000.
- The jogin, however, is not to be punished.

In Chandur village, a jogin named Kamamma threw her ghungroos at the landlord and told him to get his wife to dance. Kamamma's action caused a great deal of debate in the surrounding areas.

Sivamma of Yellareddy continued to dance in spite of Samskar's attempts to dissuade her. Her teenaged son Sailu felt both depressed and angry and so broke the pots in the house. This had a telling effect on Sivamma and she gave up dancing.

Samskar's next task was to transform the priests who were responsible for perpetuating and legitimizing the Jogin system. In 1999, the bold act of a priest gave an impetus to the efforts to convince priests to voluntarily give up their role in the system. The act was that six priests cut their hair in the presence of the then collector. Their belief was that the sanctity of pujari was in the hair which was not cut from their birth.

Efforts to Reform Potharajus

Year	*Event*
1988	Two jogin marriages arranged by Kumudben Joshi, the then Governor of Andhra Pradesh.
1991	Two jogin marriages conducted by Chelli Nilayam, Varni.
1991	Six potharajus of Borlam village of Banswada bade goodbye to their profession and cut their hair in the presence of the collector.
2001	Marriage of Raju Bai to Mallesh in the presence of the collector and ministers.
2001	About 200 potharajus voluntarily cut off their tuft of hair in the presence of District Collector Ashok Kumar.
2001	Ten jogins got married.
2001	Thirty-one potharajus voluntarily removed their tuft of hair.
2002	Forty-one potharajus removed their tuft. About 235 potharajus relinquished their trinkets and whips.

These developments facilitated the return of all the potharajus to the mainstream and the Potharaju system was almost wiped out in the district. On 12 November 2001, K. Ramaswamy, Member of the National Human Rights Commission, congratulated the District Collector Ashok Kumar on the steps taken for the rehabilitation of jogins and potharajus. The press hailed it as a "Historical Social Revolution".[1]

The Role of Potharaju in Ora Panduga

In this festival, three persons – Bindla, Potharaju and Kolupula – are important. Bindla and potharaju belong to SCs and the Kolupula (jogin) belongs to a SC or backward class. The Bindla chants the mantras and oversees the proceedings and the jogin performs the 'Rangam'. Based on her predictions, sacrifices are made.

Ora Panduga is celebrated during the monsoon season, which also gives rise to epidemics and diseases. Potharajus are the only people who can convert a girl into a jogin, as it is believed that the tuft of hair gives them divine power. It was, therefore, felt that attempts to root out the Jogin system must be preceded by the elimination of the potharaju's role. The whole village treats the potharaju as a 'guru'. His role during the festival, that is, separating the head of the sacrificed goat with one bite, was barbaric. Most of the potharajus suffer from chronic diseases like TB, cancer and asthma. Some potharajus are suspected to be sorcerers and, therefore, are not allowed to work in fields. This is one of the reasons of their backwardness. Owing to the efforts of the district administration, almost all potharajus have been rehabilitated and the obnoxious system can be said to have been totally eliminated in the district.

One potharaju said, "Despite our fairly good educational background we are unable to get jobs. We are forced to continue as caste priests initiating innocent girls as Jogins and participating in village fairs and festivals ...".[2] He recalled with anguish, "My pleas that I was not interested annoyed the village elders who issued a stern warning that I could not survive in the village if I did not continue as a caste priest".[3] Anyway, all this ended in a smooth manner.

Samskar's success in stopping the initiation of girls speaks volumes for their communication skills and persuasive power. In the neighbouring districts, the parents of young girls used to dedicate their daughters without the knowledge of Samskar. The girls, unaware of the evil practice, would tell their schoolmates, "My parents and others went to a temple where some rituals were performed including tying of a Mangala Sutra". Community members alerted Samskar about many such incidents in Nizamabad district.

In July 2001, Samskar and the National Commission of Women organized a public meeting which was attended by all district officials and 70 jogins. Samskar told the gathering about the strategies it adopted to eradicate the Jogin system. The jogins were asked to rid themselves of the wrong notion that they enjoyed their ritual status as 'Nitya Sumangali'. They were told that their dancing at funerals did not enhance their dignity and self-respect. They were advised to explore other means of livelihood.

Samskar also started an adult literacy programme for jogins aged less than thirty years. At a meeting, the Samskar team discussed various issues like health, alcoholism and the practice of sharing toddy with children. This gave the jogins confidence and improved their self-esteem. Some stood for elections and were elected as sarpanches, ward members or members of school committees.

In holiday camps, children were given an opportunity to learn many things such as magic, purse-making, drawing, making articles with waste materials, cultural activities like singing, script writing and street plays. This emboldened the children to challenge the blind beliefs of their elders.

Status of Jogins

Past	*Present*
Blind belief is a sacrosanct religious tradition that cannot be questioned.	Exploitative instrument of poor women.
Demeaning ways of addressing the women as Jogi, Lacchi.	The jogins are addressed as sisters or by their names.
Dancing at funerals was a must.	Challenged the tradition and gave up dancing at funerals.
No privacy in relationships. Some voluntarily took to prostitution.	Maintenance of privacy in one's relationships – realization of exploitative methods including prostitution.
Not respected – no sense of belonging to the family.	They enjoy respect – have an identity of their families.
Constant ill-health.	Health problems are diagnosed and treated accordingly.
Timid, voiceless.	Have become bold. Voice is raised against tradition and superstition.
Restricted mobility.	Initiative in going to banks, offices and travelling on their own and interacting with others, if necessary.
Dependence on others for their sustenance.	Self-reliance increased. Started working on farms.

It can thus be seen that by boldly challenging the traditions, the jogins have enhanced their status. Some have even come up the social ladder. For example, Kamamma has become a Director of the Agricultural Co-operative Bank of Nasrullabad.

Rehabilitation means providing a secure life. The following are among the various methods adopted to rehabilitate the jogins:

- Assignment of land.
- Fixed deposits.
- Self-help groups – setting up the Mahila Bank.
- Housing.
- Provision of health care.

It was an uphill task for the Samskar team to persuade the jogins to discard the practice of propitiating the gods for good health and prosperity and explain to them the scientific reasons for ill-health. As a result of Samskar's efforts, the jogins started giving more attention to sanitation and cleanliness. Their awareness of children's health has improved.

Samskar requested the government to build pucca houses for the jogins and helped in providing the basic amenities.

As regards agriculture, the team offered to take up issues such as:

- Identification of the land to be purchased.
- Fixation of the price of that land.
- Drilling bore wells and electrification.
- Training in crop cultivation.
- Extension of crop loans.
- Supply of inputs at the doorstep of the jogins.

Subsequently, the government provided up to to Rs 24,000 per acre. Of this, Rs 5,000 was subsidy and the balance was a loan repayable over 10 years at 4.5 per cent interest rate. Nine hundred of the 2,167 jogins have been assigned land. Land assignment and the agricultural programme are viewed as the most effective rehabilitation strategy. Samskar provided tractors, generators, seeds, fertilizers and crop loans at the doorstep of the jogins who no longer depend on moneylenders and landlords. In an evaluation in 1996, Samskar staff acknowledged that they were facing some hurdles in making the jogins self-reliant.

We cannot leave them to manage their agriculture as we help them in everything and for all decisions they have become dependent on us. As the journey time of the tractor from Varni to the land of the sisters takes time, we are unable at times to assist them in taking up timely operations. The women do not want to tap local available ploughing opportunities. We recognize that we must make them independent of us. We should only provide financial services and withdraw from other services. But the women ask us, 'if you do not help in the fields, who will? Also, you have always said you will provide us help in all matters'.[4]

These are the issues that Samskar is grappling with. As the jogins did not have sufficient experience of agricultural work, they needed time to learn agricultural management. They felt that getting trained and then taking up agriculture would be difficult. Instead, they asked for buffaloes. By 2001–2002, they were given loans totalling about Rs 11 lakh to buy livestock.

The S.C. Corporation extended its support to the jogins in the following manner:

- Assigned land to 900 jogins.
- Gave each jogin a fixed deposit of Rs 10,000.
- Gave assets worth Rs 2 lakh to each jogin.
- Built houses for some jogins.

In 1999, Samskar organized self-help groups. It was an economic activity designed to enable more than 700 jogins to escape from the clutches of landlords and money-leaders. The DWAKRA (an NGO) had, by and large, reached women of the upper castes but had made little headway among the SCs. The self-help group activity was promoted as a necessary adjunct for their sustenance. Paraspara Sahakara Podupu Sangams improved the managerial skills of the jogins. Samskar arranged training programmes for these women to develop different livelihood options. Training was imparted to 50 per cent of the members in different income-generating activities such as running a kirana shop, tea shop, vegetable-vending and livestock-rearing. Table 8.1 gives the details about the income-generating units started by 2002.

The table shows that a total of 61 income-generating activities were started with loans. This gave scope for jogins to interact with other women as well with government departments. The women started thinking seriously about the financial security. The greatest advantage is the recognition of the sisters as members of the self-help group, rather than as jogins.

Table 8.1

Income-generating units started by 2002

Programmes	*Nandipet*	*Navipet*	*Armoor*	*Yellareddy*	*Total Units*	*Total Amount (Rs)*
Kirana shop	1	5	1	2	9	97,000
Laundry shop	1	—	—	—	1	10,000
S.T.D. booth	—	1	—	—	1	10,000
Goats	1	—	8	—	9	66,000
Vegetable vending	9	1	5	3	18	5,93,000
Piggery	2	—	14	—	16	1,32,000
Bangle stores	1	—	—	1	2	25,000
Cold drinks shop	1	—	—	—	1	10,000
Tailoring machine	1	—	—	1	2	9,500
Fish net	—	—	—	1	1	10,000
Brick-making	1	—	—	1	2	12,000
Total					**61**	

For above the children of the jogins, Samskar started Ashram Vidyalayam with the object of ensuring for them a life of dignity, respect and equality. The most awkward moment for the children was when they were asked for their father's name. In this venture, Samskar received an offer from a Dutch organization called Hivos to meet the expenditure on the teachers and materials. The school which started with a primary section has now grown into a high school. It was open to not only jogins' children but to others as well to facilitate their integration. Table 8.2 shows the composition of school during 1993–2004.

Table 8.2

Composition of the school during 1993–2004

Category	*Number*	*Percentage*
Children of jogins	469	22
Other boarders	1125	52
Day scholars	580	26
Total	**2174**	**100**

Two children of jogins are now studying engineering in the Government Engineering College at Nirmal in Adilabad district. Samskar also started vocational training to ensure that the high school students learnt a vocation and became self-reliant. Training was imparted in tailoring, nursing and car-driving. Raju, a married boy, attended the training programme in car-driving. Asked for his views about the Jogin system, he said, "Every year at school I was asked who my father was and what was his name. This always made me feel bad." When he was in the 10th class, the head master wrote the boy's mother's name instead of the father's. Raju has now joined the rehabilitation programme in Medak. Samskar extended its activities to Adilabad and Medak districts in 2001. It identified 100 jogins in Adilabad and 24 in Medak.

In 1996, Samskar entered into a partnership with Plan International to expand its scope of work to focus on children in a holistic manner. These activities have a bearing on child growth and development.

Plan Sponsorship Programme - Domain

Growing up healthy-nutrition education; ante- and post-natal care; training of mothers on child care and nutrition; promotion of family planning; awareness of AIDS and health in general; supportive health care system; medical reimbursement; birth registration; physiotherapy; dental care; provision of medical kits; training on special needs to children.

An important category of the sponsorship programme was livelihood issues which consisted of

- land-based activities;
- training in agriculture;
- distribution of milch cattle;
- watershed; and
- self-help groups.

Samskar also implemented government schemes. It maintained case studies, photo exhibition and started publishing a newsletter.

As a result of Samskar's efforts, jogins have gained enough self-confidence to stand for elections. They are members of community-based organizations. They have become aware of the marriageable age for their daughters. The tough life they led has taught them to face challenges single-handedly and fight for justice. They are in a position to question the system for the wrongs done to them and ask for redressal of their grievances.

According to Samskar's Project Director K.H.S.S. Sundar, the reform and rehabilitation of jogins was high on the organization's agenda. It recognized the need for continuous social education of the jogins to ensure that they did not think of going back to their old profession. Samskar was aware that any laxity in continuing counselling programmes would prove to be counter-productive.

Many jogins are grateful to Samskar for its efforts for enabling them to lead a respectable life. Said one jogin, "It is because of Samskar that we are happy. Though our life was burnt away like a candle, we forget that phase by seeing the bright future of our children. This ray of hope is due to the efforts of Samskar alone."

Duties Organization at Nellore

In 1990, Duties Organization started its work for the cause of the disadvantaged and unprivileged sections of Nellore and Prakasam districts. It mainly worked for the cause of women. These women can be classified into three categories:

(i) Women oppressed by patriarchal ideology.
(ii) Women oppressed under untouchability.
(iii) Women dedicated to local gods and goddesses and who later became concubines or degraded themselves as sex-workers.

The organization gave top priority to the third category, i.e., the matammas. It surveyed and submitted a report to the Government of Andhra Pradesh through the district collector recommending action to rehabilitate the matangis to eradicate the system. Besides the Andhra Pradesh government, Andheri Hilfe Bonn, a Germany based organization, strengthened the hands of Duties in this programme by

(1) conducting community awareness training camps,
(2) organizing rallies of matammas to draw public attention to the problem,
(3) providing legal protection to matammas,
(4) conducting seminars on the issue,
(5) providing house sites and ritis loans for construction and pattas for both the land and house sites and irrigation facilities,
(6) arranging marriages, and
(7) starting a residential school for the children of matammas.

Since 1994, 567 matamma cases have been dealt with. Of the 567 matammas, 350 have been rehabilitated and 150 have been given houses. Loans were given to 250 matammas to buy goats, sheep or to open petty shops. While land was assigned to 100 matammas, skills like tailoring were imparted to 100 matammas to help them supplement their income. Fifty women were taught painting. For the promotion of environment and ecological balance, Duties introduced bio-gas system for farmers of all communities.

The children of matammas are getting good education at the residential school run by Duties, which is focusing on the welfare and social development of girl children. Duties has established 12 schools in 12 villages. The bridge school strength is 60 children. They will be the first generation to enjoy the benefits of education like other school children.

So far, 225 children have passed out of the residential school. Some of them have been sent to regular government schools. The special schools run by the Duties Organization have a conducive atmosphere for studies. Special attention is paid to the children's integrated development.

To enhance the status of social groups like potters, cobblers, tanners, leather and bone collectors, skill was imparted to them to do better in their respective trades. Women self-help groups were created for the amelioration of their lot. The organization also led a campaign against the atrocities on dalit women. During 2003–04, the organization started bio-gas awareness and STDs/HIV/AIDS control programme, particularly among the Hijra community, throughout the district. The organization took up multi-dimensional programmes like youth, community, public rallies, seminars and workshops, agitations against violation of women's rights, door-to-door counselling, social marriages and legal support activities. Duties also conducted 242 social mass marriages among the matammas.

To empower matamma women, the Duties Organization encouraged two women candidates to contest for the Assembly elections held in May 2004 from Gudur and Sullurpet constituencies and they got 957 and 1,172 votes, respectively.

Other activities of Duties included the running of 15 pre-schools for 450 matangi children, review meetings for the leaders of the thrift groups and organization of community gatherings.

Recommendations of Duties Organization

- Kolupulu should be discontinued.
- The custom of sacrificing animals before deities should be curbed.
- Alcoholic drinks should not be allowed in the jataras.
- Matangis should be allowed to marry mortal men.

Duties Organization is holding rallies for safeguarding Hindu culture. It is working for equality of culture, religion and caste. The organization has named its office 'Manava Nilayam' (Centre for Human Values). Its president is Nune Vengaiah.

Andhra Pradesh Jogin Vyavastha Vyatireka Porata Sanghatana (APJVVPS)

The president of APJVVPS, Grace Nirmala, said, "For centuries girl children have been converted as Jogins at Yellamma temples. When they attain puberty, these girls are used to satisfy the carnal desires of the dominant sections of society. These Jogins are considered as downtrodden in our society and Dalit women are facing humiliation and harassment in society. A woman is subjected to oppression due to this caste cadre. All jogin women are willing to lead a married life."

The aim of the Sanghatana is that no girl child should be made a jogin. With the object of eradicating the Jogin system, the organization has taken up certain activities, especially in Mahaboobnagar district. These are:

- Stopping jogin dedication. The organization has so far stopped the dedication of 10 girls and brought the matter to the notice of the government. Recently, in Ranga Reddy district, a jogin marriage was performed by a Gouda person and the Sanghatana took notice of it and is trying to rehabilitate her.
- Stopped 'Sidi' at Doma Jatara, Lingampalli Jatara, Kurumurthi and Gummumkal Jatara. For stopping the 'Sidi' at Doma Jatara in Ranga Reddy, the district unit of the Sanghatana was given the 'Swasakthi award'.
- Since 2002, the organization has performed five jogin marriages.
- The organization identified jogins in seven districts of Andhra Pradesh – 300 in Nellore, 544 in Chittoor, 2,671 in Anantapur, 2,087 in Mahaboobnagar, 1,671 in Warangal district, 4,120 in Nizamabad district and 26 in Prakasam district and rehabilitated most of them with the help of the government. Some

other organizations are showing an interest in the rehabilitation of these women.

The Sanghatana wants to organize awareness programmes. It has started four types of activities in Mahaboobnagar district and in all the districts the author has mentioned earlier. Hajamma, a jogin woman of Mahaboobnagar district, who is the convener, has received the best activist award. She participated in the international workshop "International Movement against All Forms of Discrimination and Racism" in Durban, South Africa and spoke about the problems of the jogins.

The organization has undertaken protection and safeguarding of children. It took Kalajatara on their education and with fifty jogins conducted a Padayatra. It launched a campaign against the atrocities on dalit women, conveying the message through Burrakathas. It also started legal awareness campaigns. All the members of the organization took a pledge on the following issues:

- No girl should be made a jogin.
- Provision of education to the jogins' children.

To achieve these objects, jogins/devadasis/matammas are formed into societies at village and mandal levels and federated first at the district level and then at the state level.

The Sanghatana works as a community-based organization. The jogins are organized into village communities. The leaders at the village level should have the (1) ability to speak, (2) ability to fight back, (3) ability to conduct meetings, and (4) availability in the district in times of need. The committee members have to ensure that (i) no dedication takes place in the district, (ii) children are enrolled into schools, and (iii) pattam/kolupulu is stopped.

The committee president has to lead the movement further and he or she should always be ready to discuss the issues and activities with the other members of the committee. For example, Laxmamma while discharging her responsibility as president has to see how many jogins have been rehabilitated. Table 8.3 shows where the Mandal headquarters are situated in each district.

The president, vice-president and members of the state committee are elected from the five districts. In each district, the revenue mandals are the centres for APJVVPS. The names of the leaders change from time to time, except 'Hasadi Matamma'.

Table 8.3

Headquarters in each district

District	*Mandal*	*Names*
Anantapur	Bomma Samudram	Laxmi
	Chettur	Manjula
	Kalyandurgam	Hanumakka
Mahaboobnagar	Utkoor	Susheelamma
	Dhanwada	M. Balamma
	C.C.Kunta	Ramulamma
	Narayanpet	Venkatamma
Nizamabad	Dichpally	Hasadi Matamma
	Naklur	Gurom Rog Syangu
	Nandipeta	Laxmi
		Outtan hinnakka.
Chittoor	Tirupati	Gauri
	Yerped	Radha
	Varadayyapalem	Padma
	B.N.Kandriga	Bhavani
Nellore		Thataparthi Laxmi
		Potticherla Penchalamma
		Arava Vasantamma
		Batta Penchalamma

The APJVVPS is dealing with more than 2,000 jogins in the five districts put together. It has launched programmes for their education, thrift and credit, eradication of untouchability and abolition of child marriages. It has started a quarterly magazine called *Dalita* in which all issues are discussed. Periodically, it conducts padayatras to bring awareness to the people and organizes legal awareness camps. It also holds personality development workshops to emphasize the rights of children and their education. Cultural performances are also organized. They are taking barren land from the government and distributing it among the needy people. The organization conducts mainstream marriages. Table 8.4 shows the number of jogins present in each district.

As can be seen from the table, there are more jogins in Nizamabad, Anantapur and Mahaboobnagar districts. The organization is safeguarding the interests of jogins in several ways. It is doing a commendable job. It is also developing leadership among the jogins.

Table 8.4

Number of jogins in each district of Andhra Pradesh

S.No.	*District*	*Number*
1.	Nellore	300
2.	Chittoor	544
3.	Anantapur	2671
4.	Mahaboobnagar	2087
5.	Warangal	1671
6.	Nizamabad	4120
7.	Prakasam	26

The jogin/matangi/basvi women comprise both Mala and Madiga communities. They have many sub-sects. They cultivate fields and are good at animal husbandry. These people have a strong bond with the land, but slowly the land is slipping out of their hands.

RISE and Stri Shakti Sanghatana

These two organizations were established in 1984 in Tirupati. During 1994–1995, many atrocities happened in Chittoor district. In a workshop on "Violence Against Women: Our Responsibility" held at the senate hall of S.V. University, people's associations and representatives of several NGOs demanded action against the guilty. Every newspaper in Chittoor district wrote about the dowry deaths and prostitution. There was a news report that one man made a matamma pregnant and left her to her fate.

Representatives of RISE and Stri Shakti Sanghatana (SSS) went to Karkambadi Harijanwada in Renigunta mandal and surveyed matammas there. They learnt about the injustice being done to matammas.

The two organizations met the SC Corporation officials and learnt certain facts about the life of matammas. The conclusions they arrived at after their field study are:

(i) The age of matammas ranged from 0 to 80 years and there were 332 matas in the whole of Chittoor district.

(ii) Most of the matas belonged to the Madiga community and there were also some Mala girls. Some of the backward class communities like Vadde, Yadava, Muthrasi, Washermen, Pambala and Berisetti also dedicated their girls to the local goddesses as matammas. Of the 332 matas, 234 were Madigas, 73 Malas and the remaining 25 belonged to other communities.

(iii) The literacy rate of matammas was very low. Illiterates 235; upto 5th class – 68; 6th to 10th class – 21; Intermediate only 4. It shows that after 5th class, many dropped out. This could be attributed to the ill-treatment of the girls in their respective schools and the society and the attitude of the elders in the families. Although there are 121 social welfare hostels for SCs in Chittoor district, they are not able to provide opportunity to the dalit girls, especially Matangi children. The landlords and the Jambukas are coming in the way of matammas' education and they are compelling them to perform Kolupulu during the village festivals. There was a shocking instance of a woman who was asked to perform a dance soon after she had delivered a baby.

By performing Kolupulu, matammas earn about Rs 20,000 with which they maintain themselves throughout the year. The pity is that they have to bear ill-treatment and humiliations at the hands of different people. They curse the custom and sometimes blame their own parents and the society. They are destined to suffer throughout their lives and rear the children without father.

Generally, matammas have sexual relationship with a single individual because concubinage is prevalent among them. Since the society recognizes them as village property, the entire community has a control over them. They are not traditional sex-workers. Very few have taken to prostitution as their profession.

RISE and SSS have taken up two components for plan of action – prevention and rehabilitation, and eradication of cult.

(a) Prevention and Rehabilitation

- Housing facility is the first requirement of the matammas. Houses should be constructed in the same place where they live.
- Special residential schools should be established for the dalit/matammas' children.
- Income-generating schemes should be planned to reduce their poverty. They should be provided with land. Financial assistance should be secured from the government for dairy development, sheep-rearing and for starting petty shops.
- At least Rs 10,000 should be given as fixed deposit for each mata so that they may have both social and economic security.
- Health camps should be organized periodically for check-ups for diseases like STDs and AIDS.

- Special social security schemes should be drawn up by the government.
- Marriages of matas should be encouraged by giving them monetary benefits and other incentives.
- After their marriage, the government must give them periodical support.
- Awareness camps should be organized by the NGOs for dalit women, matas and jambukas in order to root out this social evil.
- Local NGOs should constantly support them.

(b) Eradication of Cult

- Matas should be allowed to have their own names.
- Vigilance committees should be constituted with matas, social workers, academicians and officials to stop dedication of girls to the temple. The first thing they have to do is give them proper education.
- Local NGOs should organize counselling centres to persuade the matas to have legal marriage and encourage them to lead a normal life.
- Jambukas who act as local priests during the village festivals should be provided with an alternative occupation so that they do not have any role to play in the degradation of women.
- Implementation of the Dedication Act of 1988 and punishment for the violators.
- Welfare measures should be taken by the state government in collaboration with the SC Corporation.

RISE and SSS recruited two matammas in each mandal to take part in the activities relating to the rehabilitation of matammas. A vigilance committee was constituted and two matammas became its leaders. They have to supervise the distribution of milch cows, loans and sheep. The two matamma members of the vigilance committee should be given training in the implementation of the Devadasi Act and they should prevent Kolupulu in jataras.

Unfortunately, not many in the police force are aware of the Devadasi Act of 1988. RISE and SSS, therefore, went to each village and conducted awareness programmes.

These two organizations have so far arranged marriages of 74 matammas, 17 of them in 1996 alone. However, four marriages were not successful. Some matammas took part in politics and got elected as sarpanches and ward members. For example, C. Parvathi became a ward member in Bailikodimchedu.

For the education of the children of matammas and child matammas, the two organizations started Mahatma Phule Educational Centre in 1999. This residential school has a strength of 85, of whom 31 are child matammas and the rest are matammas' children.

The institution is engaged in cultural activities aimed at eradication of the Matamma cult. It distributes pamphlets explaining the evil effects of the system.

The Consequences of Matammas' Struggle

The involvement of RISE and SSS helped the matammas to secure ration cards, income certificates and caste certificates from the government. Earlier, government officials used to exploit the matammas before issuing various certificates to them.

Table 8.5

Statistics of matammas in Chittoor district which has 19 mandals

Buchi Naidu Kandrika	—	11
Chandras	—	06
Chandragiri	—	06
K.V.B. Puram	—	02
Karveti Nagaram	—	02
Nagalapuram	—	34
Nagiri	—	19
Narayana Vanam	—	08
Pichchatur	—	24
Puttoor	—	18
Ramachandrapuram	—	03
Renigunta	—	08
Satyavedu	—	27
Srikalahasti	—	29
Tirupati (Rural)	—	39
Tirupati (Urban)	—	19
Vadamalapeta	—	18
Varadayyapalem	—	06
Vijayapuram	—	49
Yerpedu	—	25

These two organizations staged a demonstration with 400 matammas before the collectorate demanding house pattas and land pattas and Rs 25,000 for each matamma for house construction. Matammas belonged to the Bailikodimchedu village in the Nagaralapu mandal; one matamma got the 'Indra Ratna' award in 2004. This awardee arranged marriages for other matammas in the village and participated in the protest movements. She was given Rs 50,000 and that Parvathi gave Rs 25,000 for the school. Table 8.5 shows the statistics of matammas in Chittoor.

It should be clear from the above figures that regardless of whether an area is urban or rural, whether it has educated people or not, whether it is developed or undeveloped, women are exploited. Superstitions and beliefs play a very important role in the continuity of the Matangi tradition.

Basvis of Rayalaseema

The Government of Andhra Pradesh declared the Basvi system illegal and started many welfare schemes such as vocational training, skill development, cattle-rearing, allotment of house-sites and construction of pucca buildings for the basvis of Adoni in Kurnool district.

Programmes Implemented in Adoni Mandal

(1) Tailoring: Recognizing that there were no employment opportunities for women in rural areas, the government started training-cum-production units in tailoring, soap-making, chalk-making, match-stick making, book-binding and spinning. In 1986, the DRDA started a garment-making factory and imparted training in tailoring to 25 basvis for one year. The author visited the rehabilitative centre known as Sankar Rehabilitative Centre, named after S.R. Sankaran, the then Principal Secretary of the Social Welfare Department. A monthly stipend of Rs 50 was paid to each trainee. The trainees were able to earn Rs 15 a day by stitching garments which were supplied to the departments of Social Welfare, Tribal Welfare, SC and ST Corporations. Twenty other basvis were given training in the same skill. However, seven of them dropped out in the middle. Table 8.6 shows the details of various programmes implemented in Adoni mandal.

Table 8.6

Details of various programmes implemented in Adoni mandal

Name of the programme	*Sponsored by*	*Period of Training*	*Stipend (Rs)*	*No. of beneficiaries*	*Year of implementation*	*Others*
Tailoring	DRDA	12 months	50	25	1985–1986	Trainees were given sewing machines free of cost
Tailoring	Social Welfare Dept.	6 months	120	13	1987–1988	-do-
Soap-making	DRDA	6 months	120	10	1986–1987	
Chalk-making	DRDA	6 months	120	10	1986–1987	
Match-stick making	DRDA	6 months	120	10	1986–1987	
Book-binding	DRDA	6 months	120	10	1986–1987	
Spinning	DRDA	6 months	120	30	1986–1987	

All these training programmes could not be run for a long time. Though basvis were imparted training, they used to get very meagre wages. Moreover, the centre could not run properly due to insufficient budget, lack of supply of raw material in time and substandard machines.

Another important factor was the difficulty in marketing the products as there was stiff competition from the local units. Also, agencies did not buy them because of their substandard quality. As regards book-binding, the production unit started functioning in 1988 and was closed down in 1990.

(2) Spinning: The training-cum-production unit was able to employ only four of the 30 trainees. It stopped functioning four months after it started because its wage structure could not attract job-seekers.

Implementation of the programmes in Alur mandal of Kurnool district also was not satisfactory. Training was provided in animal husbandry for creating self-employment. The housing scheme was not executed efficiently.

The Social Welfare Department supplied milch cows, took up construction of houses, supplied dhotis, saris to 128 people and sanctioned pension for eight basvis. Two acres of dry land was allotted to 10 people and sheep were supplied to 212 people. The beneficiaries belonged to 56 villages of Alur, Halaharvi, Chippagiri, Kouthalam, Holegunda of Adoni division. The schemes could not be continued for various reasons. The possible reasons were:

It was difficult to market the substandard goods owing to stiff competition from other manufacturers. The rehabilitation done was temporary and no long-term alternative was thought of.

Under the Jeevana Jyothi Programme, a total of Rs 1.64 crore was sanctioned and assistance was provided to each person in the form of fixed deposits and the beneficiaries were allowed to claim only the interest to meet the day-to-day expenditure. Under another economic support scheme with an outlay of Rs 10.55 lakh people were given a loan of Rs 5,000 each to start petty trades such as fruit, flower and vegetable vending. The beneficiary was asked to repay only 50 per cent of the loan in 12 equated monthly instalments with interest at the rate of 6 per cent per annum. Even these schemes could not help the beneficiaries.

These temporary schemes could not provide the required advantage to the beneficiaries. For example, while two acres of land was provided for some of the beneficiaries, they were not given the implements for cultivation nor were irrigation facilities provided.

An examination of various welfare schemes started by the district administration reveals that awareness programmes were not conducted properly and the schemes were not sufficient to bring the basvis into the mainstream. Though the beneficiaries responded to all the schemes enthusiastically, there was no commitment on the part of the officials who implemented them.

(3) Soap-making: A training-cum-production centre was started under the DRDA in soap-making. Ten basvis received the training. But the production unit could attract only three job aspirants due to its meagre wages.

(4) Chalk-making: In 1986, the DRDA took up another welfare measure, training-cum-production unit for chalk-making. A batch of 10 beneficiaries received the training. But the unit was closed down because of marketing problem.

(5) Match stick-making: This scheme provided employment to only 10 beneficiaries. Again, poor quality of the product and meagre wages led to the discontinuance of this welfare scheme.

(6) Book-binding: The district authorities took up the task of running a training-cum-production unit in book-binding in 1986. Only 10 young children of basvis received training and the unit was closed in 1990.

The government distributed sheep units among a number of basvis belonging to different villages in Alur mandal. The Scheduled Caste Corporation made arrangements for the payment of Rs 100 to each beneficiary towards subsistence allowance for month. Similarly, 77 beneficiaries received help from the government.

In Anantapur district, the author found that the plight of the basvis in the 20 villages she visited was worse than that of their counterparts in other districts. The reasons are:

(1) Anantapur is a backward district.

(2) The impact of Karnataka is felt in Anantapur district.

(3) Drought areas are more in this district.

(4) Illiteracy, poverty and superstition resulted in an increase in the number of basvis in the district.

(5) Widows and invalid children are also made basvis in this district.

(6) Very few NGOs are handling this problem.

In order to create self-confidence in the basvis under the Jeevana Jyothi Scheme, each basvi was sanctioned Rs 10,000 in the form of a fixed deposit.

In 1988, the MLAs of the Adoni constituency submitted a representation to the district administration seeking economic support for 211 basvis of Adoni Mandal. The district collector sanctioned Rs 5,000 to each basvi to enable them to take up micro-economic enterprises like fruit-vending.

On the whole, the rehabilitative programmes for the jogins, matangis and basvis were inadequate, and some of the NGOs have become commercial in their attitude and naturally they have no commitment. The results of the welfare schemes would have been better if the departments of Social Welfare, Child and Women Welfare and the SC Corporation had worked together.

Most of the programmes initiated by the government for the jogins have proved to be either inappropriate or inadequate for generating the desired results. The officials concerned should give up the mechanical way of doing things and try to emulate the work done by Hemalatha Lavanam's "Chelli Nilayam". Other organizations also would do well to take this as their model. Social reformation should go hand in hand with economic rehabilitation. What is required is not mere economic growth but the happiness of these people. The voluntary agencies should have clear-cut ideas before launching their programmes for these basvi women.

Among the many organizations devoted to the cause of jogins and their counterparts elsewhere in the state are: Social Awareness Through Learning and Training (SALT); Joint Women's Programme Team; the Environmental Education Centre, Chelli Nilayam, Arthika Samata Mandali at Vijayawada; Andhra Pradesh Jogin Vyavastha Vyatireka Porata Sanghatana at Hyderabad; Duties, at Nellore; and RISE at Tirupati.

Vimochana: Devadasi Punarvasati Sangha

In Karnataka, a social organization called Vimochana: Devadasi Punarvasati Sangha, owns its origin to a young lecturer of Shri S.M.S. College, Athani. He intended to organize a seminar at Kokatnur village of Athani Taluq on the evils of the Devadasi system in April, 1984. His intention was to prepare a research paper on the problem. After conducting a survey in 48 villages of Athani taluka, he organized a seminar on 28 March 1985 under the leadership of a young advocate B.L. Patel. A senior advocate by name M.V. Patil who spoke in the seminar said, "The seminar would have been conducted much earlier and it was indeed the need of the hour ... The place chosen for the purpose is a stronghold of the very problem. Therefore, the combined effort of a big band of youths, elders and social workers is required to make it a success". An association was formed under the stewardship of B.L. Patel who declared it as 'Vimochana: Devadasi Punarvyavastha Sangh, Athani'. Those who attended the seminar passed a resolution, "This taluka is one of the very few places in Karnataka where the Devadasi system has been in existence for centuries. It may not be out of place to mention here but with great sadness and a feeling of shame, that this is one of the very few places feeding enormously the brothels in big cities like Bombay, Pune, etc ...". Thus began the fight of the new organization against the Devadasi system.

The seminar was thus very successful and it was followed by the marriage of devadasi Nimbevva Tukaram Kamble to Srimant Bhimappa Ghata Kamble. Another person by name Ramesh Kamble came forward to marry a devadasi called Sunanda. The Karnataka State Social Welfare Advisory Board's chairperson, Savitri Gundi, wrote a letter to the Sangha saying that she would be deputing some officers to discuss with the organization different schemes for the welfare of the basvis. The officers who held discussions with 'Vimochana' were M.S. Subramanya, secretary and P. Prakash, Social Welfare Officer, advisory board, B.C. Thiagarajan, Coordinator of Christian Children Fund, Bangalore. They promised financial assistance to 'Vimochana' to carry on its activities. They registered the organization under the Karnataka State Societies Registration Act, 1960 on 4 September 1985.

Aims and Objectives of 'Vimochana'

The aims and objectives of *Vimochana* are:

- The upliftment of the women in their social, economic and cultural spheres
- Organizing of 'Holiday Home Camps', seminars, educational courses, vocational guidance and adult education centres, etc.
- To set up residential or non-residential nurseries, schools for children.
- To work for the benefit of devadasis, their children, widows, destitutes and invalids.
- To publish literature, booklets to canvas against the system.
- To implement government's policies and schemes for the upliftment of devadasis.
- To fight against the evils of untouchability.

To raise funds for the organization, the following ways were decided:

- Membership subscriptions.
- Donations.
- Financial assistance from the central as well as the state government.
- Financial assistance from semi-government and autonomous bodies.
- Financial assistance from international agencies like Christian Children Fund.

Under these schemes, marriages of devadasis were performed when men volunteered to marry them. Sponsorship was arranged for the school-going children. The Christian Children Fund assisted this scheme. Several schemes and projects were taken up by Vimochana president B.R. Patel from both the central and the state government and also from the advisory boards.

Another organization by name Sivali was run by Sushila Naik, a devadasi. 'Jalha Nirmoolana Andola' was started in Nipani with the aim of launching campaigns against dedication and for rehabilitation of devadasis. Crèches were set up for the children of devadasis. The author, along with a lecturer Malli Gandhi, Regional Institute of Education, Mysore, visited a place called Ghataprabha in 1990 where she found an organization engaged in eradicating the devadasi system in the Soundatti area.

In 1982, Karnataka enacted a law called 'The Karnataka Devadasis (Prohibition of Dedication) Act'. The Act prohibited dedication of women or girls to any deity/temple/object of worship and imposed a penalty ranging from Rs 2,000 to Rs 5,000 and/or imprisonment on any person who directly or indirectly supported dedication.

Like Yellamma of Soundatti, there is another Yellamma temple in Chandragutti in Shimoga district. This Yellamma is a nude goddess where devadasis in the nude form used to dance near the temple. Though the practice of nude dancing was banned by the government 20 years ago, it persists in some small temples in nearby villages. The author gathered this information from the people of the surrounding areas.

The Karnataka Social Welfare Department

It undertook the following activities:

- Establishment of a home for the victims of the devadasi cult.
- Special residential schools for children.
- Vocational training for devadasi women, especially tailoring and embroidery.
- Bank loans to start self-employment activities.
- Other schemes for weaker sections like Janata Housing Scheme, Bhagya Jyoti, Grahkalyan, and old-age pension, Trysem programmes are also provided to devadasi women.
- A special cell to furnish information about the rehabilitation measures.

- The NGOs were given liberal support for their fight against the Devadasi system.
- A certified school was established at Soundatti.

Some other income-generating schemes were started by various voluntary organizations.

Computer-based data is available in Karnataka about the rehabilitation programmes for the devadasis. Jogan Shankar who wrote a book called *Devadasi Cult, A Sociological Analysis* has divided his findings into four categories: (i) general findings, (ii) special findings, (iii) preventive-cum-curative measures and (iv) diagnostic measurements.

General Findings

- The Devadasi cult is non-Aryan in its structure. It is a relic of Dravidian matriarchal society. It is found throughout India with regional variations.
- 85 per cent of devadasis were dedicated to Yellama deity. At present also, it is prevalent in some small villages. Soundatti, Kokatnur and Chandragutti are the places of dedication.
- All dedications were involuntary; parents or guardians were responsible for these dedications.
- Almost all are pre-puberty dedications.
- In Karnataka, this practice is prevalent among Holer, Madar and Samagar communities.
- Priests of the Yellamma temples are Lingayats, a dominant group.
- The relationship of devadasis with the local deity Yellamma is only symbolic.

Special Findings

The special findings relate to the persistence of the cult. They are:

- The oppressive patriarchal ideology of Hinduism.
- It is concerned mainly with lower castes, especially SCs and some backward classes.
- Superstitious beliefs in the wrath and curse of Yellamma deity and religious vows – all these are myths created by upper castes for their own selfish ends.
- Abject poverty, landlessness, their dependence on upper castes, pauperization due to famines are among the causes of the persistence of this social evil.

- Illiteracy is more among the SCs.
- Prostitution due to brothels, procurers and local devadasis and gharwalis.
- Jogatis influence the parents or guardians to dedicate their children to Yellamma or to any other goddess.
- To satisfy their extramarital wants, the upper castes trap the lower castes into dedications.
- Devadasis are not aware of the Karnataka Devadasi (Prohibition of Dedication) Act, 1982.
- Commercial attitude of voluntary organizations towards the Devadasi system.
- The impact of police authorities and their intervention with the life of devadasis.
- Lack of good social workers to bring awareness among the devadasis.

Measures for Curbing the Devadasi System

(1) The humiliating and pathetic conditions of devadasis should be highlighted through media, especially electronic media.

(2) Anti-dedication campaigns and rallies should be organized in the area. Priests should declare that religion has nothing to do with the dedication and vows.

(3) The Karnataka Devadasi (Prohibition of Dedication) Act should be made known to all people irrespective of caste, creed or community.

(4) Legal action should be taken against the priests, procurers, gharwalis for the breach of law.

(5) The young girls who are dedicated to the goddess or god should be accommodated in shelter homes or state homes.

(6) The priests or the village accountants should bring the incidents of initiation to the notice of the police authorities.

(7) Rehabilitation centres should be opened in the areas around the Yellamma temples and these should be run by committed social workers.

(8) These rehabilitation centres should become income-generating units with small-scale industries. They should impart training to the devadasis and give them an opportunity to live on their own incomes.

(9) Residential schools should be started for the children of devadasis so that they can be kept away from their mothers and other devadasis.
(10) Simplification of the lengthy marriage procedures. Voluntary organizations should take the responsibility of their marriages.
(11) Devadasis should be married to sincere, hard-working and reliable persons after proper investigations.
(12) A special officer who can understand the devadasi position should be appointed with adequate staff.
(13) Acquired Immune Deficiency Syndrome (AIDS) is seen among the devadasis of Belgaum district and so a thorough medical check-up is required.

Diagnostic Measures

- Survey and study of devadasis should be done both at micro and macro levels.
- The mindset of men and the reaction of women members should also be studied.
- Backward and SC women's status should be studied comprehensively to know why the system exists only among these women.
- Every voluntary organization should have a research wing with trained personnel.
- Folk music and dances of these people should be preserved.
- Data-based study of the whole state is required.

Since its inception in 1985, Vimochana has been striving hard to eradicate the Devadasi system in northern Karnataka. It believes that the most effective way to fight this social evil is through the children of devadasis by educating them and giving them health care, vocational training, employment, marriage, to ensure their rehabilitation and integration into the mainstream of society.

Vimochana's Achievements

- Adopted 1,024 children from 960 families spread over 73 villages of Athani taluka.
- Provided free medical aid to many families.
- All the children, both boys and girls, are given free education, books, uniforms, food and medical care.
- Established Vimochana Multi-purpose Cooperative Society (1992) for devadasis with a share capital of Rs 5 lakh. The present membership is 600.

- Assistance to girls for marriage. So far, 180 girl children of devadasis have been married.
- Housing assistance given to 282 devadasis.
- Conducted awareness programmes for devadasi families and holiday home camps for their children every year.
- Organized two AIDS surveillance camps.
- Computer education for high school children.
- Ambulance service.

Vimochana has published and distributed 36 books and papers and has started the following income-generating activities:

- Self-employment programmes.
- Dairy units.
- Garment unit – Training-cum-production centre.
- Rope-making unit – Training-cum-production.
- Medleri Charaka unit – Training-cum-production.
- Handloom development centre.

For all these activities, financial assistance is given by some international agencies. Vimochana has started the following new ventures:

- Vimochana Institute of Technology, Athani.
- Vimochana Institute of Nursing, Athani (Diploma course in general nursing and midwifery).
- Herbal garden at Malabad.
- Watershed Development Project in Anantapur taluka.
- Vimochana Institute of Self-Employment Training, Malabad taluka, Athani.

In August 1995, with the blessings of H.H. Shri Mahanta Swamiji of Chittargi, Izkal, the Shri Guru Basava Prasad Trust started a trust at Malabad. Its aims and objects are to provide boarding facilities for the children of Vimochana Residential School and to start educational institutions.

Devadasi Rehabilitation project – Belgaum (Myrada Devi), Ghataprabha and Karnataka State Women's Development Corporation Limited started this programme in 1991. The main objective of the project is to eradicate the Devadasi system and to improve the socio-economic status of devadasis in Belgaum district. As per the survey conducted in 1991–1992, there were about 3]300 devadasis in the district. Of them, 35 per cent are aged and have migrated to red-light areas. This organization Kerala State Women's Development Corporation (KSWDC) Myrada, started working with 2,200 devadasis living in Belgaum. Myrada, a voluntary organization, started the project 'Devi' (Devadasis Efforts towards Voluntary Initiatives) in August 1991, mainly to support the Devadasi Rehabilitation Project of KSWDC, Myrada. Myrada programmes are focused on organizing the devadasi women and the community to make them initiate a movement to bring about changes in society whereas KSWDC is engaged in providing alternative livelihood for women who have been exploited under the Devadasi system.

Approach and Programmes

(1) **Self-Help groups:** The goal of both DRP and Devi is organizing self-help groups. A total of 78 such groups are functioning in their respective villages.

(2) **Grama Sabha:** To gain support from the entire community in implementing eradication programmes and also to involve them in planning and implementing action-oriented programmes against this evil system, meetings were held with community people, representatives of various local-level associations and several steps against the Devadasi system were initiated.

(3) **Intensive awareness programmes:** Awareness programmes are organized in annual fairs (Soundatti, Kokatnoor and other villages). Awareness is being created through communication media like TV, pamphlets, posters, announcements, street plays and jataras.

(4) **Economic support:** To improve the economic status of devadasi women, training in various skills is being imparted. Loans are arranged and income-generating activities are taken up.

(5) **Mobilizing government benefits:** House sites, housing, old-age pensions were given to the devadasis.

(6) **Collaboration:** Both KSWDC and Myrada are jointly combating the Devadasi problem.

Some other organizations are working at Gulbarga, Chandragutti, Bijapur and other places for the same cause.

In Maharashtra, due to the interventions of the NGOs and welfare measures undertaken by the Maharashtra government, the muralis have stopped dedicating their girl children to the deity Khandoba and are sending their daughters to school. Today's category of scheduled castes comprises largely of the socially disadvantaged groups which are the creation of the caste system.

In Goa, both kalavantins and bhavins are rendering services in the temples. Kalavantins sing songs and perform dances in temples. The Saraswat Brahmins, who are the priests, keep the kalavantins as their concubines.

The Gomantak institutions in Goa are arranging marriages of bhavins and kalavantins. They have taken the responsibility to educate girl children of these two communities.

The Polki festival takes place in the Shanta-Durga shrine during Navaratri. The purohits decorate the Palki and Makhar in shrine. On festival days, the image of the deity is placed in a decorated palanquin and taken around the temple courtyard accompanied by musicians and devotees. After every few steps, the procession halts and a devadasi sings a few verses in praise of the deity. This procedure is followed until the procession comes back to the temple.

Bhavins do some menial services in the temples. They sweep the temple floor and fan the deity and clean the vessels. However, of late, their number has decreased. In each temple of Goa, there are one or two bhavins.

Thus, the jogins, matangis and basvis of Andhra Pradesh, muralis of Maharashtra, devadasis or jogitas of Karnataka, mariammas of Tamil Nadu and bhavins of Goa hail from the poorest families. They are regarded as the collective property of the village.

Suggestions to Eradicate this Evil Practice

- The rehabilitation programme may form an important part of the special component plan for the scheduled castes and the department of woman and child welfare.
- All organizations and departments, both at the centre and in the states, may be associated with the programme of rehabilitation of jogins and their counterparts in South India.
- A state-level committee may be formed for the implementation of the programme. It should be chaired by an eminent social worker and consist of officials, researchers, NGOs and leaders among the jogins and their counterparts as members.
- At the district level, a joint committee of officials and non-officials should be formed for the implementation of the programme. Just as a sustained campaign helped eradicate the Jogin system in Nizamabad district, similar efforts should be made in other places too.

- The state-level committee should have an autonomous status and there should be no interference by official agencies.
- Ashram schools should be set up in the districts where this problem exists.
- Training programmes through income-generating schemes are required in the areas where religious prostitution is prevalent.
- Pensions should be given to the aged among these women.
- Poverty alleviation programmes should be implemented in these areas.
- Women students of institutions of social work as well as women students of the universities and social workers and researchers of this particular subject should visit these places now and then to educate the exploited women.
- Thus, a congenial atmosphere should be created to protect the self-respect and dignity of these unfortunate women.

Notes

1. Potharaju is responsible for Jogin system. To wipe out the system is very important in the context of eradicating Jogin system. Cutting the tufts of potharajus is an achievement, so the press hailed this incident as a "Historical Social Revolution".
2. Potharajus who are initiating Jogins also know that they are doing obnoxious work. Even if they do not like the work which they are doing, the feudal lords do not allow them to leave the job. Secondly, jobs are not provided for them either in the government or in private establishments. Some of the potharajus are feeling for this state of affairs.
3. Same potharaju recalled his past memory how the village elders wanted potharajus to continue the Jogin system in the village. This system is advantageous to the village elders and also to some of the male members of the village to satisfy their lust and the extramarital life with that of the Jogins. To perpetuate the same system, potharajus should not leave their posts.
4. The organizers of Chelli Nilayam took a decision that they should provide the financial help and also implements to cultivate the land. But Jogins are unmarried and there is no support from the men who make these people as concubines. They are not responsible fathers to their children. So they requested the organization to help them. It is a demand from Jogins.

CHAPTER 9

Conclusion

Womanhood, despite being an outstanding object of adoration, has not been free from the stains of exploitation. This is the paradox of the socio-cultural milieu of the world. The struggle for women's liberation in the today's world setting, therefore, is a struggle against exploitation, tyranny and indignity.

Nowhere else in the world has any name been more sullied, any idol more tarnished, any term more misinterpreted and religion more desecrated than in the Jogin system. The origin of the system is shrouded in the mists of history; and since the practice was accepted and institutionalized, it was never questioned. Whenever epidemics struck, or whenever there was a drought or flood, it was the innocent villager who was expected to offer his first or best offspring to appease the gods.

After the girl is made a 'jogin', she becomes a whore to be used by the rich men. Herein lies a dichotomy. On the one hand, she is married to a deity and on the other she is a concubine to a rich landlord. There is no doubt it is a handiwork of the privileged who have perfected a system whereby prostitution becomes an accepted form of life. This concubinage is sometimes just for a day and sometimes for one or two years, depending upon the jogin's physical attractiveness. Moreover, it is a status symbol among the rich to have more than one mistress.

By becoming jogins, girls belonging to Mala and Madiga castes and backward classes like Goundla, Dommara and Boya communities have to satisfy the carnal desires of the rich. This obnoxious practice, a social anomaly, is as deep-rooted as untouchability. Since the practice stems from superstition, the first thing to be done is disabuse their mind of the notion of divine wrath and other false beliefs. As the girl is dedicated to the temple by dasaris, jangams, ayyavarlu or potharaju, these people should be reformed first.

It is awkward and embarrassing to talk about potharajus. These belong to the Mala community. When the villagers sacrifice a buffalo to gods, potharaju should be naked. The nerves of the buffalo are used to adorn potharaju's neck. Some parts of the buffalo's body are put into his mouth and the dung is kept in a basket which he has to carry. By following this tradition, they run the risk of contracting asthma, cancer or tuberculosis or any such disease. The bangles of potharaju's wife are broken and toe rings and mangalasutra are removed as if the potharaju might not survive. The potharaju is required to kill the sacrificial sheep or goat with one bite. This horrid thing is known as 'Gavupattu'. Sometimes, this act even leads to the death of the potharaju.

The scheduled caste girls are married to Goddess Yellamma or Pochamma and inducted into prostitution. These marriages are meant for warding off catastrophes like drought or epidemics. The child bride does not know that she is being condemned to a life of exploitation, slavery, bonded prostitution and poverty. Satiating the lust of the landlord is the last phase of her transformation into the Jogin system.

The landlord who burdened Ganga with two children in a span of a few years paid a total of Rs 200 as a token to her parents. Diseased, deprived of honour and existence as a free human being, Ganga was passed from one landlord to another only to meet a horrible death at the age of 30. While Ganga's children are begging, the landlord has taken to another jogin for pleasure and prestige. In no other part of the world is found such a horrible traditional institution where the children are dedicated to the so-called gods and goddesses and abused by men. This strange marriage to the immortal has the sanction of the priest and society as well as the families of jogins. Thus, thousands of outcaste women are vegetating as marginal women in the whole of South India except Kerala. This is a widespread paranoic paedophilia. One jogin said, "I never went to the doctor because I saw illness as a curse of Goddess Yellamma." Thus, robbed of human dignity, the young girls were made sacrificial goats. They exhibit their obedience to religion and subordination to man. The jogins, who are victims of religious bigotry and are toyed with as sex dolls by the rich people of the village, should be rescued and saved from the situation.

The task is stupendous and unless rehabilitative measures are taken, solutions to the problem will continue to remain a mirage.

The convention of 1987 held at Delhi makes the following recommendations:

(1) This programme may form an important part of the special component plan for the SCs. State government departments dealing with the welfare of the SCs and women's welfare should forthwith formulate schemes for rehabilitation of jogins from the annual plan of 1987–88 onwards. They may be treated as a specially vulnerable group for whom even the special assistance provided by the Ministry of Welfare may be utilized.

(2) The Planning Commission, the Department of Woman and Child Welfare, the Central Social Welfare Board, the All India Association of Social and Moral Hygiene, the National Institute of Social Defence and other organizations concerned may be associated with the programme of rehabilitation of jogins. Towards this end, a seminar was planned at an early date at Varni in Nizamabad district.

(3) Media, particularly television, can be the most effective channel for raising consciousness among jogins and the community at large. Eminent and committed film directors like Girish Karnad and Govind Nihilani may be approached to produce and direct a telefilm on the problem of jogins.

(4) A state-level committee may be formed for the implementation of the programme. It should be chaired by an eminent social worker like Hemalatha Lavanam and it should comprise academicians, officials and non-officials.

(5) At the district level, a joint committee of officials and non-officials should be formed for the implementation of the programme. It should be headed by a prominent social worker.

(6) This committee should be autonomous in character.

(7) The jogins in the age group of 5–14 years should be taken away from their homes and admitted to residential schools but not in their own districts. These residential schools should also admit students from other sections of the society for social integration.

(8) For jogins in the higher age-group, say 14 to 30, schemes should be drawn up for training them in various skills. The trainees

should be given stipends. After the training period is over, these women should be given financial assistance to enable them to get gainful employment.

(9) The jogins who are aged and or not in a position to undergo any training may be given special stipends of Rs 600 per month.

(10) The adult members of the families of the jogins may be given preference in selection as beneficiaries under different poverty alleviation programmes like IRDP, RLEGP, NREP. The representatives of jogins must be associated with the programmes at all levels.

(11) Women students of social work and universities must organize camps in the villages of jogins to educate them and help them in rehabilitation.

There should be counselling sessions followed by interaction with them in an effort to know what they are good at. For example, Gangamani who was given an acre of agricultural land, is a successful farmer.

"It took me a month to realize that I could choose not to be a jogin", Gangamani said when she was cultivating the field. It is heartening to know that initiations have come down considerably in the last six years, not only in Nizamabad but all over South India. While some people have become leaders, jogins in villages like Govvur, Rudrur and Chandpur villages continue to be sex workers because of abject poverty. Sobha, Syamala, Sunita and others in their 20s and early 30s continue to be in flesh trade. Some have already sold away their plots given by the government. Some work as daily wage earners in Nizamabad and solicit clients at construction sites. Sunita said, "Earlier, young and old alike would come and force them to satisfy their carnal desires", but at present the jogins are worried about HIV and, therefore, reject men who refuse to use condoms.

Even now in some circles, they do not allow people to intervene in things pertaining to their customs and traditions. Samskar chairman Lavanam says social reform needs active persuasion and passive control. Punishment is not the only answer; bringing about social change needs constant endeavour.

The real scourge is abject poverty. Though social change has come into these villages, the jogins' economic condition continues to be bad. K.H.S.S. Sundar, development activist in 'Chelli Nilayam', sees children like Swapna as harbingers of hope. He hopes that no one of the third generation will speak of jogins.

The findings given by Jogan Shankar are valid for the transformation of jogins joining the mainstream. They are:

- The evolution of the Devadasi cult can be traced to a period earlier than the entry of Aryans in India. It is a relic of Dravidian matriarchal society.
- The girl children are dedicated to Yellamma, Maisamma, Pochamma in Telangana districts; Mathamma in coastal Andhra; and Yellamma, China Obulesu and Sunkalamma in Rayalaseema. These people visit Kokatnur temple. In Karnataka 85 per cent are dedicated to Yellamma and in Maharashtra, Muralis to Khandoba; Mariammas and Thayammas in Tamil Nadu.
- All dedications were involuntary. Parents or guardians and indirectly the landlords were responsible for their dedication.
- Almost all the dedications are done at pre-puberty age.
- The practice is prevalent among the SCs and very few backward classes in all the South Indian states except Kerala.
- Priests of the Yellamma temples in Karnataka who are Lingayats, an upper caste, potharajus in Telangana and Baineedlu in coastal Andhra are responsible for tying 'tali' to the bride.
- The functional relationship of these jogins, matangis or devadasis is only symbolic and their importance is recognized during jataras and other religious festivals.

The following factors are responsible for the persistence of the cult:

- The oppressive and exploitative nature of patriarchy in Hindu hierarchy.
- Ethnological susceptibility among the members of lower castes.
- Superstitious religious beliefs, in the notions of wrath and curse of the deity.
- Economic factors: abject poverty, famines, droughts, landlessness and dependence on landlords.
- Educational backwardness: illiteracy and ignorance.
- Lure of easy money and affluence derived from prostitution in urban areas.
- Influence of old devadasis.
- Selfishness of parents and guardians.

- Extramarital sexual needs of the men of the upper castes.
- Women are generally not aware of the Devadasi (Prohibition of Dedication) Act, 1982 of Karnataka and the Devadasi (Prohibition) Act, 1988 of Andhra Pradesh.
- The police department does not seem to take these Acts seriously.
- The government's rehabilitation policy is not uniform in all the states. Moreover, a humane approach is missing in its implementation.
- Commercial attitude of some of the NGOs in implementing the rehabilitative programmes.
- Dearth of committed social workers. Persons like Lavanam and Hemalatha Lavanam in Andhra Pradesh and B.P. Patel of Vimochana in Karnataka state are extremely rare.
- Women's organizations in Karnataka have not shown much interest in these programmes.
- Lack of active cooperation of exploited devadasis to start a movement to end this oppression, exploitation and slavery.
- In order to root out this inhuman system, the following suggestions may be considered:
- Education is the vehicle through which the problem can be solved. The emancipation of women occupies a pivotal role in the social reform movements in India. For centuries, women in general lived in social bondage. They suffered because of: (i) want of social liberty, (ii) infant marriages, (iii) polygamy, (iv) enforced widowhood, (v) devadasi system, (vi) dowry system, and (vii) lack of education.
- The backwardness of women was attributed to their lack of education. It was a deep-rooted belief for centuries that women should not be educated. People feared that it would bring misfortune to families whose girls were educated. The popular belief was that female education was meant only for devadasis who had to learn the fine arts and literature and perform dances in temples on public occasions.
- Frequent anti-dedication campaigns and rallies should be organized wherever the practice is prevalent. In Andhra Pradesh, this is being done by organizations like 'Chelli Nilayam', APJVVPS, 'Duties' organization, RISE and SALT organizations. In Karnataka, 'Vimochana', the Devadasi

Rehabilitation Project and Myrada Ghataprabha and in Pune there are some social service organizations which have taken up the rehabilitation of these unfortunate women.

- The Karnataka Devadasi (Prohibition) Act, 1982 should be propagated among all people at all levels in Karnataka and the Devadasi (Prevention) Act, 1988 should be propagated among the people in Andhra Pradesh.
- Legal action within the purview of the Acts should be taken and priests like potharajus should be rehabilitated properly.
- Sympathetic treatment should be given to devadasis of the younger age group.
- Government officials and NGOs should be made responsible for stopping the initiations.
- Rehabilitation and correction centres should be started in rural areas wherever religious prostitution is prevalent. Social workers should be made in charge of those centres and the centres should be periodically inspected by the government.
- Under the rehabilitation scheme, small-scale units should be set up to enable these innocent girls to earn their livelihood through respectable and gainful employment.
- As the children of devadasis are vulnerable to the devadasi system, they should be moved to decent places and taught some skills.
- The procedure for the marriages of these people should be simplified. The government should give them incentives to lead a good life and at least one of the partners should be given employment so that they can lead a happy, dignified life. Otherwise, the marriage may prove futile, driving them back to the old pattern of life.
- A permanent office should be established in the state capital to monitor the progress in regard to the rehabilitation of jogins at various centres.
- An analytical study of SC women should be made from legal, political and economic angles at different levels.
- A research cell should be established wherever voluntary organizations are active.

The Project Director of Chelli Nilayam, K.H.S.S. Sundar, in his paper 'Jogini reform and Jogini children: Need for continuity in post-reform era' wrote how Samskar had made an entry into the field of jogins' reform movement and mentioned a few important components of the social and cultural life of jogin sisters followed by rehabilitative aspects. They are:

- Top priority to reform and rehabilitate jogins to enable them to live as human beings.
- The first generation of the reform forms the last generation of the direct victims of this social evil. Their children to some extent can breathe free air on the one hand and become indirect victims of the last generation.
- The reformed jogin has a split personality – of reform and change. Her 'changed personality' is more important for social monitoring, especially her health aspects. This gives them the much-needed 'social caring effect'.
- Any laxity in counselling programmes may prove counter-productive.
- Education and continuation of the programmes are crucial for the children of jogins.

They should be guided and encouraged to explore other avenues for self-sustenance.

Thus, the children of jogins deserve protection in terms of immunization, nutrition and primary education. They should have normal family relationships in their childhood. These girls are made to believe that even their free labour is a sacred service for the sake of their 'human consort', namely, the landlord.

The government has taken many positive steps for the rehabilitation of jogins, but a lot more needs to be done as it is a problem of not only women but also of the entire Hindu society.

Glossary

Akkammas	=	Sapta Matrikas, Seven Sisters
Arisina Honda	=	Tank of turmeric powder or bandaru
Arundhatiwada	=	Madigawada (Arundhati belongs of Madia community)
APJVVPS	=	Andhra Pradesh Jogin Vyavaslka Vyatireka Porata Sanghatama (Mahaboobnagar)
Ant-hill	=	Snake pit or the place of birth of Yellamma, Pochamma or Poleramma, the children of Siva and Parvati
Bandens	=	A division of devadasis in Goa
Baila Deiras	=	Devadasis in Goa
Bhavin	=	A devotee of the God in Goa
Booralu, Daralu, Runjalu	=	Musical instruments used in Matangi Kolupulu
Baineedlu	=	A pujari belonging to Mala caste recites the story of Yellamma
Cidi	=	A type of rope used in a jatara for Ora panduga.
Chedwas	=	A division of devadasis in Goa
Chekkiliyar	=	A category of backward classes in Tamil Nadu
Chelli Nilayam	=	An NGO where rehabilitation started in Nizamabad district. Chelli means "sister"; brother and sister relationship is brought out between jogins and other employees of the organization

Female valour	=	Courage of a woman
Dhavina	=	A woman who left the temple and settled as a prostitute
Divine prostitution	=	Religious prostitution
Dedication	=	A person is dedicated to the service of any deity
Darshan	=	Cowrie shell chain
Funeral dance	=	Dance before the corpse
Goravaiah	=	A kurama devotee of Mallanna
Gavu pattu	=	Adamant action killing a scarifying animal with bare teeth by Potharaju, the brother of the Seven Sisters
Hennu basvi	=	Basvi existed in the erstwhile state of Mysore
Hennuma duvude	=	Consummation of a basvi after puberty
Joga or Jogu	=	Begging
Jatara	=	Village festival before a deity
Jogula Bavi	=	A place where Yellamma took her bath
Jogtis	=	Devadasis in Karnataka
Jogavva	=	A devotee of Yellamma
Jogi pattam	=	Dedication ceremony of a girl by Potharaju before the village deity
Jagartha deities	=	Deities have the power to fulfil the wishes of the people and protect them in times of need
Jagaran	=	Chain breaking ceremony to bless the newly married couple in Maharashtra by Vaghya Murali
Jogaiah	=	A male person dedicated to Yellamma
Kasabi	=	Devadasis in Karnataka
Kolupulu	=	Dance in a jatara during village festival by a Matangi
Kolla	=	Valley
Kumkuma Honda	=	Tank of kumkuma powder
Landa	=	Where the leather is kept in a Madiga house where Renuka is given shelter in a Madiga house
Madisi kondavalu	=	Devadasis in Karnataka

Mailapattam	=	Consummation ceremony with the landlord after puberty of the jogin
Mariamma	=	Goddess of small pox in south India
Matangi Makkalu	=	Children of Matangi
Muni Raju	=	Giri Raj, father of Parvati
Murali	=	A devotee of Khandoba in Maharashtra
Muthu Mangalasutra	=	Used for devadasis in Karnataka
Muthu katti Kondavalu	=	Davadasis in Karnataka
NISA	=	National Institute of Social Action
Nitya Sumangali	=	A wife of the God hence, no widowhood to her
Nagna Kabandha	=	Nude girl of Indus valley civilization
Nude squatting goddess	=	Mother Goddess or Shameless goddess
Neeradi	=	A village employee one who waters wetlands
Orapanduga	=	Village festival
Potharaju	=	Brother of Seven Sisters or deities
Patam	=	Designs used during the Kolupulu of Goddess. It is called Saka
Pedda Golla	=	Head of the Yadava community. Plays a major role in Matangi system
Pinna pedda	=	Head of the dalit community in Matangi system
Public woman	=	A woman available to all men for sexual purpose
Rabildry	=	Vulgar language
RISE	=	An NGO working for Matangi rehabilitation at Tirupati
Reulinas	=	A division of Devadasis in Goa
Self-flagellation	=	Flogging the self
SSS	=	Stree Sanghatana Shakti
Samskar	=	An NGO with an aim of reformation at Vijayawada
SHG	=	Self-help Group
Sankarnagar	=	NGO in Adoni named after S.R. Sankaran
Saka	=	Drawing used in a Matangi kolupulu
Tayamma	=	Mathamma in Tamil Nadu

Tolu Billa	=	A piece of sacred leather used as a Mangalasutra which is tied to a Matangi girl
Vimochana	=	An NGO in Karnataka
Vaghya	=	A male devotee of Khandoba in Maharashtra
Xens	=	Girl initiated in the profession of devadasis
Yenu Honda	=	Tank of oil

Appendices

Appendix I

Case Studies of Religious Prostitution in Andhra Pradesh (South India)

In South India, we have the Jogin system and its counterparts such as the Basvi system in which the girl child is dedicated to a deity, be it a god or a goddess. How did this custom originate? Some of the possible theories emerging from the studies are as follows:

- The custom of dedicating girls to temples emerged as a substitute for human sacrifice to gods and goddesses to appease them for the sake of them whole community or the village.
- The Devadasi cult simply represents the licentious worship offered by people, subservient to the vested interests of the rich landlords or to satisfy the priestly class.
- This is a custom created by upper castes to exploit the lower castes. The upper castes have influenced the establishment of the system of prostitutes who are licensed to carry on their profession under the protective shield of religion. This system makes it easy for the high-caste men to have extramarital flings. This results in the destruction of the self-respect and dignity of lower caste women.

This cult is prevalent even today throughout India with some regional variations. That means it was a pan-Indian phenomenon in the past. The girls/women dedicated to deities are called jogins, matangis and basvis in Andhra Pradesh; muralis in Maharashtra; devadasis or basvis or jogatis in Karnataka; mariamma and thayamma in Tamil Nadu and bhavins in Goa. Whatever be their name, the system is a blot on society. This cult appears to be a relic of the Dravidian matriarchal system mentioned in the earlier chapters.

The author would like to present a few case studies which include different types of individual accounts of the devadasis concerned. These are not biographical accounts but empirical accounts of these women. These accounts have a great socio-cultural value and humanistic significance. A salient feature of the case studies is the common thread of illiteracy and economic backwardness coupled with blind religious superstitions. How girls are dedicated to the various gods and goddesses has already been described.

Case Studies in Nizamabad district

1. Thirty-year-old Dasari Pedda Gangamma belongs to Ganpur village in Varni taluka. Her parents dedicated her to the village deity Pochamma. The reason for the dedication was her brother's sickness. When she attained puberty, she became a prey to the lust of the village landlords. Because of her intimacy with many people, she gave birth to two children who were not legitimately fathered by anybody, although it was public knowledge who their father was. Gangamma lost her youth, her health and everything and no one came to her rescue. She worked as a coolie to feed her two children.
2. Kanchapati Poshavva was dedicated to Pochamma even before she was born. When her mother was pregnant she had fallen ill and had vowed that if she was blessed with a female child, she would dedicate it to the goddess. She had taken the vow on the advice of a soothsayer. Accordingly, when the child was born she was dedicated to the goddess. And when the girl grew up, traditional dancing skills were imparted to her. Poshavva became a good dancer and the real Dasi of the village elders, i.e., the upper caste men. Her attractive physical appearance prompted the village to exploit her joginhood.
3. Malakamma Kamavva of Bhamma Undevalli in Beerkur mandal fell sick when she was just three months old. Immediately, her mother took her to a Pochamma temple and dedicated her to the deity. Suddenly, the child got well. When she attained puberty, she was inducted into prostitution. She then became the mistress or the 'kept woman' of one Sailu and gave birth to two children. On Sailu's death, Kamavva returned to abject poverty.
4. Another unfortunate story is that of Gyni Bhoolakshmi of Rudrur village in Varni mandal. Her selfish parents dedicated her as a jogin. Bhoolakshmi was in love with a man called Raju and wanted to marry him against the tradition of the Jogin system. Despite the opposition from her parents and society, she became intimate with Raju. Consequently, Bhoolakshmi became pregnant and they both moved to another village. Her bad time started with the child's birth when Raju left her. Bhoolakshmi went back to her old profession to rear her child.
5. In the case of Posani Gopu of Govuru village, it was an epidemic that resulted in her becoming a jogin. Gopu was born in a Harijan family and lost her mother when she was just two years old. As joginhood was prevalent in untouchable families, she never knew who her father

was. When an epidemic struck the village, the village elders thought that the only solution lay in dedicating Gopu to the village deity. She was exploited not only by the rich landlords of the village but also by men of her own caste. She gave birth to three children. Gopu was destined to live the rest of her life on the coins thrown at her when she was performing a funeral dance or when she was begging. Strictly speaking, jogins' children should be treated as a casteless community but they revert to the lowest caste by social compulsion.

6. Many young Harijan girls were inducted into 'Joginhood' during natural calamities and epidemics. Neeradi Lakshmi was nine years old when one day, the cattle in her village were hit by an epidemic and three animals died. As soon as this news spread, the so-called elders met and decided to dedicate one girl as 'jogin' to Pochamma. The choice fell on Lakshmi for various reasons. Her parents were poor untouchables steeped in blind beliefs and the 'upper caste' elders expected very little resistance from them. Once the decision was taken by the elders, Lakshmi's parents fell at their feet entreating them to change the decision. But their pleas were ignored.

   When Lakshmi attained puberty, she became the common property of the village and as a jogin, she never had to bear the brunt of untouchability. As she led the life of a jogin, Lakshmi's beauty and health faded. She gave birth to a number of children, and again became an outcaste and had to resort to begging.

7. A girl of six years by name Ganga underwent the marriage ceremony of a jogin. The child-bride in her innocence did not know that she was being condemned to a life of exploitation, slavery, bonded prostitution and poverty.

   She was dressed and decorated like a bride. A large number of Madigas sat in the marriage pandal which was decked with flowers and mango leaves. Some drank arrack and some danced. Only one person was missing – the bridegroom. Potharaju, the master of ceremonies, filled in for him and tied around the girl's neck a Mangalasutra or tali made of leather.

   When Ganga became 14 year old, Dora, the local landlord, went to her hut one night and took her away. Satiating the lust of the landlord was the last phase of her transformation into a 'jogin'. The landlord paid Rs 200 to her parents and burdened Ganga with two children in a span of a few years. Diseased, deprived of honour and freedom Ganga, was passed from one landlord to another only to meet a harrowing death at the age of 30. Ganga's children took to begging and the landlord took to another jogin for pleasure and prestige.

   Ganga's is not an isolated case. There are thousands of Gangas in South India condemned to the infamous life of jogins or jogatis. The young jogin after her marriage to the goddess is called 'Nitya

Sumangali'. This is her chance to become the mistress of the rich village landlord or she may have to go to all and sundry to keep her body and soul together.

8. It is festival time for the people of Chandur village. There is a 'Pondal' and a goat is tied to it with a garland in its neck – the poor thing looks proud of the attention bestowed on it. The priest, 'Potharaju', strides in with a scary whip in his hand and lashes himself to drum beats.

   Seventeen-year-old Bhagirathi is about to be made a jogin. Potharaju finishes drinking toddy and starts performing his rites and becomes instrumental in making Bhagirathi the property of the villagers to satisfy their sexual needs. Despite the social workers trying hard to stop the marriage, the marriage took place and the girl was taken away into the village head's room.

9. Balavva is young and only till the previous day she used to be called to dance in front of corpses as is the custom in Telangana areas. When the news of the death of a prominent personality in the neighbouring village reached Ballavva, she was attending an adult education class. She refused to accompany the callers.

   The village panchayat chastised her. She hit back: "If I go to work, I get a few rupees. If I dance in front of a corpse, all that I get is a bottle of 'kallu' (toddy), and a few paise. Why should I go there?"

   In rural areas, people are victims of elders' abhorrent practices. "And so, we made her a jogin so that we could get a few rupees to live," said her parents. That is the way how parents look at their girl's future!

   When the girl attains puberty, the village head sleeps with her first. She is paid the 'princely' sum of Rs 116 and forced into prostitution.

10. Anumadi Sydavva of Chunduru village was excommunicated by the village elders as she refused to take narcotics and "dance before the dead bodies" as a jogin. She migrated to another village, Bodhan. There she came in contact with one Tulasi Ram, a band boy who was attracted to her and wanted to marry her.

    NISA, Hyderabad took the initiative of getting them married. The marriage was solemnized in the presence of the then Governor of Andhra Pradesh, Kumudben Joshi, in January 1987 at Raj Bhavan in Hyderabad.

    Pandle Anjali of Sangam was a volunteer who fought against the Jogin system. After her dedication to Yellamma by her parents, Anjali refused to be inducted into the Jogin system. Today, she is one of the most vocal among the voluntary workers of the Chelli Nilayam organization. Like her, Malakamma Kamavva also rebelled against the system. Even as a jogin, she refused to dance at funerals and consume intoxicants. She saved many girls from becoming jogins.

    During the interaction with the jogins in Chunduru and the neighbouring villages, the author asked a jogin, Yellamma why did she become a jogin. Yellamma answered, "What do I know? Do I remember all that happened when I was so young?" To the question, who was the first male to contact her, Yellamma said, "That also I do not remember. All I know is that I have to serve them, otherwise the goddess will be angry". Another jogin, Sanamma, was asked if she refused to dance in front of the corpses, won't she be doing something against the rule of the village; Sanamma replied, "What do I care? I do not want to drink toddy and dance." A potharaju said, "Born into the profession, these girls have to carry on the tradition".

11. Thokala Muthyamma, a jogin, aged about 25 years belongs to Badguna village of Nandipet mandal. She was the only female child in her family and loved by every member of the family. This deep affection prevented her from going. Her childhood was full of joy. When Muthyamma grew up, she did not know that she had been dedicated to a goddess. One day Samskar members went to Badguna to offer a fixed deposit of Rs 10,000 to each jogin. It was then that for the first time she learnt she had been made a jogin. She started abusing the Samskar brothers saying, "Why have you come to our house to give the money? Go away." She also started fighting with her family members. She would abuse anyone who tried to speak to her. Her parents told her, "We dedicated you to the goddess when you were ill and about to die." She shouted at her parents, "You should have allowed me to die, instead of dedicating me." People in the village thought that Muthyamma had gone mad and advised her parents to take her to the hospital. She replied, "You people have gone mad. You don't have brains at all; you do all meaningless practices and say that I have become mad." Muthyamma decided to free herself from the stranglehold of the system.

    Days passed and Muthyamma was engaged in beedi-making along with other women of the village. One day she saw a boy crying. She asked him why he was crying. The boy replied, "I was beaten by my school teacher for not revealing my father's name." This boy was the son of a jogin who was Muthyamma's colleague in the beedi factory. This incident made Muthyamma think, "why is the society playing with the lives of some people in the village. What wrong have they committed? Why does such a system exist?" With such thoughts, she visited Samskar's "Chelli Nilayam" and met mother Hemalatha. Muthyamma found a comforting, consoling and helping friend and above all an understanding mother, who understood her pain and agony. The 'mother' gave her a small job in Chelli Nilayam and told her to stay in Chelli Nilayam. Since then Muthyamma has been living there.

    Some days later, her parents and brother decided to dedicate her niece (brother's daughter) who was blind. Muthyamma's brother came to her to take her opinion. There itself, she scolded her brother, went home and abused her parents for trying to make the same mistake again. She took her niece to hospital for treatment. Her niece is not blind anymore. Muthyamma's family members are happy.

Now, Muthyamma is a free woman and is treated with respect in society. For the past three years, she has been working at Samskar's Chelli Nilayam on a salary of Rs 3,000 a month. Now she is altogether a different woman, with a bright future ahead.

12. Erupula Yadamma of Tandur village in Nagireddypet mandal is a jogin aged about 30 years. Her daughter is studying in the fourth standard in Samskar Ashram School at Varni. Her mother is also a jogin. During festivals and at funerals both used to dance and beg in villages. Whenever elders of the village called them, they would go. This continued for some years. Samskar has changed them completely through awareness and counselling.

    The change was good, but sustenance of the family became difficult as there was no one to earn. This spurred Yadamma to take a bold step. She decided to approach Samskar and ask for financial assistance to start a general store or a bangle store. Samskar agreed and gave her Rs 15,000 to open a bangle store. The cluster manager personally took her to Nizamabad and bought her all the items needed for the shop. The shop was opened on Sunday, 28 April 2002. She has been managing the shop properly and earning Rs 50 per day on an average since then. She is thinking of developing her bangle store. Yadamma, once a helpless woman, is now economically independent and leading a normal and respectable life. "All this is because of the help of Samskar," says Yadamma.

13. Pulinte Devapala, a jogin of Komangpalli in Velpur mandal, aged about 30, belongs to a scheduled caste. When she was still a child, her father made her a jogin thinking that she would look after him in his old age. Even villagers encouraged Devapala's father saying "you don't have male children to look after you". Days passed, and Devapala was forced to stay with a man called Parthy Balaiah. Within a year, Balaiah left for Dubai and Devapala gave birth to a baby girl. Some days later, Devapala was again forced to stay with another man called D. Rajanna. She gave birth to two more girls. Both men who fathered these children had promised to help Devapala but deceived her. Devapala faced many hardships in life.

    Samskar met Devapala and created awareness with regard to her past, present and future life, and advised her to think of her children's future. Samskar also advised her to take up vegetable-vending and gave her financial assistance for the purpose. Devapala started selling vegetables and earns Rs 100 to Rs 150 per day on an average. She sells vegetables in three nearby villages, going on foot. Seeing her enthusiasm, Samskar helped her by providing her with a push-cart.

Devapala says, "I have saved a considerable amount and villagers come to me for financial help. Now I am leading a respectable life." She says that thanks to the counselling by Samskar, she is bold enough to face any hardship and problem. She narrated an incident: "One day it so happened that a man deliberately dashed against me thinking that I was a jogin. I just caught hold of him and slapped him. Since then, people started respecting me more. I am grateful to Samskar for helping me to come out of the Jogin system and do vegetable-vending," she says.

14. Nagaram Savithri, a jogin of Akbar Nagar village of Varni mandal, aged about 35 years, belongs to a scheduled caste. Those were the initial days of jogin reformation by Samskar and the Jogin system was normal and no one considered it an evil practice. Indeed, people were afraid to speak against the system or practice, because it was being done in the name of the goddess. Samskar started its reformation work in Akbar Nagar. Its representatives met Savithri and persuaded her to break away from the bondage. A man called Pedda Gangaram of Vijayawada came forward to marry her. Samskar was happy with his response and performed the marriage. For Pedda Gangaram, who also belongs to a scheduled caste, it was a second marriage. This was the first marriage performed by Samskar as a part of its reformation work in Nizamabad district.

    To quote Savithri, "My husband comes from the non-Jogin cult. We are happy with this life. Before marriage, my life was filled with darkness. Samskar has brought light into my life. Now I boldly say, I am leading a respectable family life. Samskar has helped me with building material worth of Rs 8,000 to build a house, and one acre of agricultural land. I am grateful to them."

15. Devara Chinnamma of Rudrur village in Varni mandal is aged about 45 years and belongs to the fishermen community, a backward class. When she was still a child, her parents dedicated her to the local goddess. Now she has two daughters, both studying. The elder one has completed the 10th class and the second is in the 4th. Chinnamma is illiterate and says, "In those days, my parents did not send me to school."

    Devara Chinnamma's situation was better than that of other jogin sisters. She says, "The entry of Samskar has changed the picture of jogin completely. Earlier, a jogin was looked upon as public property but now jogins are seen as sisters and fellow human beings. It is because of Samskar that we are leading a normal life like others. Now people address us as sisters and treat us as human beings. Our economic condition has improved and it is more secure. More importantly, I have been elected as Gram Panchayat ward member. This itself shows that we are in the mainstream and society is accepting us."

16. Thirty-year-old Mamidi Savithri, also of Rudrur village in Varni mandal, belongs to a scheduled caste and was made a jogin in her childhood. With the awareness created by Samskar, Savithri understood the evils of the Jogin system and decided not to follow the system any more. Samskar gave her one acre of agricultural land (government land).

    Meanwhile, she had developed friendship with a person called Prabhakar. Savithri informed "mother" at Chelli Nilayam of her friendship with Prabhakar. Mother suggested that she should marry him. Prabhakar was happy with this idea, and agreed to marry Savithri. With the support of Samskar and with the mother's blessings, Savithri and Prabhakar got married. Savithri, once a jogin, is now leading a normal married life. She says, "I am happy now that I am married. As a jogin, I didn't have any hope of a good future. The marriage has brought hope into my life and given me a social status." She further says, "I am thankful to Mother, brothers and all Samskar people. It is because of them that my life has been restored, I am no more a jogin but a normal married woman in the mainstream of society."

17. Siriga Balamani is wife of Raju, Saloor Village, Bodhan Mandal. In Saloor village on 18 April 2006, Balamani danced before a corpse. This news spread among the sisters and immediately they informed the field officer who went to the village and met her and spoke to the people gathered in front of Jangam Gangadhar's house.

    Siriga Balamani has two daughters. The elder daughter Roja and the second daughter Savitri are studying in V and III class, respectively. Four staff members – M. Kistaiah, Ramesh, R.K. Marni and Srinivasa Goud – left for that village and went to Gangadhar's house. Tents had been put up. Women were there with the corpse. Then four people brought Balamani in a jeep. She said she had been forced to drink and dance. Though she told the villagers that she was sorry, the whole village wanted to execute Balamani and Jangam Gangadhar. But, the Samskar people did not allow it.

    If Samskar volunteers had not intervened, there would have been great unrest in the village – the SCs and BCs would have clashed, the wife and husband would have got separated and new problems would have arisen.

    Subsequently, Balamani married Raju, a band master. Samskar gave them one acre of land and built a house for them. Samskar involved Balamani in all its welfare activities.

18. Another case study relates to Potti Balamani who lived with Salim but there were differences between them.

    Potti Balamani's daughter Ganrama belongs to Pitla village. In her 6th year, she was made a jogin. When she was 13, she was married to someone in Turkapalli village. That man had another wife and there used to be clashes between them and therefore she left him. Her brother died from drowning and the people blamed the family for it. Ganrama decided to continue her life as a jogin. Her mother, meanwhile, had sexual relations with another man who deserted her after she had lived with him for two years.

Balamani and Salim started living together without marrying. They were blessed with a baby girl, who is now going to school. They started a brick-making unit. After some time, Balamani's family members came to know that Salim had a wife and an affair with a Harijan girl. When Balamani questioned Salim, he said he was a man and could afford to have relations with as many women as he liked. Infuriated by this reply, Balamani thrashed Salim and this became a big issue between Harijan and Muslim families. The two parties met at a mosque. All agreed that Salim was wrong in having relations with a Harijan girl and compelled him to marry her. They also told him to give Balamani Rs 1,600 every month – Rs 600 for her maintenance and Rs 1,000 for the marriage of her daughter.

The village people blamed Balamani saying that her character was not good and asked her family members to excommunicate her. They paid Rs 3,000 to the Panchayat. Later, Balamani's mother died under Salim's tractor. Salim agreed to give her Rs 65,000 as compensation and gave her Rs 7,500 as the first instalment. He sold his tractor and became a pauper. Balamani is now a daily wage-earner. In 1998, Salim again deserted Balamani. Balamani claimed money for her maintenance. Salim accepted that and asked for some time to give that money.

19. Ramalalavva's first daughter was made a jogin on 4 June 1999 at Renjal village. Samskar activists went to Renjal and enquired about it.

    Ramalalavva is the daughter of Balaiah and she has two daughters, Pallevva and Nagamma. Pallevva is also known as Renuka. Renuka was made a jogin in Viranna Gutta. For the initiation ceremony, she was dressed as a bride and given finger rings. Ramalalavva was fined Rs 500 and Balaiah took away the finger rings and mangalasutra from Renuka.

20. When Mandalal Parvathi Raju of Chepur village in Armoor mandal was five years old, she was taken to Vemulawada and dedicated to the Rajarajeswara temple there. At that time, her parents were in Bombay. Her father had lost his eyesight. His regaining the sight was the reason for her dedication to the temple.

21. Baddenna had a daughter, aged 18 years. He believed that she was a gift from his family deity "Baddedamma". He therefore wanted to dedicate her to the deity and borrowed Rs 3,000 for the ceremony. He requested Digambar to perform the initiation ceremony. Digambar, influenced by Samskar, declined and informed the organization. Samskar volunteers persuaded Baddenna to drop the idea.

22. Harika was a student of 4th class. She was the daughter of Bombayu Sayulu Koni Raju. Their four other children had died and the couple had taken a vow that they would dedicate Harika to the Rajarajeswar temple of Vemulawada.

    Sayulu had gone to Muscat and had come to India for Sivaratri. His whole family went to Vemulawada and took a house on rent. On the morning of Sivaratri, they went to the temple with Harika and performed puja and with the help of Jangams, and they made her a jogin. Devathi Laxman tied tali to Harika to signify Harika becoming a jogin. Everybody fasted that day. On returning to their village, they arranged a feast for the whole village. Everybody participated in that feast including the deputy sarpanch. Thereafter, Bombayu Sayulu left for Muscat.

23. Pushpa belongs to Sirpur village. She was sick in her childhood. Her parents had then taken a vow that they would dedicate her to Goddess Chinnamma if she survived. When Pushpa was 18 years old, her parents started looking for a bridegroom for her. Meanwhile, Pushpa again fell ill. Her grandmother thought the cause of her illness was non-fulfilment of the vow to the goddess. She insisted that she be made a jogin. Accordingly, she was taken to Mudukapalli village and the purohit tied a tali to her and she was made a jogin.

24. J. Padma, aged 32, was made a jogin in her childhood. She told the volunteers what the jogins had to go through before the advent of Samskar. The jogins had to dance during Ora Panduga and at funerals. They would beg at harvest time. But what they got was not sufficient for their needs.

    After Samskar told them how their superstitions had destroyed their self-respect, they realized their mistakes and decided to educate their children. Thanks to Samskar's intervention, they are leading a respectable life.

    At present, Padma is sharing her life with a Muslim who is working in the forest department. Her two daughters are going to school.

25. Bhumavva was the daughter of Parvaiah of Yellareddy village of Yellareddy mandal. Many people had left this village but this family did not. Somebody set fire to her house when they had all gone out to work. She informed Varni office of Samskar of this incident. The Cluster Manager went there and examined the situation and gave her Rs 4,000 on behalf of Samskar.

26. Laxmi was Gajjara Bhagiratha's sister. They belonged to Chikli. In 1994, one Gangaram came from Nanded. Laxmi and Gangaram lived together. Gangaram told Laxmi's mother that he wanted to be an in-house son-in-law (illarikam). Bhagiratha wanted to arrange their marriage. Meanwhile, Laxmi became pregnant and some months later

Gangaram deserted her. A male child was born to her. Bhagiratha went to the Samskar office.

27. Mugalavva, daughter of Kasubai, belongs to Komulancha village of Nizamsagar mandal. She has two sons and one daughter. The daughter discontinued her studies after the seventh class. The elder son is married. They don't have a pucca house. Mugalavva goes to work as a coolie everyday. When coolie work is not available, she and her son catch 20 kg of fish and sell it in the market.

    They did not have good nets and they could not afford plastic nets. So, the Cluster coordinator requested Samskar to help her financially.

28. Pushpa is a beautiful girl. Until she was 10, like all other girls, she went to school and played with her mates. Suddenly, her father fell ill. His condition started deteriorating. Pushpa's mother and other relatives decided to dedicate the 10-year-old Pushpa to Goddess Yellamma hoping that Pushpa's father would recover.

Case Studies of Mahaboobnagar District

Mahaboobnagar is a backward district. Jogins revealed their heart-rending events to the social workers. If these girls went to school against the will of the villagers, other students as well as the teachers harassed them by asking questions such as "who is your father?" In Bairamkonda village, the headmaster refused to give transfer certificate to the children of jogins on the ground that their father's name had not been mentioned.

Recently, the Supreme Court gave the verdict in mothers' favour. Social service organizations especially insisted that children of jogins be allowed to mention their mother's name, instead of father's or God's. However, the tradition is deep-rooted in remote, backward areas of the state.

(1) Hajamma's experiences: Here is an account of Hajamma in her own words:

"I am Hajamma. I belong to the Madiga community, a dalit community in India. We follow the ritual of dedicating girls to Goddess Yellamma in our community. A girl so dedicated is ritually a goddess, but lives a life lower than other dalits or any other human being. My story is the story of thousands of dalit women dedicated as 'devadasi/jogin' – the handmaid of Gods."

"I joined the village school thanks to the keen interest and efforts of a local dalit teacher but dropped out when I was in Grade VI. When I was 11 years old and had not attained puberty, all of a sudden, for reasons unknown to me, there was talk of dedicating me as a jogin. Within a week, everything was decided and arranged. The landlord gave Rs 5,000 towards the expenses."

"A jogin's marriage is a formality. It does not matter whom she is married to. It is a passage which allows her to be used by anyone for sexual enjoyment. The man who visits her, however, has no obligation either to her or to her children. He does not accept the children as his. There is no one to question him if he ill-treats her, comes home drunk at any time of day or night, and does not give her any money."

"They asked an old man to marry me, but he refused saying his daughter was studying in my class. Another one also refused. Finally my mother's brother's son Sankarappa agreed to marry me. He was already married and had three children."

"An old jogin, close to my family, supported me when I refused to be made a jogin. I had neither the knowledge nor the courage to stand up against my family and village. But I refused to be made a jogin in the temple, as it places severe restrictions on me. Finally I was made a jogin in our home."

"The man who marries the jogin has the right of the first night with her. Shankarappa did not, however, insist on this. But he was goaded by others in my village to exercise his right. One night he tried but I pleaded with him not to have sex with me. Next day, he left the village."

"As a young girl, I remember picking up quarrels with many men in the village. From old to young, from dalits to upper castes, they would come to our house, saying they would give me a bag of paddy, half a kilogram of silver and clothes if I agreed to have them for the nights. While I did not understand what they meant, I was hurt at being singled out for this humiliation among other girls of my age."

"When I was about 18 years old, I studied Intermediate in our village. As marrying a jogin was not acceptable, we ran to Maharashtra to settle there. But the harsh reality would catch up with us – that I am a jogin, that I am already married to another man, that I am a keep for Lakshmaiah."

"Every time we visited our village, the people would hold a meeting to fine us. I wanted to marry and live with my husband but it became impossible for me. I was pregnant and had a son. There was tremendous pressure from Lakshmaiah's kin that he marry someone else as they believed that any man living permanently like a husband with a jogin would die. At one point of time I agreed to let go Lakshmaiah to marry some other woman."

A jogin's life ends when she is about 35 years old. Her health fails and she has no means of support as no one would go to her to help her out. Many end up as prostitutes, selling their bodies for less than Rs 10 a day or go to the red-light areas of our cities.

While a jogin learns to face these problems, it is her children who are hit hard as they have no rightful father. At school, as they do not fill up the form requiring them to mention the father's name, they become the butt of taunts and sarcastic remarks. This pains them beyond words.

While the system has been legally abolished, the practice persists. Hajamma's life began with sorrow and continued to be sorrowful. But, she did not lose her courage. She joined an NGO, Andhra Pradesh Jogin

Vyatireka Vyavastha Porata Samiti (APJVVPS) and is now a leader. She told her mother that she would not like to perform 'trance dance' or beg for the basic needs of life.

Participating in the Durban conference she argued against the Jogin system. In the Geneva conference she said, "If we are not there, the deity has no money." She married someone she was in love with. She attended conferences at Mumbai, Hyderabad, and other places. When she was asked whether Jogin practices were going on, she said, "they are still going on secretly. The person who tied the tali to me should divorce his wife and live with me".

(2) K. Satyamma's experiences: Jogin Kantipapa Satyamma, aged 40, of Perapalli village in Narayanpet mandal, belongs to a backward community. She has two daughters and three sons – Ambamma, 20, and Renuka, 11, is in the 5th standard, Balraj, 18 (coolie) studied up to 5th standard, Krishnaiah, 13, is in the 8th standard and Parushuram, 7 years, 1st standard. Satyamma does not own any piece of land.

Satyamma's family depends upon daily wages for livelihood. Satyamma works as a coolie. In a month she gets work for 10-15 days. She and her children are dependent on these earnings. They were leading a deplorable life. She was in such a state that she could not afford to buy rice from the fair price shop.

She approached an APJVVPS committee member and took a loan of Rs 20,000 from a bank (subsidy Rs 10,000, loan Rs 10,000) under the Income Generation Scheme. With the loan amount, she bought a chilly-grinding machine. This helped her earn Rs 70 to Rs 80 per day. She charges Rs 10 per kg. Her financial position steadily improved and she was able to repay the bank loan. She said, "I am glad to say that I can afford to give proper education to my children. We are leading a good life and also planning to set up a tea-stall."

Matammas

(1) Let me see the smile of my sisters ...

Venkatamma, a child matha, is from Abbabatlapalle in Srikalahasti mandal. She is the elder child in her house, she has one younger brother.

Her parents are agricultural labourers. She studied up to the 2nd standard in her village, and stopped going to school due to teasing by other children as Matamma. In a survey by a social worker, she was identified as Child Mata, and advised to join a school. Accordingly, she sought admission in the 3rd standard. When she was in the 4th standard, her mother fell ill and to take care of her she again discontinued her studies. She remained one year in the house. One day, her maternal uncle offered to marry her. Even though she expressed herself against the offer, her parents agreed to it.

On God's marriage festival at Srikalahasti, without informing the school authorities, her parents performed her marriage to her mother's brother, Subrahmanyam, an illiterate farmer. For some time, he maintained normal relations with her. Later, he started scolding and beating her. One day, her mother went to Subramanyam's house and took her back to her house.

Venkatamma was thus separated from her husband in just 8 months after marriage. As she had been made a Mata when still very young, she was robbed of the joys of childhood and made to undergo many bad experiences. She said, "Today I am telling each and every sister in my school about my life experiences, thereby helping the innocent children understand the evil of child marriage. I am telling the parents that they should not marry their daughters at an early age." Venkatamma participated in a protest against child marriages in Srikalahasti with RISE and SSS teams."

She said, "Now, I am studying in the 5th standard in MPLC School, and also learning music. God has given me a sweet voice. My aim is to become a good singer so that I may share sweet tunes and melodious songs with my hapless sisters and other oppressed women."

(2) ***By early marriage, I lost the chance to study***

"I am Saroja, 18 years old. When I was a child, as I was afflicted with chickenpox, my parents dedicated me to Goddess Matamma. Thus, I am a child Mata. My father expired in my childhood and my mother started living with another man who was younger to her. I studied upto the 5th standard and then quit school as the other children teased and taunted me for being a matamma. In a 1999 survey, social workers identified me and admitted me to MPLC School in the 6th standard. After passing the 10th standard with the financial support of RISE, I joined the nearby Vadalamalapet Junior College. I live with my mother. When my mother was not around, my stepfather used to misbehave. I didn't know how to tackle this problem and I didn't tell anyone about it. Fortunately, I met Munuswamy, my neighbour, and we started loving each other and married secretly. But elders from both sides disregarded our marriage. Subsequently, caste leaders and youth leaders went to our college and met the Director. After that, RISE Director organized our marriage in the bridegroom's house."

"I am living in my husband's house with my in-laws. My father-in-law is the only earning member, and all others are depending on him. My husband is not employed. Since my marriage, I have been facing so many problems from my in-laws. They do not allow me to participate in ceremonies and festivals. Because I am a Mata, they have restricted my participation in religious rituals."

"Now I want to continue my studies. My family members are not cooperating with me. They are treating me as a servant. Even though life is full of ups and downs, I am determined to complete my education. I often tell my dalit sisters and friends that marriage will curb their educational opportunities. So, they should be careful."

(3) ***Timely helping hand ...***

"I am Prasanthi (14) studying in the 9th class in MPLC School. I participate in all the activities conducted by the school. My aim is to become a nurse because service to man is service to God. With this motto, I am studying hard."

"I tell you briefly about my family. My mother died when I was a child and my father married a second time. I have two brothers and one step-sister. Social workers identified me as a child Mata and admitted me to school in 1999 in the 4th class."

"When I was preparing for the annual examinations on February 25th, 2005 my paternal aunt came to the school and said that my father was ill and wanted to see me immediately. Taking permission from the headmistress for 3 days, I went to my village with my aunt and was shocked to hear that my marriage had been fixed with my paternal aunt's son on March 8 2005 (International Women's Day). They had even distributed wedding cards."

"I strongly opposed the marriage. But my father started blackmailing me emotionally, saying if I refused to marry he would commit suicide. My relatives and others in the village forced me to marry. Fortunately, for me, on the day of my scheduled wedding in March 2005, Madam sent a watchman to my village to find out why I had not been attending school. The watchman saw the situation and he asked me the details and immediately telephoned the school and gave information about my marriage. At that time, all my relatives gathered in my house. Feast was ready, clothes and other jewellery had been purchased. In the evening, we were to leave for Srikalahasti, which is famous for mass marriages on the eve of God's own marriage."

"At 12.30 pm on March 8 2005, suddenly a four-wheeler stopped in front of my house. I saw Madam Suseela, Project Co-ordinating Officer (PCO) and Vijayalakshmi, social worker rushing to my house with a big team. They pushed me into the vehicle, despite the relatives and some villagers trying to prevent them from taking me away. Suseela Madam shouted at my father and my aunt and warned them that she would file a police complaint against child marriage. Scared of stopping my marriage, the villagers tried to drag me out. My aunt who sat in the vehicle came with us to Tirupati. PCO Madam, headmistress and social worker had given a police complaint in women's police station, Tirupati. We went to MPLC School at 6.00 pm. At 8.00 pm, some of my relatives, Sarpanch (village head) and villagers came to school but the watchman not only did not allow them in but also scolded and sent them back."

"The social worker and headmistress advised my parents and my aunt about the disadvantages of child marriages and advantages of education. Now, I am studying happily. Timely help saved my life. My sincere thanks to them. Now I am leading a peaceful life which justifies my name (Prasanthi means very peaceful)."

(4) ***Failures taught me how to achieve success ...***

"I am Haritha (17), studying plus two, higher secondary education in Science group (Biology, Physics, Chemistry). My aim is to become a doctor. I am working hard to reach my goal. My parents are daily-wage earners. We are three siblings. I am the eldest one. My father is a drunkard. When I was in the 9th standard, i.e., in pre-puberty age, I was married to my maternal uncle on Nov 10 2001. I was not prepared mentally and physically for the marriage. Hence, I faced many problems with my in-laws, though they are my grandparents. My husband is a tailor by profession. He had all bad habits. He used to drink and beat me every day. He suspected me whenever I talked with men in the village. My grandparents also would scold me daily saying that I was not cooking well. Sick of all this, one day I attempted to commit suicide by taking sleeping pills. My parents then took me back to Tirupati. But I told them that I wanted divorce and want to be freed from my husband's clutches and that I wanted to continue my studies. Appreciating my predicament, my parents admitted me to the MPLC School in the 10th standard. I got second division in the 10th standard examination. RISE Director admitted me to a college and RISE is giving financial support for my studies, and providing accommodation in hostel. I participated in sports and was selected as a member of the zonal cricket team. I was also included in the district kho-kho team."

"I got an opportunity to participate in inter-district games competition. Though we lost, I had the satisfaction of meeting several players. Once a victim, I am now recognized as a good pupil, player and person."

Case – 1

One landless agricultural family lost four children due to some disease. They attributed the deaths to the wrath of Goddess Yellamma and dedicated the next girl when she was just two years old to Yellamma of Kokatnur. The girl's paternal aunts were also devadasis.

Mangalasutra was tied to her by a rich, middle-aged Lingayat of a neighbouring village. She lived with him for two years. He then deserted her but gave her clothes, a bag of jowar, but never any money. It, thus, became her responsibility to take care of her parents and other children. "I thus felt forced to become a prostitute", she said.

Because of her good looks and pleasant manners, she attracted a number of persons and became rich and bought five acres of land. She sent her brother to the college, and deposited Rs 10,000 in the local Grameena

Bank. She had only one son whom she wanted to see as an officer. She expressed her opinion that the government should come forward to help these women by launching income-generating schemes. She thought that would solve the problem.

Case – 2

An eight-year-old girl had a skin disease. Her parents thought that it was due to the wrath of their family deity Yellamma. To appease the goddess, they dedicated the girl to Yellamma at Soundatti when she was 12. A Lingayat landlord deflowered her. For a few days, she maintained her relations with him and later she took to other men. As she was attractive, even Kulkarnis and Patils went to her. She earned considerable wealth and her parents and brothers enjoyed the property. They took to vices and became extravagant. When she was 40 years old, she lost all property and adopted a girl from a poor family. That girl was 8 years old. She was also dedicated to Yellamma.

Basvi worships the goddess. Once in a week, she goes to five houses for customary begging. She does not even have a proper house. She was a beneficiary of the spinning scheme under which she was given employment in a training-cum-production unit for six months and a stipend. However, due to unavoidable circumstances this work was discontinued.

The basvi came to know about the Devadasi Act. She expressed her willingness to discontinue the temple service and wanted to educate her children and lead a decent life.

Case – 3

Another basvi belonged to the Madiga community. She was an illiterate woman, dedicated to Yellamma at the tender age of 9 years. The initiation ceremony took place on a Tuesday. Bayannayana officiated at the function and tied the mangalasutra around her neck.

She started living as a concubine to her maternal uncle, an agriculturist. She begot one male and two female children. The children were educated well. The basvi is unhappy with her life. She wanted to arrange the marriages of her daughters. She availed herself of the government's welfare measures.

Case – 4

Interestingly, some basvis seem to be happy with their lot. For instance, a basvi of Adoni belonging to the Mala Dasari community was dedicated to Vrukunda Veeranna.

She is patronized by one person. She seldom goes for customary begging. She is a casual labourer and the government sanctioned a house for her. She learnt tailoring in six months during which period she was paid a stipend. She is happy with the dispensation.

Case – 5

A woman's life is often a saga of sacrifice either for herself or for her family. A basvi of Alur was dedicated to Tikkalakshmamma, a woman saint at Adoni, at the age of 11 years to ward off her elder brother's illness. She has one elder brother and two sisters, one elder and the other younger, both married. Her sister's husband tied the tali to her. This basvi lives with her elder sister's husband who ekes out his livelihood by working as a labourer. She does customary begging every now and then.

Case – 6

In some cases, many factors are responsible for the dedication of girls as basvis. Poverty, patriarchy, customs and traditions, superstitions and absence of a male heir in the family are responsible for a family making a girl a basvi.

In one case, a 10-year-old was dedicated to Mallayya. The marriage badge was tied to this girl by the chief functionary known as Goravayya. At the time of her initiation, a Muslim patron gave her Rs 300, a saree and other gifts.

This basvi lived with her Muslim paramour for four years and had children. After that, another Muslim took her for a concubine. The result was the birth of six more children. This basvi started begging for five days in a week and earned Rs 10 as wages everyday.

Case – 7

Another girl belonging to the Madiga community was dedicated to Pedda Uligamma at the age of seven years. Her elder sister was also made a basvi. Absence of male issues in the family was the root cause of making these two girls basvis.

The second girl was made a basvi in the Jatara of Uligamma. Bayannayana was the chief official who tied the mangalasutra on behalf of Uligamma. Her maternal uncle, a farm labourer, became her paramour. She participates in the Jatara of Uligamma. Customary begging was compulsory for her. She worked in a cotton-ginning factory at Adoni for six months and also sold firewood to supplement her income. Later, she became disabled due to an accident.

Her sixth daughter did not go to school because of poverty and her mother's physical disability. She made one of her daughters a basvi despite being aware of the Act of 1988.

Case – 8

This is an account of a basvi of Madiga caste. Daughter of a basvi of Alur, this girl was dedicated to her family God Anjaneya, at her house. Dasariah officiated at the function and tied the tali on behalf of the deity.

A local mason gave her Rs 200 as a gift. Her sexual relations with her Harijan husband lasted for only nine months. Later, another patron belonging to the Uppara community started living with this basvi and she begot three female children.

For her, begging for alms was not only customary but necessary as well. The government gave her a good house and she opened a petty shop which fetched her Rs 207 per day. She also learnt tailoring to supplement her income.

Case – 9

Another Madiga girl of Alur was made a basvi when she was 10 years old. She had one younger brother and three younger sisters. The dedication was done by her parents. Her maternal uncle acted as the bridegroom and tied the tali. The two lived together for two years and then he deserted her. By then, she had one male child. Another paramour of the Boya caste started going to her and she bore him two female children.

This basvi used to perform dances during Yellamma Jatara. She was a daily wage-earner. As she had neither a house nor any landed property, she resorted to begging in her old age. The district administration allotted her a house site and a sheep unit as she was interested in income-generating activities.

Case – 10

Another Madiga woman living in Holigunda village had two sons and one daughter male and female children. When she was 10, she was dedicated to Pedda Uligamma. Her grandmother was also a basvi.

The Bayananayana acted as a religious functionary and tied the tali to her on behalf of the deity. She became a farm worker's concubine and begot four children. She was then deserted.

Every Tuesday and Friday, she would collect alms. She was a regular participant in the Uligamma Jatara. She had no landed property and her income as a casual labourer was meagre.

Case – 11

Another Madiga woman of Holigunda dedicated her 16-year-old daughter to Vrukunda Veeranna in the hope that this God would take pity on her and save her to-be-born children. Her other children had died soon after birth.

Her maternal uncle who had tied the tali around her neck at the initiation ceremony deflowered her and kept her as his concubine. She collected alms regularly and did not participate in the Yellamma Jatara.

Though she had two acres of dry land, she worked as a casual labourer. She was given a house site and a sheep unit.

Case – 12

Another Madiga woman of Adoni town was a basvi. Both her mother and grandmother were basvis. When she was 12, she was dedicated to Yellamma. Her maternal uncle did the initiation ceremony in the village temple and tied mangalasutra to her.

This basvi's maternal uncle, a postal employee, regarded himself as a protector of this tradition and kept her as a concubine and she remained that throughout her life. She seldom did the customary begging, but participated in the annual jataras.

Her two sons were then in the high school and her daughter was in the 6th standard. She was a daily wage-earner and her economic condition was pathetic. Though unaware of the Devadasi Act, she wanted to free herself from the bondage.

Appendix II

The Andhra Pradesh Gazette
Part IV-B Extraordinary
Published by Authority

No. 161

Hyderabad
Thursday, March 31, 1988

Andhra Pradesh Acts, Ordinances and Regulations, etc.

The following Act of the Andhra Pradesh Legislative Assembly which was reserved by the governor on the April 24, 1987 for the consideration and assent of the President received the assent of the President on March 25, 1988 and the said assent is hereby published on March 31, 1988 in the Andhra Pradesh Gazette for general information:-

ACT No. 10 of 1988

An Act to prohibit the dedication of women as Devadasis in the state of Andhra Pradesh.

Whereas the practice of dedicating women as Devadasis to Hindu deities, idols, objects of worship, temples and other religious institutions or places of worship exists in certain parts of the state of Andhra Pradesh; and

Whereas such practice, however ancient and pure in its origin, leads many of the women so dedicated to degradation and to evils like prostitution; and

Whereas it is necessary to put an end to the practice.

Be it enacted by the Legislative Assembly of the state of Andhra Pradesh in the Thirty-ninth Year of the Republic of India as follows:-

Short title, extent and commencement

1. (1) This Act may be called the Andhra Pradesh Devadasis (Prohibition of Dedication) Act, 1988.
   (2) It extends to the whole of the state of Andhra Pradesh.
   (3) It shall come into force on such date as the government may, by notification in the Andhra Pradesh Gazette, appoint.

Definitions

2. In this Act, unless the context otherwise requires,
   (a) "dedication" means the performance of any act or ceremony by whatever name called, by which a woman is dedicated to the service of a Hindu deity, idol, object of worship, temple or other religious institution or place of worship and includes tying "tali with jakini" to a woman or tying a woman by a garland to a Garuda Khambham, dhaarana and deeksha;

(b) "Devadasi" means any woman so dedicated by whatever name called and includes Basvi, Jogin, Parvati, Matamma and Thayamma;

(c) "Government" means the state Government;

(d) "Notification" means a notification published in the Andhra Pradesh Gazette and the word "notified" shall be construed accordingly.

(e) "Woman" means female of any age.

Dedication as Devadasi to be unlawful

3. (1) The dedication of a woman as Devadasi, whether before or after the commencement of this Act and whether she has consented to such dedication or not, is hereby declared unlawful and void; and any woman so dedicated shall not thereby be deemed to have become incapable of entering into a valid marriage.

(2) Any custom or usage, prevailing in any Hindu community such as the Bogum, Kalavanthula, Sani, Nagavasulu, Devadasi, Kurmapulu, Basvi, Jogin and Parvati and the like, that a woman of that community who gives or takes part in any melam (nautch), dancing or music performance in the course of any procession or otherwise is thereby regarded as having adopted a life of prostitution and becomes incapable of entering into a valid marriage, and the performance of any ceremony or act in accordance with any such custom or usage, whether before or after the commencement of this Act and whether the woman concerned has consented to such performance or not, are hereby declared unlawful and void.

Marriage of Devadasis

4. No marriage contracted by a woman in accordance with any law, custom or usage shall be invalid and no child of such marriage shall be considered as illegitimate by reason only of such woman being a "Devadasi".

Penalties

5. Any person who performs, promotes, takes part in or abets the performance of any ceremony or act for dedicating a woman as Devadasi or any ceremony or act connected therewith shall on conviction be punishable with imprisonment of either description for a term which may extend to three years but which shall not be less than two years and with fine which may extend to rupees three thousand but which shall not be less than rupees two thousand:

Provided that where the person referred to in this section is a parent or guardian or relative of a woman so dedicated, he shall on conviction be punishable with imprisonment of either description for a term which may extend to five years but which shall not be less than two years and with fine which may extend to rupees five thousand but which shall not be less than rupees three thousand:

Provided further that the woman who is dedicated in such ceremony or act or in respect of whom such ceremony or act is performed shall not be punishable.

Punishment for propagation

6. Whoever propagates the practice of dedication of women as Devadasis shall on conviction be punishable with imprisonment of either description for a term which may extend to three years but which shall not be less than one year and with fine which may extend to rupees five thousand but which shall not be less than rupees two thousand.

Powers to be conferred on Collector

7. The Government may confer such powers and impose such duties on the Collector or any other Officer of the Revenue Department not below the rank of Mandal Revenue Officer, as may be necessary to ensure that the provisions of this Act are properly carried out and may specify the local limits within which such powers or duties shall be carried out by such Officers.

Duties of Collector and other Officers

8. It shall be the duty of every Collector and other Officers specified under Section 7 to inquire whether after the commencement of this Act, the system of Devadasi is being practised and if, as a result of such enquiry, any such practice is found to exist, he shall forthwith take such action as may be necessary to put an end to such practice.

Offences to be tried by Executive Magistrates

9. The Government may confer, on an Executive Magistrate, the powers of a Judicial Magistrate of First Class or of the Second Class for the trial of offences under this Act; and on such conferment of powers, the Executive Magistrate, on whom the powers are so conferred, shall be deemed for the purposes of the (Act 2 of 1974) the Code of Criminal Procedure, 1973 to be a Judicial Magistrate of the First Class, or of the Second Class, as the case may be.

Offences under the Act to be cognizable and non-bailable

10. Every offence under this Act shall be cognizable and non-bailable.

Power to make rules

11. (1) The Government may, by notification, make rules for carrying out all or any of the purposes of this Act.

(2) Every rule made under this Act shall immediately after it is made be laid before the Legislative Assembly of the state if it is in session, and if it is not in session, in the session immediately following for a total period of fourteen days which may be comprised in one session or in two successive sessions and if, before the expiration of the session in which it is so laid or the session immediately following the Legislative Assembly agrees in making any modification in the rule or in the annulment of the rule, the rule shall, from the date on which the modification or annulment is notified, have effect only in such modified form or shall stand annulled, as the case may be; so however that any such modification or annulment shall be without prejudice to the validity of anything previously done under that rule.

Repeal and Saving Act XXXI of 1947

12. (1) The Andhra Pradesh (Andhra Area) Devadasis (Prevention of Dedication) Act, 1947 is hereby repealed.

Act 1 of 1891

(2) On such repeal, the provisions of sections 8 and 18 of the Andhra Pradesh General Clauses Act, 1891, shall apply.

P.V. VIDYA SAGAR
Secretary to Government,
Law and Legislative Affairs,
Law Department.

Appendix III

A Summit of Judiciary on Devadasi/Dedication Cult

On September 3, 2005, very special visitors visited MPLC School to hear matammas and their children's problems. They were Sri M.V.N. Pathrudu Garu, Member Secretary, Andhra Pradesh – State Legal Services Authority, Sri Appa Rao Garu, District Magistrate, Chittoor and Sri S. Ravi Kumar Garu, III Additional District Judge, Tirupati. They interacted with our MPLC children and matammas. Our matammas explained their problems with the community, lack of basic minimum needs of housing, ration cards, lands, etc. They listened to their problems very patiently and asked them to submit their requirements in a form of memorandum during the Devadasi Summit which was to be held on September 10, 2005 at Tirupati. They enjoyed watching our children's cultural programmes and were very much impressed and appreciated the children, also permitted us to perform a 20-minute cultural programme during the Summit. They enquired about the school and its activities, went round the school, residential campus, and the kitchen. They felt very happy spending an evening with our children. They promised us that they would visit our school whenever they came to Tirupati. They appreciated the RISE team and our HEKS donors for their efforts in the implementation of the programme as well as in the eradication of this social evil.

September 10, 2005 was a very special day for RISE as well as the matammas in Chittoor district because the national and state-level magistrates had called for a one-day summit on Devadasi system to eradicate the evil.

The National Legal Services Authority (NLSA) and the Andhra Pradesh State Legal Services Authority (APLSA) had organized this one-day summit with magistrates from four states (Andhra Pradesh, Tamil Nadu, Karnataka and Maharashtra) along with the matammas of four districts and NGOs who are working with this vulnerable group in the above-said states. A total of 150 judges from four states participated in the summit. The significance of the programme is that most of the high court judges from the four states attended and gave their messages. The organizers of the programme successfully gathered 1,500 vulnerable women and their children.

RISE had the opportunity to be part of the programme committee along with the National Legal Service Authority to make a success of the programme and had been with them in the preparatory and implementation process.

Mr D. Ramakrishna, Director of RISE, had submitted a set of recommendations to all the magistrates along with our research study report of the Mata Cult. Mr Ramakrishna made a five-minute speech on the Matamma cult and the major problems of matammas. He also recommended a set of policy matters for alternative measures for matammas. Our cultural team performed a Dappu programme which was appreciated by the chief guests and everyone else.

The matammas of three districts spoke about their problems and requested for sanction of pensions.

Justice Sri Sabharwal Garu, Judge of the Supreme Court and Executive Chairman of NALSA, expressed his deep anguish over the prevalence of the Devadasi system in the country and called for a strict timeframe to banish this social evil. Strict punishment should be awarded to those who promote this social evil. He also recommended a set of measures to root out the Devadasi system. The Judge suggested a three-pronged strategy to eradicate the evil:

- Urgent measures to de-stigmatize devadasis.
- Mere enactment of laws and legislations not enough.
- Legal teams to be set up at the district level to bring about awareness.

High Court Chief Justice Bilal Nazki said immediate steps should be taken to implement the government order on increasing the relief package of fixed deposits for matammas from Rs 10,000 to Rs 20,000.

The next day, all the district magistrates visited the school again and appreciated our RISE team and cultural team for their participation and performance. They distributed blankets, sweets and savouries as their contribution to all our children and spent half a day at the school. They promised to extend their support in future in legal matters as well as financial support.

It was a memorable day for our children and RISE team because they had an opportunity to get onto the dais to speak and dance in front of VIPs.

Sri Pathrudu, Chairperson of Andhra Pradesh State Legal Service Authority observed that "it is not just a school, it is a social temple to serve the child."

Appendix IV

News Clippings

CUS

Photos: C Kesavulu

Poonni thus become a Jogin at the age of nine. Five sheep were slaughtered for the feast that followed; today while she is the wife of god Pothuraju, she is also the mistress of the village landlord. And the story of exploitation continues...

WOMEN OF GOD AND RICH MEN

Newstime's Edroy writes after an extensive tour of Nizamabad district...

Let Us Give'em A Chance

No one may be better equipped to talk about the Jogins, than Ms Kumud Ben Joshi, Governor of Andhra Pradesh. She has been instrumental in bringing together various voluntary organisations to fight this evil, and giving the problem a national exposure...

With the Governor taking such keen interest, can the Jogins hope for the better...

TELANGANA

GODDESS, LET TH

Slave to religious prostitution, Telangana's joginis get to discover there's life beyond

EM GO

And Laxmi Was A Jogin ... One Out of Hundreds!

6-year-old Susheela from a traditional Jogin family. Will she too grow into one ...

Jogin has a child. The children of Jogins invariably become Jogins themselves; and they are half orphaned at birth. The father does not accept his responsibility, and it is left to the mother to look after her offspring. This has two reasons. One, the landlord would not be burdened with the task of feeding another mouth, and the other, it keeps the Jogin system alive by adding fresh blood to it.

Devamma, aged 30, refused to become a Jogin and her parents broke both her legs. Today, she walks with the help of crutches, and is blamed for all the troubles befalling the family or the village. Balamma was not made a Jogin by her parents despite the advice of the village elders. The very next year she was struck by Polio, which left her handicapped. The villagers explained that this was the 'wrath of god.' They cite this as an example of what would happen if young girls are not made Jogins.

But while all this happens in the villages, the city dweller has shown just how vulnerable he is to caste considerations. When the rehabilitation centre was first opened in Nizamabad town, neighbours objected to having scheduled caste Jogins in their midst. The opposition from the 'enlightened' citizens was so great that the Collector had to shift the rehabilitation home to a secluded place outside the town, where the pure souls of the area may not be contaminated by these untouchables. Such is our concern for Jogins

It would not seem wrong to say that had not a sanction in the form of Jogin system existed prostitution would well have taken the place of an occupation in a set-up where there is no scope for income-earning employment for the village woman ...

her unseeing eyes, and each visitor threw some money on to the body. She was a Jogin. One out of hundreds Bodhan village of Nizamabad district in Andhra Pradesh. This last fact, was what brought us to her funeral...

There are over 5000 women like her in the district of Nizamabad alone, and the number may well exceed 25,000 when one takes into the account the fact that they exist in Karimnagar, Medak, Adilabad and Kurnool districts of the State as well. Laxmi was made a 'Jogin' woman when she was four following a vow taken by her parents during a drought. This is the story of all the other Jogins too, caught in a whirlpool of misery, they cannot escape the weight of history.

Gangamani, aged 27, of Bodhan has five brothers and two sisters. After her conversion to a Jogin she was kept by a landlord who is now dead. "I would like to get married and lead a normal life," she said echoing the sentiments of most other Jogins. But things are not as simple.

While Gangamani and her ilk may seem to be the average Jogin, there is another breed which defies efforts of rehabilitation simply because they never had it so good. Yellamma belongs to this fold. Being quite pretty, she is today the proud owner of a tractor and some paddy fields. She was the mistress of a rich landlord who left her some land after his death. People like Yellamma are more the exception than the rule. And that makes others hope against hope. It is the economics of survival.

The structure of the village economy is one of subsistence. The main crops there are paddy and sugar cane, both seasonal. So where does the village woman go for regular work. It would not seem a wrong argument to say that, had not this sanction existed, prostitution would have well taken the place of an occupation.

Now, her father's decision is was taken with the idea that she would become the breadwinner for the family once he was too old to work. This decision is basically economic, because in a village where there is no sustained employment, sanctioned prostitution may well be the easy way out. This is a fact for, many a time it is the parents who oppose efforts to rehabilitate Jogins.

The Jogin system not only suits the poor peasant, but obviously makes things easier for the rich landlord too. Everything is fine until the

Union, it may well give an ... as to why nobody was really serious about the problem, after all it was a Harijan problem.'

This theory is compounded by the fact that many of the Village Officers Tahsildars and other officials were aware of this obnoxious practice, but chose to keep quite because it was a "Harijan problem."

Any change can therefore come about only if it is treated as a human problem, on all levels. This is a social anomaly as deeprooted and serious as untouchability itself because it affects only one community. Since the practice stems from superstition, the first thing to be done is to educate them. Says Mr Simhadri, deputy director of social welfare: "Improved educational facilities, medical care and above all an understanding of the problem is what is essentially required." He agrees that there are no preventive measures, and that prevention at this stage can come about only subtly. "One cannot force these people to give up something that they have been living with all their lives," he said.

In all this, there is some hope. The case of Gangamani is a pointer. She is only nine years old, and does not know what the future has in store for her. She was dedicated to the Goddess Yellamma by her parents and would have ended up as a whore, had not the District Collector, Mrs Murthy, intervened. Her brother who was with her at the time of the Collector's visit to the village refused to let her go to the rehabilitation centre, saying that the wrath of the goddess would descend on his family. But the collector could convince him. And today, Gangamani is in a social welfare hostel, leading a normal life. She is a lucky one, because for every Gangamani there are a hundred others who are forced into wretched existence by circumstances.

A feeling of insecurity may well be another reason for the continuation of the practice. When a woman is made a Jogin, she cannot marry and therefore for her, the relative security of being somebody's mistress is much better than being without a man for the whole of her life. "What will the government give me, I have everything I want," says Lalitha, who points out that she earns more and has a man when her sisters in the rehabilitation home do not have that privilege. But this is where we must step in, for rehabilitation is not for the ... who have something

her unseeing eyes, and each visitor threw some money on to the body. She was a Jogin. One out of hundreds Bodhan village of Nizamabad district in Andhra Pradesh. This last fact, was what brought us to her funeral...

There are over 5000 women like her in the district of Niza-

Union, it may well give an ... as to why nobody was really serious about the problem, after all it was a Harijan problem.'

This theory is compounded by the fact that many of the Village Officers Tahsildars and other officials were aware of this obnoxious practice, but

DECCAN CHRONICLE SUNDAY FEBRUARY 4 1990

Governor Kumudben Joshi blessing the couple after the marriage of a Jogin at the Atheist Centre in Vijayawada on Saturday. Mrs Hemalata Lavanam, a social reformer, who adopted the Jogin Mrs Sudini before she was given in marriage to a farmer is also seen.

Jogin gets married

From our bureau

VIJAYAWADA, Feb 3

Garlands of vegetables

From our bureau

VIJAYAWADA, Feb 3

JUNE 24, 1999 HINDU

REGI

Yet another Jogini enters wedlock

By Our Staff Reporter

HYDERABAD, JUNE 23.

The Governor, Dr. C. Rangarajan, and his wife, Haripriya Rangarajan, greeting the newly married couple — Anjaiah and Bhojamma — at the Raj Bhavan Community Hall in Hyderabad on Wednesday.

Rs. 10-crore project for rehabilitation of Joginis

HINDU 24/6/99

By Our Staff Reporter

NIZAMABAD, JUNE 23. The Social Welfare Minister, Mr. Kadiyam Srihari, has said that the Government has evolved an action plan to rehabilitate about 6,000 Jogini women in the State by earmarking Rs. 10 crore for their welfare.

Addressing the District Development Review Committee (DDRC) meeting at the Pragati bhavan auditorium here, Mr. Srihari referred to the reports appearing in newspapers about four young SC girls being initiated into the Jogini system. Expressing his anguish at the age-old practice being revived in the district despite the best efforts of the Government and the Non-Governmental organisations (NGOs) in the district, the Minister made a fervent appeal to the public to collectively oppose the evil practice.

He said after reading the news reports, he held a meeting with the Excise Minister, Mr. Mandava Venkateswara Rao, and the Housing Minister, Mr. P.Srinivas Reddy, who were here to attend the DDRC meeting and reviewed the situation. He said the Government and Samskar, the NGO working for the uplift of the Jogini women, were confident that the system was on the decline but were shattered by the happening. He pointed out that the Government had even launched an ambitious plan to rehabilitate the reformed women by giving them houses under the Indira Awas Yojana, putting Rs. 10,000 per head as fixed deposit in banks and also handing over an acre of land each belonging to the Nizam Sugar Factory, Bodhan.

Mr Srihari directed the District Collector and the Joint Collector to visit the places where such cases were reported and wanted them to submit a report within a week. He also issued a stern warning to the Village Administrative Officers who failed to inform the District Collector about the incidents. He said if in future the VAOs failed to do their bit in not alerting the district administration, action would be taken against them.

The Social Welfare Minister also referred to the rehabilitation package for the 'Potharajus', the caste priests, who are instrumental in initiating the girls into the system. He said the Government would soon finalise a rehabilitation package for them so that they desisted from doing the same job. He asked the Collector to prepare an action plan for their rehabilitation. He said if any Potharaju was found guilty, he would be punished. The Minister wanted the administration and the NGOs to take up a massive awareness programme in the district so that within six months, the evil system would be wiped out.

He called upon the media to play a positive role in highlighting the plight of the Jogini women and encourage them to lead a normal life. The Government would highlight the evils of untouchability, atrocities against weaker sections, harassment of persons by branding them sorcerers and the Jogini system.

The Social Welfare Minister later reviewed the functioning of various welfare measures like Mundadugu, Cheyuta, Chaitanyam, Apathabandhu, Aadarna being implemented by the Government. The DDRC meeting saw the elected representatives complaining about vacant posts of doctor and paramedical staff in several hospitals. The Minister directed the District Medical and Health Officer, Dr. R.Hussain Reddy, to fill the vacancies. The Minister also asked the Collector to fill the backlog posts reserved for the SCs by the month-end.

The ZP chairperson, Mrs. Sharada Suryakant, the Government whip, Mr. N.Anjaneyulu, the Bodhan MLA, Mr. Basheeruddin Babu Khan, the Kamareddy MLA, Mr. Gampa Goverdhan, the Nizamabad MLA, Mr. Satish Pawar, the District Collector, Mr. R.M.Gonela, and others were present.

Bibliography

Government Reports

Archival Sources Report, Andhra Pradesh State Gazetteer, A Manual of Kurnool district in the Presidency of Madras, Hyderabad, 1922 (1886).

Bog, G.T. (ed.), Census Report of India, 1921, Vol. B, Part II, Madras, 1922.

Census of India 1881–1951, Reports relating to Madras Presidency, H.E.H. Nizam's Dominions, Hyderabad, Bombay and Mysore states.

Francis, W. (ed.), Census of India, 1901, Vol. IX A, Part II, Madras, 1902.

Government of Bombay, Gazetteer of Bombay State, Bijapur, Vol. 123, Bombay, 1884.

Government of Bombay, Gazetteer of Bombay State, Dharwad District, Bombay, 1959.

Macangi, Census of India, 1961, Vol. VI, Andhra Pradesh, Office of the Department of Census, New Delhi.

Molony, J.C. (ed.), Census Report of India, 1911, Vol. 12, Part II, Madras, 1912.

Books in English

Altekar, A.S., *The Position of Women in Hindu Civilisation,* Delhi, Motilal Banarsidass, 1956.

Assayag, Jackie, "Modern Devadasis: Devotees of Goddess Yellamma in Karnataka" in Gabriella Elchimgar and Ferro/Luzzi (eds) *Rites and Beliefs in Modern India,* Delhi, Manohar Publications, 1990.

Bachofen, Johann Jakob, *Myth, Religion and Mother Right: Selected Writing,* London, Routledge and Kegan Paul, 1967.

Banerjee, Sumantha, "Marginalisation of Women's Popular Culture in 19th Century Bengal" in Kumkum Sangari and Sudesh Vaid (eds), *Recasting Women: Essays in Colonial History,* New Delhi, Kali for Women, 1989.

Basham, A.L., *A Cultural History of India*, Oxford University Press, Delhi, 1954.

——, *The Wonder That Was India*, New York, Grove Press, 1954.

Basu, N.K., S.N. Sinha and Rita D. Sil (eds.), *History of Marriage and Prostitution (Vedas to Vatsyayana)* New Delhi, Khama Publishers, 1992.

Bhattacharya, N.N., *The History of the Tantric Religion: A Historical, Ritualistic and Philosophical Study,* New Delhi, Manohar Publications, 1982.

Briffault, Robert, *A Study of Origins of Sentiments and Institutions,* Vols. I, II, III, London, George Allen and Unwin, 1927.

——, *The Mothers: A Study of Origins of Sentiments and Institutions,* Vol. 2, London, George Allen and Unwin, 1927, Latest edition, 1969.

Balon, Carol R., *Forms of Goddess Lajja Gauri in Indian Art,* Pennsylvania: Pennsylvania State University Press, 1992.

Chakrabarti, Kakolee, *Women as Devadasis: Origin and Growth of Devadasi Profession,* New Delhi, Deep and Deep Publication, 2000.

Chakravarthi, Uma, "What Ever Happened to the Vedic Dasi Orientalism, Nationalism and a Script for Past" in Kumkum Sangari and Sudesh Vaid (eds), *Recasting Women Essays in Colonial History,* New Delhi, Kali for Women, 1989.

Chakladar, H.C., *Social Life in Ancient India: Studies in Vatsyayana's Kamasutra,* Delhi, Bharatiya (India) Limited, 1954.

Chandra, Moti, *The World of Courtesans,* New Delhi, Vikas, 1973.

Chandramouli, V., *Jogin: Girl Child Labour Studies,* New Delhi, Sterling Publishers, 1992.

Chatterjee, Santosh, *Devadasi (Temple Dancer),* Calcutta, The Book House, 1945.

Chattopadhyaya, Devi Prasad, *Lokayata: A Study in Ancient Indian Materialism,* Sixth Edition, New Delhi, People's Publishing House, 1985.

Chintamani, C.Y., (ed.), *Indian Social Reform: Being a Collection of Essays, Addresses, Speeches,* Madras, Thompson and Co., 1901.

Clough, Emma Rauschenbusch, *While Sewing Sandals: or Tales of a Telugu Pariah,* London, Hodder and Stoughton, 1899.

Dedutt, Pattanaik, *Devi: The Mother Goddess, An Introduction,* Bombay Vakils, Feffer and Simons Limited.

Dhere, R.C., *Lajja Gauri,* Pune, Sri Vidya Prakashan, 1978.

Doshi, Saryu (ed.), *Dedications to the Altar: The Devadasi Tradition* by Ramesh Chandra Sirkar, Goa, Marg Publications, 1983.

Dubois, Abbe, *Hindu Manners, Customs and Ceremonies,* London, Oxford University Press, 1909.

Dumont, Louis, *Homo Hierarchicus: The Caste System and Its Implications,* Chicago, The University of Chicago Press, 1980.

——, *Religion, Politics and History in India: Collected Papers in Indian Sociology*, The Hague, Mouton, 1971.

Ehrenfals, O.R., *Mother Rights in India*, Hyderabad, 1941.

Elmore, W.T., *Dravidian Gods in Modern Hinduism*, New Delhi, Asian Educational Services, 1984.

Engels, Frederick, *The Origin of Family, Private Property and the State*, Moscow, Progress Publishers, 1977, (reprint).

Francis, Hamilton, *A Journey from Madras through the Countries of Mysore, Canara and Malabar* (Three Volumes), London, T. Cadell and W. Devis, 1807.

Frazer, James, *Adonis, Attis, Osirs*, London, 1907.

——, *The Golden Bow: A Study in Magic and Religion*, Vol. I, *Magic of Art*, Vol. II, New York, London (1911) MacMillan and Co., 1992, 1966.

Fuller, C.J., *Servants of the Goddess, the Priest of a South Indian Temple*, Cambridge, Cambridge University Press, 1984.

Fuller, Marcus B, *The Wrongs of Indian Womanhood*, Edinburgh, 1900.

Gurumurthy, K.G., *Devadasi Custom in Peasant Context in Indian Peasantry*, Delhi, B.R. Corporation, 1982.

James, E.O., *Cult of the Mother Goddess: An Archaeological and Documentary Study*, London, Thomes and Hudson, 1959.

James, J. Preston, *Cult of the Goddess: Social and Religious Change in a Hindu Temple*, New Delhi, Vikas Publishing, 1980.

Jogan Shankar, *Devadasi Cult: A Sociological Analysis*, New Delhi, Ashish Publishing House, 1990.

Kadetod, N.K., *Yellamma Jogatiyaru Hagu Devadasi Paddhati*, (Jogatis of Yellamma and Devadasi Custom), Dharwad, Karnataka University, 1983.

Kamble, Uttam, *Devadasi Ani Nagnapuja*, Bombay, Lok Vanimaya Griha, 1988.

Kapoor, Subodh (ed.), *The Indian Encyclopaedia: Biographical, Historical, Religious, Administrative, Ethnological, Commercial and Scientific*, Vol. VI, New Delhi, Cosmo Publications, 2002.

Karkhanis, G.G., *Devadasi: A Burning Problem of Karnataka*, Bijapur, Radha Printing Works, 1959.

Kaushik, Susheela, (ed.), *Women's Oppression*, New Delhi, Shakti Books, 1985.

Kersenboona, Saskia C., *Nitya Sumangali: Devadasi Tradition in South India*, Delhi, Motilal Banarsidass 1987.

Kingsley, David, *Hindu Goddesses: Vision of the Divine Feminine in the Hindu Religious Tradition*, New Delhi, Archives Publishers, 1987.

Krishna, Reddy, B. and Malika J. Srujana , "Welfare Measures for the Emancipation of Basvis of Kurnool district of Andhra Pradesh" in C. Chakrapani and S. Vijaya Kumar (eds), *Changing Status and Role of Women in Indian Society*, New Delhi, M.D. Publication, 1994.

Krishna, Sastry H., *South Indian Images of Gods and Goddesses*, Varanasi, Bhartiya Publishing House, 1916.

Kumar, Pushpendra, *Shakti Cult in Ancient India with Special Reference to the Puranic Literature*, Varanasi, Bharatiya Publishing House, 1974.

Lakshmi, Raghuramaiah, K., *Night Birds: Indian Prostitutes from Devadasis to Call Girls*, Delhi, Chanakya Publications, 1991.

Lavanam, Hemalatha, Samskar Organization, Varni, Andhra Pradesh, Chelli Nilayam.

Manjunath, Bevinakatti, *Matangi*, Hampi, Kannada University, 1996.

Marglin, Apffel Frederique, *Wives of the God-King: The Rituals of the Devadasis of Puri*, Delhi, Oxford University Press, 1985.

Mayo, Katherine, *Mother India*, London, 1927.

——, *Slaves of the Gods*, London, 1929.

Muthulakshmi, Reddy, S., *Autobiography of Dr S. Muthulakshmi: A Pioneer Woman Legislator*, Madras, N.H.J. Press, 1964.

Nandi, R.N., *Religious Institutions and Cults in the Deccan*, Delhi, Motilal Banarsidass, 1973.

Omvedt, Gail, *Dalits and Democratic Revolution: Dr Ambedkar and Dalit Movement in Colonial India*, Delhi, Sage Publications, 1994.

Penzer, N.M., "Sacred Prostitution", Appendix IV in Charles Henry Tawney Jr. and N.M. Penzer (eds), *The Ocean of Story*, Vol. I, Delhi, Motilal Banarsidass, 1968.

Prasad, A.K., *Devadasi System in Ancient India: A Study of Temple Dancing Girls of South India*, Delhi, H.K. Publishers, 1991.

Ramakrishna, V., *Social Reform in Andhra 1848–1919*, New Delhi, Vikas Publishing House, 1983.

Sarma, Nagabhushana, *Folk Performing Arts of Andhra Pradesh*, Hyderabad: Telugu University, 1995.

Singh, Nagendra Kumar, *Divine Prostitution*, New Delhi, A.P.H. Publishing Corporation, 1997.

Sinha, S.N. and Basu N.K., *History of Prostitution in Ancient India*, Vol. I, Calcutta, Bengal Social Hygiene Association, 1933.

Sontheimer, Gunther-Dietz, *King of Hunters, Warriors and Shepherds: Essays on Khandoba*, Edited by Anne Feldhaus, Aditya Mallik, Heidrun Bruckner, New Delhi, Manohar Publications, 1997.

Srivastava, M.C.P., *Mother Goddess in Indian Art, Archaeology and Literature*, Delhi, Agam Kala Prakashan, 1979.

Stanley, John M., "Capitulation of Mani: A Conversion Myth in the Cult of Khandoba" in Alf Hiltebeitel, *Criminal Gods and Demon Devotees*, New York, SUNY Press.

Subrahmanyam, V., *Mother Goddess and Other Goddesses*, New Delhi, Ajanta Publication, 1993.

Sundara Raju M., *Prostitution in Madras: A Study in Historical Perspective*, Delhi, Konark Publishers, 1993.

Syamala, Parama, Sivaiah G.R., Rajagauda P.S. and D.S. Rajendra (eds), *Soundatti Yellamma*, Karnataka (n.d.).

Thurston, Edgar and K. Rangachari, *Castes and Tribes of South India*, Vol. III, Madras, Government Press, 1909.

Trivedi, Harshad Ramachandra, *Scheduled Caste Women: Studies in Exploitation*, Delhi, Concept Publishing, 1976.

Whitehead, Henry, *The Village Gods of South India*, Calcutta, Association Press (YMCA), 1921.

English Articles/Papers/Proceedings

Anandam, K., "Matamma Thirunallu", *S.V. University Oriental Journal* January-December, Vol. 25, No. 1, Tirupati, 1982.

Anandi, S., "Representing Devadasis 'Dasigal Mosavalai' As a Radical Text", *Economic and Political Weekly*, March 1991, Bombay, 739–746.

——, "Women's Question in the Dravidian Movement (1901–1948)", *Social Scientist*, Vol. 19, No. 586, 1991.

Artal, P.O. "Basvis in peninsular India", *Journal of Anthropological Society of Bombay*, Vol. 9, No. 2, 1910.

Assayag, Jackie, "Women Goddess, Women Distress: Yellamma Goddess' Devotees in South India", *Man in India*, Vol. 69, No. 4, 1989.

Bang, B.C., "Current Concepts of the Smallpox Goddess Sitala in Parts of West Bengal", *Man in India*, No. 53, 1973.

Barse, Sheela, "Rights of the girl child", *The Indian Journal of Social Work Special Issue on the Girl Child*, Vol. C 11, No.1, 1991, Bombay, Tata Institute of Social Sciences.

Chakrapani, C., "Jogins of Telangana", *Eastern Anthropologist*, Vol. 45, No. 3, 1992.

Chandra, Moti, "Studies in the Cult of Mother Goddess in Ancient India", *Bulletin of Prince of Wales Museum* (1–2), Western India, 1968.

Fawcett, "Basvis Women Through Dedication to a Deity Assume Masculine Privileges", *Journal of Anthropological Society*, Vol. II, 1892, 322–345.

Gulvadi, Santosh Kumar, "Handmaidens of God", *The Illustrated Weekly*, 1978, 19–21.

Gurumurthy, K.G., "Devadasi Custom: March of Karnataka", Vol. 21, No. 8, Bangalore: Karnataka Government Publications Division, 1983.

Hegde, Odeyar D., "A socio-economic Strategy for Rehabilitating Devadasis", *Social Welfare*, Vol. 29, No. 11 and 12, 1983.

Jambagi S., "A Study of Prostitutes in Belgaum", *Social Welfare*, Vol. 17, No. 6, 1970.

Jamnadas, K., "Devadasis were Degraded Buddhist Nuns", *Dalit Digest*, Chandrapur.

Khare, G.H., "Khandoba: A Popular Deity of South India", proceedings of Indian History Congress, 21st Session, 1958.

Lalitha, V., "Empowerment of Women", paper presented in National Seminar on Strategies for Development of Women, 9 and 10 June, 2000, DSRF, Hyderabad.

——, "Religious Prostitution: The Problem of Jogins in Telangana", proceedings of the Indian History Congress, 49th Session, 1988, Karnataka University, Dharwad.

——, "Strategies for Combating Violence Against Dalit and Weaker Sections Women", National Seminar on Dalits, paper presented, 1999, DSRF. Hyderabad.

——, "Yellamma Worship – Village Deity: A Case Study of Jogins in Andhra Pradesh", proceedings of Andhra Pradesh History Congress, Warangal, 1990.

——, G. Hema, Ravi D'Souza and A.V. Ramani, "Indian Women's Employment", Kuchibhotla Vasanthi Foundation, Kakinada, 20th March, 2001.

Linda, J., "EPP Dalit Struggle: Nude Worship and Chandragutti Incident", *Sociological Bulletin*, Vol. 41, No. 1–2, 1992.

Mahale, Prabha, "Basavis of Karnataka: The Daughter Endowed with Masculine Privileges", *Eastern Anthropologist*, Vol. 39, No. 2, 1986, 125–130.

——, "Women in the Service of God", *South Asian Social Scientist*, Vol. III, No. 1, 1987, 17–30.

Malik, Bela, "Untouchability and Dalit Women's Oppression", *Economic and Political Weekly*, Vol. 34, No. 6, 1999, 323–324.

Mario Cabral, e Sa, "The Evolution of a Community: Devadasis of Goa", *in Illustrations from India Portuguese* A. Lopes Mendes, 1986.

Murthy, M.L.K. "Ethnohistory of Pastoralism: A Study of Kuruvas and Gollas", *Studies in History*, New Delhi, 1993.

Outlook, "You Are Being Watched: Tales of Sex, Sleaze and Dirty Talk Shake the Political Class. Have We Become a Nation of Peeping Toms?", 6th February, 2006.

Parasher, Aloka and Usha Naik, "Temple Girls of Medieval Karnataka", *The Indian Economic and Social History Review*, pp. 69–78 New Delhi, Sage, 1986.

Patil, B.A., "The Jogati", *Man in India*, Vol. 57, No. 1, 1977.

Patil, B.R., "The Devadasis", *Indian Journal of Social Work,* Vol. 35, No. 4, 1975.

Patil, M.B., "Emancipation of Devadasis from Age-old Shackles", *March of Karnataka,* Bangalore: Karnataka Government Publications Division, December, 1988.

Prasad, A.K., "Devadasis in Karnataka", proceedings of Indian History Congress, Bardhaman, 44th Session, 1983.

Rajyalakshmi, P., M. Suryanarayana and D.P. Mukherjee, "The Basavis in Chittoor District of Andhra Pradesh", *Man in India,* Vol. 56, No. 4, 1976.

Ranjana, "Devadasis: The Girls Dedicated to Temples", *Social Welfare,* Vol. 29, No. 11 and 12, 1983.

Sandhya Rani, B. and B. Suguna, "Rehabilitation of Child Matammas: A Study of Poly Learning Centre at Jeevakona", paper presented at National Seminar on Socially Sanctioned Gender Violence, November 29-30, 2001, Tirupati, S.V. University.

Sen, Amartya, "Many Faces of Gender Inequality", *Frontline,* Vol. 18, No. 22, 2001.

Sontheimer, Gentheir "Scriptural Religion and Folk Religion in India, A Case Study of Rudra, Shiva and Khandoba", paper presented in International Seminar at Cuttack, Orissa, 1978.

Tata, Madhavi, "Goddess, Let Them Go: Slave to Religious Prostitution, Telangana's Jogins Get to Discover there's Life Beyond Outlook", *Weekly newsmagazine,* Vol. XLVI, No. 5, 2006.

Thorat, Sukhadeo "Oppression and Denial: Dalit Discrimination in 1990s", *Economic and Political Weekly,* February 9th, 2002, pp. 572–578.

Telugu Books

Arudra, Visalandra, *Gudilo Sex,* Hyderabad, Bhagavathula Sankara Sastri, 1994.

Lavanam, Hemalatha, *Mruthyorma Amrutham Gamaya* (Autobiography), Hyderabad, Anupama Printers, 2004.

Mohan, Laxmi Kantha, *Yellamma Katha,* First edition 1984, Secunderabad M. Seshachalam and Co., (Telugu Poetry).

Nayani, Krishna Kumari, *Telugu Janapada Geya Gadhalu,* Hyderabad: Telugu Akademi, 1990.

Prabodha, Shanti, *"Jogin" – Taratarala Duracharam pai Samagra Kadhatmaka Rachana,* Hyderabad, Praja Sakti Book House, 2004.

Radhakrishna, Murthy Mikkilineni, *Teluguvari Janapada Kalarupalu,* Hyderabad, Telugu University, 1992.

Rama Raju B. and Krishna Kumari Nayani, *Janapada Geyalu,* Hyderabad, Sanghika Charitra, (n.d.).

Rama Raju B., *Telugu Janapada Sahityam*, Hyderabad, Andhra Rachayitala Sangham, 1958.

Reddy, Ramakrishna, *Godavariseema Janapada Kalalu, Kridalu, Vedukalu*, Peddapuram, Telugu University, 1991.

Sundaram, R.V.S., *Andhrula Janapada Vignanam*, Hyderabad, Andhra Pradesh Sahitya Akademi, 1983.

Tapi, Dharma Rao, *Devalayamulo Boothu Bommalenduku*, Hyderabad, Visalandra Publishing House, 1994.

Telugu and Kannada Articles

Gurumurthy and Khadetotad N.K., "Devadasi Paddhati", *Manavika Bharathi*, 1981.

Lalitha, V., "Matangi Vyavastha", *Samkshema*, Hyderabad, 2003.

——, "Devadasi Nunchi Joginiki Marina Paristhiti", *Samkshema*, Hyderabad, 2003.

——, "Matangi Vyavastha – Andhra Pradesh", proceedings of the Andhra Pradesh History Congress, Guntur, 1996.

Shettar, S., "Maduve Vondu Sankole Yella Sudha", *Kannada Weekly*, 1976.

Suhasini, Laxmi, "Matamma System is a Blot on the Society", *The Mahila Margam*, Bulletin 4, 6 October to December, 1992.

Tirumala Rao, Jayadhir "Matangi Vyavastha: Light and Dark", *Vartha*, 27.1.2002.

——, "When did Parasurama's Murder Happen? Who Killed Yellamma History?", *Andhrabhumi*, 11.7.1999.

Reports

Jandhyala, Kameshwari, "Empowering through Reform and Rehabilitation", Samskar's Journey of Working with the Jogins in Nizamabad District, Andhra Pradesh, 2003.

Lakshmaiah, D., "Jogins", An Unpublished Report, Research Officer, Tribal Cultural Research Training Institute, Hyderabad, 1989.

Lavanam, "The Need, the Challenge and the Dynamics of Social Reforms", National Convention on Jogin Welfare, New Delhi, February 16 and 17, 1987.

RISE (Rural Institute for Social Education) Documentation Unit, "Matha Cult in Chittoor District, Andhra Pradesh" Tirupati, 1998.

SALT (Social Awareness Through Literature and Training), "The Humanised Call", UNICEF, Hyderabad.

Samaram, "Jogini: A Deep-rooted Social Problem with Social, Economic and Cultural Ramifications", paper submitted to National Convention on Jogin Welfare, New Delhi, 1998.

Subrahmanyam, P., "Socio-Economic Rehabilitation of Jogin/Basavi Women", a report submitted by Sub-Collector to the Government of Andhra Pradesh, 1987.

Dissertations

Aruna, S., "An evaluation of the Implementation of Government Programmes: A Case Study of Matamma Rehabilitation Programme in Chittoor District", Master of Arts in Women's Studies, Sri Padmavathi Mahila University, Tirupati, 1997.

Gadlock, Norma Elaine, "Ant-hills. Split Mothers and Sacrifice: Conceptions of Female Power in Mariamman Tradition", PhD Thesis, University of California, Berkeley, USA, 1994.

Kambli, N.D., "Devadasis in Belgaum District: A Sociological Study", PhD Thesis, Shivaji University, Kolhapur, 1988.

Kannabiran, Kalpana "Temple Women in South India: A Study in Political Economy and Social History", PhD Thesis, Jawaharlal Nehru University, Delhi, 1992.

Nandi, R.N., "Social and Religious Developments in Deccan", PhD Thesis, University of Patna, Patna, 1969.

Priyadarsini, Vijayasree K., "Patterns of Sacred Prostitution in Colonial Andhra", M.Phil. Dissertation, Jawaharlal Nehru University, Delhi, 1997.

Srujana, Mallika J., "A Socio-cultural Study of Basavi System in Kurnool District of Andhra Pradesh", PhD Thesis, Sri Venkateswara University, Tirupati, 2001.

Srujana, Mallika J., "Basavi System in Andhra Pradesh with Special Reference to Kurnool District", M.Phil. Dissertation, Sri Krishnadevaraya University, Ananthapur, (A.P.), 1990.

Subrahmanyam, Ravi, "A Critical Analysis of Mathangi in Chittoor District", MA Dissertation, University of Hyderabad, Hyderabad, 1997.

Suresh Kumar, K., "Basavi Literature: A Sociological Analysis", PhD Thesis, University of Hyderabad, Hyderabad, 2001.

Personal Papers

Bhagyareddy, Verma M., Papers Collection Under the Possession of his Son M.B. Gautham, Hyderabad.

Chinthamani, C.Y., Papers 1924–1941, Nehru Memorial Museum Library, New Delhi.

Newspapers and Periodicals

English

Deccan Chronicle, "Collector Calls for Rooting Out Untouchability: Promises Rehabilitation, Employment for Jogins, Distributes Cheques", Karimnagar, 4.11.2001.

Deccan Chronicle, "Eighteen-year-old Jogin Gets Married", 24.6.1999.

Deccan Chronicle, "Jogin Gets Married", Vijayawada, 4.2.1990.

India Today, "Shatabdala Duracharampai Samaram", 27.7.1999.

Indian Express, "Furore Over Jogins Issue Resented", Vijayawada, 4.2.1997.

Indian Express, "Vengal Rao Offers to Take up the Cause of Jogins", Vijayawada, 18.2.1987.

The Hindu, "Action Plan for Jogin Women Being Prepared", Nizamabad, 22.7.1999.

The Hindu, "Package for Jogin's Rehabilitation", Varni, 28.1.1997.

The Hindu, "Shunned Then: Shining now", 11.7.2004.

The Hindu, "Women Victims of Tradition", 17.2.1987.

The Hindu, "Wronged Women get new lease of life", 1.2.1987.

The Hindu, "Yet another Jogin enters wedlock", 24.6.1999.

Telugu

Andhra Bhoomi, "Central Government's Act is a Must for the Eradication of Devadasi System – Suggestion of NHRC", 25.10.2004.

Andhra Bhoomi, "Foreigners Came to Utkur to Survey Jogin System", 1.3.2002.

Andhra Bhoomi, "Vrutthini Manukunna Joginula Jeevanampai Germany Brundam Adhyayanam", Nizamabad, 19.7.2003.

Andhra Jyothi, "Jogin Duracharanni Rupumapadaniki Krushi", Nizamabad, 19.7.2003

Andhra Prabha, "Yellareddy Mandalamulo Paryatinchina Germany Brundam", Nizamabad, 19.7.2003.

Andhrabhoomi, "Jadalu Vipputunna Jogin Vyavastha", 22.6.1999.

Andhrabhoomi, "Nutikokkaru: Hemalatha Lavanam", 1997.

Andhrajyothi, "Heyamyna Jogin Duracharam", 9.1.1987.

Andhrajyothi, "Ika joginulu Urummadi Asthi Kadu", 10.8.1999.

Andhrajyothi, "Jogini Vyavasthanu Protsahiste Charya; District Collector Heccharika" Nizamabad, 25.6.1991.

Andhrajyothi, "Joginula Bagogulu", 16.7.1989.

Andhrajyothi, "Joginula Bratukullo Kalyana Vasantham", Vijayawada, 2.2.1987.

Andhrajyothi, "Samaja Sravanthilo Joginulu", 8.6.1987.

Dalita Bulletin (Trymasika Patrika), "2 APJVVPS", September, 2005.

Dalita, Prarambha Sanchika (Trimasika Patrika), "APJVVPS", June, 2005.

Eenadu (Sunday), "Kutumbam Andhamaina Podarillula Undaali, Hemalatha Lavanam – Toduneeda", Nizamabad, 11.1.2004.

Eenadu, "Armoor Pramhamlo Jogini Duracharampy Chaitanya Shibiralu", Nizamabad, 22.6.1999.

Eenadu, "Balya Vivahanni Apina Samskar", Nizamabad, 5.3.1997.

Eenadu, "Duracharam Nndi Vivaha Bandhamloki", Nizamabad, 9.7.1997.

Eenadu, "Governor Samakshamlo Nedu Joginula Pellillu", Nizamabad, 28.10.2001.

Eenadu, "Jogin Rachapundu Chaitanyame Virugudu", Eenadu Charcha Vedika.

Eenadu, "Jogin Vyavastha Nirmulanaku Samishti Krushi", Nizamabad, 10.6.2001.

Eenadu, "Joginula Jeevithallo Velugu", Nizamabad, 5.4.2001.

Eenadu, "Joginula Punaravasamlo Jogutunnaru", Nizamabad, 1992.

Eenadu, "Kalmoktha Dora, Nunchi Adhikara Peeta Varaku Joginula Adhikara Prasthanam", Nizamabad, 2003.

Eenadu, "Kanureppe Katesthe", Nizamabad, 16.3.2001.

Eenadu, "Nadu Joginulu – Nedu Rythulu", Nizamabad, 1993.

Eenadu, "Pratibhavantulu; Thandri Peru Nilipina Tanaya Hemalatha Lavanam", Karnataka, 19.10.2004.

Eenadu, "Samaja Rugmathalanu Paradrolali", Nizamabad, 29.1.2001.

Eenadu, "Samskaranaku Sanmanam Jarigina Vela", Nizamabad, 1997.

Eenadu, "Yellareddy, Mandalamulo Germany Brundam Paryatana", Nizamabad, 19.7.2003.

Nalupu, "Hemalatha Lavanam", 16.12.1990.

Netinijam, "Sama Samajam Asadhyam Kadu", Samskar Plan Vyavasthapaka Karyadarshi, Nizamabad, 4.1.2002.

Varhta, "Mantralam Jatara – Recurrence of Another Social Evil", 18.3.2002.

Vartha (Chelli), "Athmiyatha Asalyna Chirunama: Amma", 22.9.1998.

Vartha, (K. Sajaya) "Joginula Jeevana Punarnirmanam: Bhoomilabhinchindi, Jeevitham Shobhinchindi", Nizamabad, 2.9.2002.

Vartha, "Abhagyula Andhrajyothi", Nagireddypeta (Ningi Sailoo), 5.12.1990.

Vartha, "Dalit Women Speak on Jogin System", 25.8.2002.

Vartha, "Father's Name is God – Mother is the Protector", Mahaboobnagar, 5.12.1999.

Vartha, "Hunger and Humiliation Left for Them: Difficulties Faced by Potarajus in the Framework of Superstitions", Nizamabad, 30.8.2001.

Vartha, "Jogin Sthitigatula Adhyayaaniki Germany Brundam Paryatana", Nizamabad, 19.7.2003.

Vartha, "Joginula Sthitigatula Parisheelana", Nizamabad, 2.5.1999.

Vartha, "Lingampalli Yellamma Jatara", 4.2.2004.

Vartha, "Rajadhani Chenthane Jadalu Vippina Jogini", Nizamabad, 15.6.1997.

Vartha, "Samskar Palana Vyavaharalu Hemalathaku Appagimtha", Nizamabad, 31.10.2002.

Vartha, "Samskar: Helpage Tarapuna Dikku Mokkuleni Vruddhulaku Chyuthanamdistunna Chairman Hemalatha Lavanam", Nizamabad, 1999.

Vartha, "Velugu should Get the Solutions to the Problems of Poor Collector", Narayanapeta Town, 5.11.2004.

Vartha, "Work for the Eradication of Jogin System", 13.2.2003.

Vartha, "Yellamma Jatara – Thousands of Dvotees", 20.2.2002.

Vijetha, "Mahila Millennium Lonu Kanabadutunna Jogin Vyavastha Nimmavargala Mahilalapy Lyngika Niyamtrutvam Idi" Interview with Lalitha V, 2.1.2001.

Interviews

Asha Murthy, IAS, the then Collector of Nizamabad District, June, 1985.

Grace Nirmala – President, APJVVPS, Hyderabad, June 10, 2005.

Haripriya Rangarajan, Social Science Researcher and Historian, July 20, 2006.

Hemalatha, Hyderabad, June 20, 2006.

Jayadhir Tirumala Rao, Hyderabad, April 20, 2004.

Kumudben Joshi, the then Governor of Andhra Pradesh, 1987.

Lavanam, Hyderabad, June 20, 2006.

M.L.K. Murthy, Hyderabad, June 16, 2005.

Nune Vengaiah – President, Duties Organization, Nellore, Andhra Pradesh, February 20, 2006.

P. Subrahmanyam, IAS – the then Sub-collector of Nizamabad District, Nizamabad, July 10, 1987.

Ramakrishna – President of RISE Organization, May 8. 2006.

S.R. Sankaran, IAS, the then Principal Secretary whom the author of this book often consulted and found his advice and secured his valuable auggestions.

Suseela – President, SSS, Tirupati, May 8, 2006.

Index